BIBLE NATION

BIBLE NATION

THE UNITED STATES OF HOBBY LOBBY

Candida R. Moss and Joel S. Baden

PRINCETON UNIVERSITY PRESS
PRINCETON AND OXFORD

Published by Princeton University Press,
41 William Street, Princeton, New Jersey 08540

In the United Kingdom: Princeton University Press,
6 Oxford Street, Woodstock, Oxfordshire OX20 1TR

press.princeton.edu

Jacket design by Faceout Studio, Jeff Miller; jacket art courtesy of Shutterstock

ISBN 978-0-691-17735-9

Names: Moss, Candida R., author. | Baden, Joel S., 1977–author.

Title: Bible nation : the United States of Hobby Lobby / Candida R. Moss and Joel S. Baden.

Description: hardcover [edition]. | Princeton, NJ : Princeton University Press, 2017. | Includes bibliographical references and index.

Identifiers: LCCN 2017014809 | ISBN 9780691177359 (hardcover : alk. paper)

Subjects: LCSH: United States—Church history—21st century. | Evangelicalism—United States. | Christianity and culture—United States. Green family. | Christianity—Influence. | Museum of the Bible. | Hobby Lobby (Firm)

Classification: LCC BR526 .M675 2017 | DDC 261.70973/09051—dc23 LC record available at https://lccn.loc.gov/2017014809

British Library Cataloging-in-Publication Data is available

This book has been composed in Sabon and Helvetica Neue

Printed on acid-free paper. ∞

Printed in the United States of America

10 9 8 7 6 5 4 3 2 1

CONTENTS

PREFACE

THIS BOOK BEGAN WITH A SINGLE CONVERSATION: AN INNOCUOUS catch-up chat with a friend from graduate school, the eminent New Testament scholar Brent Nongbri, in a conference center lobby four years ago. It was supposed to be the usual old friends reuniting and updating one another on their lives. But when he mentioned in passing that the Green family, better known as the owners of Hobby Lobby, were collecting biblical manuscripts, the nature of the conversation changed. "Tell me about that," I said, as I removed my laptop from its case. "This is the first time a friend has taken notes during a social chat," he joked. And this was how we first learned about the Greens of Oklahoma City.

At the time, we had no idea how expansive the influence of the Green family was; our interest was piqued entirely by the sheer peculiarity of it all. This was in 2013, before plans for the Museum of the Bible in Washington, D.C., were widely known, before the Greens' lawsuit against the U.S. Department of Health and Human Services took over our national stage via the Supreme Court, before their Bible curriculum chartered a course through the Oklahoma education system, and before a significant number of biblical scholars—our colleagues and, in some cases, our friends—signed up to work privately on the artifacts acquired by the Green family. The collection had been quietly gathering momentum for a few years, but the wheels of the Museum of the Bible organization were only just beginning to turn.

Initially, we were merely curious: why would a crafting family be interested in these artifacts? What would their collection mean for the academy in general? Our curiosity turned to concern when a number of papyrologists (specialists in ancient manuscripts), most prominently Roberta Mazza, began to voice concerns about the origins of the artifacts in the Green Collection and the qualifications of those handling them. Now we wondered if this prominent and secretive collection was properly documented or if it contained illicit artifacts that should never have been brought into the country. We remain, however, interested primarily in why these initiatives appeal to the Greens at all—in how their understanding of the Bible influences their decisions, and in the worldview that stands behind that understanding.

Our intent is to tell, with as much empathy and fairness as we can, the story of the Green family's efforts to use the Bible to shape the religious climate of the United States. Over the course of the last decade, the Green family have quietly become one of the most significant and powerful religious forces in this country. They have, as we will show, ambitions reach to a global audience. The lawsuit for which they are so well known, and which we barely graze in this book, is to our minds no more important than their work to shape the religious consciousness of Americans, and arguably the world, through various Bible-related initiatives.

The purpose of this book is not merely to describe what they have done and plan to do, or even to survey the manifold problems with those initiatives, but also to explain the beliefs—religious and otherwise—that inform their actions and the principles that guide them. This book is about the Greens, but it is also about a set of American values, in which success in business is viewed as a qualification for success in any area of life; in which the United States is first and foremost a Christian country and religious freedom is the magnanimous gesture of that powerful majority; and in which individualism and property rights trump free access to and public ownership of knowledge and learning.

This book—which covers the global antiquities market, efforts to place an apologetic view of the Bible in public schools, the construction of the world's largest Bible museum, and the privatization of the academy—would not have been so engaging for us were it not for the personal charisma and sincerity of the Green family themselves. This story is more complicated and nuanced than a fiction-worthy conspiracy theory. It is precisely because we respect and admire their sincerity that we found their story so compelling.

PREFACE

This is a book about the power and influence of one billionaire Christian family and the cultural commitments that have made them so powerful, but it should not be understood as an effort to discredit their motivations.

The past four years have taken us on a journey of discovery: we have learned a great deal about antiquities-collecting; the tax codes governing charitable organizations; evangelical subculture; a variety of laws, governing religious freedom, education, and customs; and, most of all, human nature. This journey would not have been possible without the generosity and assistance of hundreds of colleagues, professionals, and interested parties who gave freely of their time and learning and some of whose names are listed below. Among them are a number of members of the Green family, as well as administrators and employees of the Museum of the Bible. We remain grateful for their willingness to meet or correspond with us.

Particular thanks are due to Lance Allred, Christian Askeland, Roger Bagnall, Paul Baylor, Lee Biondi, Douglas Boin, Sarah Bond, Neil Brodie, Scott Carroll, Mark Chancey, Randall Chesnutt, Ray Clemens, Tasha Dobbin-Bennett, Eugene Donadoni, Ellen Doon, Josephine Dru, Robert Duke, Craig Evans, Michelle Farmer, Jeffrey Fish, John Fitzgerald, Brad Gregory, Michael Holmes, Michael Johnson, Brice Jones, John Kutsko, Karl Kutz, Steven Green, Ron Hendel, Hugh Houghton, Jennifer Larsen, Roberta Mazza, Christoph Markschies, Mark McKenna, Lauren Green McAfee, Michael McAfee, Suzanne Mekking, William Noah, Brent Nongbri, Jerry Pattengale, Edouard Planche, Rebecca Raphael, Harley Roberts, Melanie Ross, Caroline Schroeder, Marcel Sigrist, W. Andrew Smith, Cary Summers, Emanuel Tov, David Trobisch, Dan Wallace, Peter Williams, and Lisa Wolfe.

In addition to those named above there were many scholars, students, officials, and former employees of Hobby Lobby or the Museum of the Bible who agreed to speak with us on the condition that they remain anonymous. In keeping with the standards and best practices of investigative journalism, we want both to honor their contribution and respect their wishes. They are not named here, but this book would have been impossible without them.

We are grateful for the work of our editor Fred Appel, our agent Joe Veltre, and Princeton University Press, all of whom believed in this project and our desire to write something that was not mere muckraking. Two anonymous readers from Princeton University Press were unfailingly helpful and supportive of the project, and we are grateful to them for their comments and suggestions. Before we came to Princeton two news outlets—*The Atlantic Monthly* and *The Daily Beast*—published forerunners to this story. We remain grateful to them for their trust and commitment. In particular we want to thank Noah Shachtman, executive editor of *The Daily Beast*, who truly treated us as family.

Finally we are thankful to our families, both personal and academic, for humoring us with this project, which very much fell in our path but which we could not help but pick up. Special thanks here are due to Gillian Eversman, Zara Baden-Eversman, Iris Baden-Eversman, Justin Foa, Max Foa, Luke Foa, Alice Robb, Meghan Henning, David Cohen, Kathryn Paget, John Cunningham, Catherine O'Malley, Jessica Baron, Christopher Baron, Blake Leyerle, Jeff Berger, Autumn Henry, Lauren Harris, Nathan Gurr, and Grace Watkins.

While Bible scholars might seem to be all of a piece, we are not the kind of academics most directly affected by the Greens' actions. We are neither specialists in ancient manuscripts nor especially concerned with the transmission of those texts. We could happily conduct our own research without ever feeling the need to consult the Green Collection. We have not, unlike some of our colleagues, had to make hard choices between access to resources and complicity with an organization we find, broadly speaking, unethical. This book is written for our colleagues; with profound gratitude to those who first spoke out and with admiration for those who have taken principled stands. Our hope is that, in the future, others will not have to make these choices.

BIBLE NATION

INTRODUCTION

IN 1804 A YOUNG MAN NAMED WILLIAM COLGATE, LOOKING FOR work, arrived in New York City. His family had come to the United States from Kent in southeast England and had settled in Hartford County, Maryland. They purchased a farm there, but the title to the property was found to be illegitimate. It was the first in a long line of heavy financial losses for the Colgates, such that at the tender age of seventeen William became the breadwinner for the family.

He began life as a clerk, offering to work for free in the principle chandlery in the city. He soon rose to the rank of manager and at twenty-two opened his own firm. Business was a pleasure to him, as well as an opportunity to do good. From the very beginning he committed himself to donating 10 percent of his earnings to charitable causes and often surpassed this goal, donating 20, 30, and eventually 50 percent of his earnings each year. For his remaining fifty-one years he lived a life of industry, application, and philanthropy, attending a Baptist church for much of his life.

This story was published first in Colgate's *New York Chronicle* obituary and then in abbreviated form for the first volume of *The Young Men's Magazine*, a Christian publication intended for the moral benefit of its titular audience.[1] Colgate's is one of a generation of hard-working Protestant success stories, men for whom hard work and religious piety were closely linked, for whom directing profits into charity was a moral obligation, and for whom education was the primary goal. His legacy is still felt today, not only at Colgate University but at the many other institutions of higher learning he supported.

Colgate represents one of many rags-to-riches stories that undergird and illustrate the American Dream. His Christian principles, proudly displayed, made him different from the robber barons who profited from the railways. He became—for readers of *Young Men's Magazine*—a model to be emulated. He was not only wealthy, he was devout. His home, as his obituaries stated, was a pillar of the state and a "nursery for the Church." His piety, his patriotism, and his business acumen were all folded together into a single recipe for success.

As remarkable as his story is, Colgate was just one of a cadre of successful Christian businessmen who intermingled religion and entrepreneurship. The evangelical leader Dwight L. Moody, eponym and founder of the Moody Bible Institute in Chicago, is another example. A shoe salesman, Moody explicitly sought to bring his business acumen to bear on the spread of a socially activist evangelicalism.[2] John Wanamaker, the Philadelphia department store magnate, combined religion and retail into a powerful notion of Christian stewardship.[3] Beginning in the last third of the nineteenth century, stories like these became typical for popular books and articles that identified Christianity and capitalism.[4] Alongside success stories like Colgate's ran books like Bruce Fairchild Barton's *The Man Nobody Knows*, a life of Jesus that portrayed the Savior as the "founder of Modern Business."[5] Colgate and men like him credited God for their success and invested in the divine plan. And in exchange for tithes, God repaid them with capital gains and success. "If you will allow me to make money to be used in Your service, You will have the glory," Henry Crowell, the founder of Quaker Oats, put it.[6] Their theology of tithing anticipated what would later be called "the prosperity gospel."

If he had been born a century later, William Colgate might have been friends with the Green family of Oklahoma City, owners of the crafting empire Hobby Lobby. Like Colgate, the Greens are devout Christians, businessmen, and patriots, and, also like Colgate, they are seen as living embodiments of the American Dream.

In his youth, David Green felt inadequate. The current chairman of Hobby Lobby was born in Emporia, Kansas, in 1941, one of six sons of a small-town preacher, but he was the only one who didn't follow his parents into the ministry. Not having that call, he felt for years that he was, in his own words, the "black sheep" of the family.[7] He thought that God had passed him over. When he called his mother to tell her that he was the nation's youngest manager in the chain of five-and-dime stores, TG&Y, she was unimpressed: "Oh yeah, what are you doing for the Lord?" As a child he grew up poor—dirt poor. His father migrated from one small congregation to the next, never preaching to churches larger than fifty or seventy-five people, before landing in Altus, Oklahoma. The family survived on small donations from congregants, sometimes going for weeks without eating meat.

Green's path was not ministry; retail was in his heart. In 1970, following a brief stint in the Air Force Reserve designed to make him eligible for management positions, the twenty-nine-year-old Green borrowed $600 (about six weeks' worth of his wages) to buy a molding chopper and form Greco Products, a company that manufactured miniature picture frames.[8] His home became a makeshift factory: his wife Barbara oversaw operations at the kitchen table and his young children Steve and Mart were paid seven cents apiece to assemble the frames. Barbara would do most of the manufacturing herself and would take their infant daughter Darsee in her carrier to ship the frames.

In 1972, David and Barbara opened their first store, in a snug studio-apartment-sized space in Oklahoma City. A mere three years later, on the back of the hippie obsession with beads, the Greens were able to acquire a second, 6,000-square-foot store. Against the wishes of his wife, Green quit his job at competitor TG&Y, and in the next thirty years took his company from annual sales of $100,000 to more than $3 billion. TG&Y no longer exists; many of its former retail locations are now Hobby Lobbies.

What began as a living-room family photo-frame assembly line grew into a retail giant. By 2012, Hobby Lobby had 520 superstores in 42 states, and the Green family, which owns 100% of the company, was ranked at number 79 on the Forbes list of the four hundred richest Americans, with an estimated net worth of $4.5 billion.

Every step along the way Green quietly stayed true to his religious beliefs, often at the expense of company profits. The company pays for public printing of images of the biblical stories of

Christmas and Easter in the local paper of every town with a Hobby Lobby store; these stores are closed on Sundays in order to give employees time to attend church. The company employs three Christian chaplains, who dispense financial as well as spiritual advice, and offered a free health clinic to staff at its headquarters long before free healthcare came into political vogue.

Green has raised the minimum wage for full-time employees by a dollar an hour every year since 2009, with the result that their minimum hourly wage is currently $15. It's a gesture that he grounds in his religious beliefs. He told Forbes in 2012, "God tells us to go forth into the world and teach the gospel to every creature. He doesn't say skim from your employees to do that."[9]

As is to be expected with any company of this size, there are some murmurings of discontent. In 2013, a Jewish blogger inquiring about the lack of Hannukah-themed merchandise at a New Jersey Hobby Lobby was told by a salesperson, "We don't cater to you people."[10] A local representative can hardly be said to speak for the Green family themselves, but the absence of Jewish items can be contrasted with the interest in Christmas decorations. For the first twenty years of the company's existence, David and Barbara Green personally selected the Christmas items that were sold in stores. Amid public accusations of anti-Semitism and discrimination, the family was forced to apologize, citing their donations to Israel's Holocaust museum, Yad Vashem, for example, as proof that the company respected Judaism.

The incident appeared to be isolated. But there are rumblings that all is not well for those working inside the gates of the Greens' Kingdom. In the past the Greens have proudly stated that they have never been sued by disgruntled former employees. Yet lawsuits have indeed been filed: for gender discrimination, discrimination against those with disabilities, lengthy work hours, and improper documentation of work hours.[11] These kinds of accusations are standard for large corporations, but, unusually, those leveled against Hobby Lobby have been withdrawn under threat of countersuit.[12] The reason: all Hobby Lobby employees sign an agreement that they will not sue the company, even in cases of sexual harassment.[13] Instead they agree to either secular or religious mediation, the results of which remain private.

Throughout, the Greens have seen God as the ultimate owner and director of the company. In 1985 the company lost $1 million, and its bank was threatening to foreclose. The company had aggressively expanded in the '70s and early '80s, but it was a period of false security: the stores were stocking expensive gifts and high-end luggage, both of which failed to sell with the economic downtown. David Green recalls praying at his desk on a daily basis, asking God to tell him where they had gone wrong. In retrospect, he says, they had gotten prideful, and so God left them to manage the company alone. That feeling, he says, lasted about a year; since then he has depended on the Lord for guidance.

The sharp side of divine management was felt again when Hobby Lobby decided to cease Sunday trading. The decision was taken so that employees could put God first in their lives, but in the late '80s, when they decided to close the stores, they were doing around $100 million worth of business on Sundays alone. Today, that number would be in excess of $250 million. While the family collectively felt that God was instructing them to cease Sunday trading, they "didn't have enough faith to close them all." So the rollback was staggered state by state. Nebraska, home to three stores, closed first, and Texas, which then housed around sixty stores, closed last. During this period when they were "halfway obedient" sales started to slump. It was only when all of the stores were closed that things picked back up. "We had done what we were supposed to do, then at that time we saw things were going in the right way." There was a direct correlation between fulfilling God's commands and company profits.

The principle had been instilled in David Green as a child. Despite his family's poverty and itinerant lifestyle, any gift they received—either from their garden or from congregants—they tithed; that is, they gave a tenth back to God. He has said that "if we picked cotton and we made a dollar, we would give a dime of it to the church, so that's just something that was bred in us. We think that God would reward that."

As a result, like Colgate and other Christian moguls, the Green family is committed to dedicating a substantial portion of their revenue to charity. They started small, supporting the distribution of Bible tracts around the world. In keeping with David's missionary church roots, evangelization was the soul of their charitable work. Most of the primary recipients of Hobby Lobby funds—charities like One Hope, Need Him, Every Home for Christ, Every Tribe Every Nation, and Wycliffe Translators—are concerned with spreading the Word of God and promoting Christian evangelization.[14]

Hobby Lobby donates half of its pretax earnings to charity and invests them in a portfolio of evangelical ministries. The total sum of charitable contributions is unknown, but estimates by Forbes in 2012 placed the company's total giving at upwards of $500 million.[15] If Hobby Lobby were ever to be sold, the structure of the company is such that 90 percent of the proceeds from the sale would go to ministry work. Dedication to philanthropy has kept the Hobby Lobby stores privately owned; in an interview in 2009 David Green said that the most important reason he declined to take the company public was that it would have prevented him from donating company profits to missionary endeavors. Missionary work, Green has said, is his contribution. He never became a minister like his siblings, but as Hobby Lobby has prospered the family has become convinced that Green's business acumen is both God-given and providential. Had David been a newspaper man, his son Steve told us, they would be in a very different position today, given the precarious state of the print media. The historian Darren Dochuk describes the evangelical acceptance of this link between business success and faith-based giving as a "corporate formula, which at its essence meant: more money, more ministry."[16]

Involvement in Hobby Lobby's charitable projects comes with the kind of strings that many philanthropists attach to their gifts. Like the Ford Foundation, the Rockefeller Foundation, or the Bill & Melinda Gates Foundation, the Greens have expectations of those with whom they work. Unlike those organizations, Hobby Lobby's requirements are religious: beneficiaries must pass a doctrinal vetting process, "which includes questions about the Virgin Birth."[17] Only about one in ten ventures that approach the Greens passes muster, both for doctrinal and financial reasons. In deciding how to allocate funds, Green distinguishes between causes that are merely "good" (like building hospitals, or improving childhood literacy) and causes that are "great" (like the dissemination of God's Word).[18] This conviction gives a laser-sharp focus to Hobby Lobby's philanthropic work. The Greens focus exclusively on spreading the Good News: they have sponsored a free Bible app, multiple international evangelical Christian missionary endeavors, and programming that helps children understand the Bible even if they are unable to read.

If Hobby Lobby's choice of causes seems impractical, it is a choice that David Green would sincerely make for himself. He has said, "If I die without food or without eternal salvation, I want to die without food."[19]

The Greens are poster children for the American Dream. David and Barbara have enjoyed a lengthy and successful marriage. Their sons—the current CEO, Steve, and Chief Strategic Officer, Mart—are family men who have been married to their respective wives for over thirty years. And their daughter, Darsee Lett, is Creative Director for the Hobby Lobby stores. Together this family, as a family, turned their small business into an empire.

But there is one key aspect of the Green family that sets them apart: they didn't just want to turn their mom-and-pop home-crafts store into a billion-dollar empire, or even merely to give back to society once they had made it big. They wanted to play a role in the course of human history. As Mark Rutland, the former president of Oral Roberts University, put it, "the Greens are Kingdom givers."[20]

Indeed, David Green aspires to personal cosmic impact. "I want to know that I have affected people for eternity," he said. "I believe I am. I believe once someone knows Christ as their personal savior, I've affected eternity. I matter 10 billion years from now."[21] Green has been clear that God is the author of his success, but there's no shortage of ego here, either.

Almost all of the Greens' philanthropic activity once took place without fanfare and out of the eye of the general public. They could walk the streets of Oklahoma City, Steve Green told us, and nobody knew who they were. In Christian circles, however, things were very different. They were well known as the largest Christian philanthropists in North America: everyone from the celebrity evangelist Jerry Falwell to enterprising Bible scholars beat a path to their door. They receive hundreds of charitable requests each month.[22]

With a much-publicized lawsuit against the U.S. over the provision for birth control in the 2010 Affordable Care Act, the Greens were suddenly transformed into public figures on a national scale, transitioning from salt-of-the-earth billionaires to iconic patriotic Christians. Their Supreme Court case, *Burwell v. Hobby Lobby*, which the Greens won in June 2014, played out on the world's stage. Hobby Lobby was represented by the Becket Fund, a nonprofit legal organization that specializes in religious freedom cases. This was the same firm that in 1999 successfully fought for the rights of two Sunni Muslim police officers to be exempted from their government employer's no-beards policy and in 2009 defended the right of a Santeria priest to perform animal sacrifice in his own home. The Greens' lawsuit too was about religious principles; more specifically, it was about their rights as owners of a closely held company to refuse, in accordance with their religious beliefs, to provide insurance covering certain medical procedures.

The crux of the issue for the Greens was that the regulations issued under the 2010 Patient Protection and Affordable Care Act (more popularly known as "Obamacare") required them, as owners of the privately held company Hobby Lobby, to provide abortion-inducing drugs and devices to their employees. In their original complaint, they stated that their "religious beliefs forbid them from participating in, providing access to, paying for, training others to engage in, or otherwise supporting" four medical devices: Plan B One-Step (the "morning-after pill"), Ella (another emergency contraceptive pill), and two forms of intrauterine devices.[23] The Greens maintain that life begins at conception and that, inasmuch as these devices interfered with pregnancy after that moment, they were abortifacients.[24] In insisting that they provide medical coverage for these products, the government mandate, the Greens argued, forced them "to violate their deeply held religious beliefs under threat of heavy fines" ($1.3 million per day) and that doing so was unconstitutional and a violation of the "American traditions of individual liberty, religious tolerance, and limited government." As evangelicals who ran their company in accordance with biblical principles, they requested an exemption from the mandate on the grounds that it violated their First Amendment rights and also the terms of the 1993 Religious Freedom Restoration Act. The Free Exercise Clause of the First Amendment states that Congress shall not pass laws prohibiting the free exercise of religion; the RFRA maintains that the federal government is responsible for accepting additional obligations to protect religious exercise.[25]

The case travelled from the U.S. District Court for the Western District of Oklahoma, to the U.S. Court of Appeals for the Tenth Circuit, and finally to the Supreme Court, where it was consolidated with another case, *Conestoga Wood Specialties v. Sebelius*. The 2014 Supreme Court decision, which was split 5–4, sided with Hobby Lobby.[26] Writing for the majority opinion, Justice Alito stated, "The companies in the cases before us are closely held corporations, each owned and controlled by members of a single family, and no one has disputed the sincerity of their religious beliefs." The Court's decision did not address Hobby Lobby's constitutional claims under the Free Exercise Clause of the First Amendment, but in addressing the statutory claim noted that for-profit corporations could be considered persons under the RFRA. Because there were other ways that the government could guarantee access to cost-free contraception, the Supreme Court judged that the HHS contraceptive mandate placed a substantial burden on Christian companies like Hobby Lobby and, thus, violated the RFRA.[27] While the lawsuit was won on the basis of the RFRA, the Greens continue to describe themselves as exercising and defending the First Amendment rights guaranteed to them by the Constitution.[28]

It was a case fought on statutory and constitutional principles, but a hefty part of the Becket Fund's legal strategy involved telling a particular story about the Greens. That story was one of a Christian family from Oklahoma who lived the American Dream and whose livelihood was under threat because of an aggressive antireligious government health mandate. In a statement to the press in 2012, David Green said, "Our family is now being forced to choose between following the laws of the land that we love or maintaining the religious beliefs that have made our business successful and have supported our family and thousands of our employees and their families. We simply cannot abandon our religious beliefs to comply with this mandate."[29]

It was not just the Greens who were on trial: it was the American Dream itself. A promotional video posted on the Becket Fund's website for the Hobby Lobby lawsuit began with the rags-to-riches story of David and Barbara Green before pronouncing: "What's at stake here is whether you're able to keep your religion when you open a family business."[30] In 2017, David Green described himself as politically disinterested: "I like to be left alone as a businessman and do my business without the government interfering. And so we had to sue the government or take life, that was our two choices. And so we didn't want to sue our government, we love this country, but we were forced to do that and now we're back to running our business."[31]

The lawsuit introduced the Green family and their company to America. Many Americans regarded their lifestyles, now greatly scrutinized, as a pleasing medley of aspirational and down-home: they fly in private planes, but they eat Panera and Chik-Fil-A. When we interviewed Steve Green in 2015, he greeted us in an off-brand golf shirt, Levis, and sneakers. To many observers it seemed that these, the most wholesome of the superrich, were being targeted precisely, and solely, because they were Christian.[32]

As the lawsuit progressed, and even more so once it had been won, the Greens became Christian celebrities. They speak regularly at evangelical conferences, and even their political endorsements become national news.[33] They are paradigmatic examples of the kind of politically influential evangelical lay leaders discussed by Lydia Bean in her book *The Politics of Evangelical Identity*, and simultaneously part of the kaleidoscope of responses to the crisis of authority that historian Molly Worthen has identified in her work on evangelical communities.[34] In March 2016, David Green endorsed Marco Rubio for the GOP presidential nomination. Green's endorsement was announced the same day as that of Mitt Romney, and yet it still received attention. In an interview on Fox Business, Green was presented as a "man of God," his authority buttressed by his dual credentials as billionaire and famous Christian culture warrior. In the wake of the Trump tidal wave, Green, like many evangelical leaders, changed his position; it is yet another indication of his prominence that his endorsement of Trump was published as an op-ed in USA Today.[35]

Their transition from entrepreneurs to political taste-makers may seem strange, but from the time of Andrew Jackson onward, success in one sphere of American life—at first the military, later business—came to be seen as evidence of universal competency. In a country founded on the explicit intention of replacing inherited status and aristocracy with individual democratic opportunity and meritocratic accomplishment, the blistering success of families like the Greens is generally understood as a transferable qualification. The backdrop for the Greens' particular understanding of the intersection of business success and adherence to the Bible is a peculiarly American brand of what since World War II has been called "prosperity gospel." At its core, prosperity gospel is the belief that God intends for humans to enjoy physical and financial good health, and that this kind of flourishing can be secured by, and even guaranteed to, those who possess faith and support the appropriate kind of religious causes. The roots of the American prosperity gospel go back to early twentieth-century Pentecostalism but are intertwined, as Kate Bowler has shown in her study of the movement, with the ideals of pragmatism, individualism, and upward mobility so prized by traditional articulations of "the American Dream."[36] This "new gospel of wealth," as historian Darren Dochuk calls it, brought conservative fiscal beliefs into the pews, and, momentously, reshaped the nature of Southern evangelicalism itself: it was, as Dochuk says, "no longer the poor person's religion."[37]

A much wider circle of evangelicals and nonevangelicals holds to the same basic structure of expectation even if they are not part of the particular subset of Pentecostal preachers that coined the term. Thus, though Pentecostalism was somewhat unusual for Oklahoma City, David Green's family held beliefs that were shared by many varieties of American Protestants; his household had practiced tithing and trusted in the almost contractual nature of faith as a means of securing God's protection. This is the central thesis of David Green's 2017 book *Giving It All Away . . . And Getting It Back Again*, in which he argues that the God-given rewards of philanthropy and Christian business are protection in times of stress, stable and joyful family life, and a familial legacy that goes beyond mere wealth.[38] Many of the Greens' discussions of professional failings and success are set against the backdrop of trusting in divine guidance and support. It is a belief system that guided their decision to cease Sunday trading, their interpretation of their financial losses in the 1980s, their Supreme Court battle, and their philanthropic work.

The Greens have been quite open about their belief that business, religion, and government are not separate and distinct spheres. In 2006, years before their famous lawsuit, they ran an Independence Day advertisement featuring quotes from founding fathers about the centrality of religion to education, governance, citizenship, and law. The poster—reprinted regularly since—clearly articulates the belief that the United States is a Christian country; it condemns legal measures that have prohibited prayer in public schools and ties Christianity to the founding of the United States. Unlike the biblical quotations in their Christmas and Easter advertisements, the purpose of which, according to the Greens, is to witness publicly to the truth and primacy of the Gospel message for its own sake, the Independence Day ads openly evangelize for the biblical foundations and Christian character of the Unites States. The 2006 advertisement, which has run seven times, included quotations about the Christian character of the country from a plethora of founding fathers, Supreme Court justices and rulings, U.S. presidents, and foreign commentators. In its original iteration it included quotations from the 1636 Harvard and 1737 Yale Student guidelines about the necessity of religious education and religious educators. It also added commentary to the 1892 *Church of the Holy Trinity v. U.S. Supreme Court* decision that declared that the United States is a Christian country. This decision, the commentary notes, "cited dozens of court rulings and legal documents as precedents to arrive at this ruling; but in 1962 when the Supreme Court struck down voluntary prayer in schools it did so without using any such precedent." The quotation that follows the commentary is from the decision in *Vidal v. Girard's Executors* (1844) which encouraged that the Bible "be read and taught as a divine revelation in [schools]." It is difficult to read these statements as anything other than a critique of the current religiopolitical climate.

What these advertisements represent is a particular understanding of the relationship between the founding of America and the Bible, and between America's biblical foundations and the political obligations of today's legislators and citizens. This narrative is not unique to the Greens—it is a commonly held belief with roots in the colonial New England Puritans' sense of chosenness. That regional belief became national at the time of the American Revolution, when patriots saw their war for independence against Britain as particularly blessed by God.[39] This belief helps explain the Greens' explicitly stated interest in using their wealth and influence to educate the public, and especially legislators, about the centrality of the Bible. For the Greens, this is not an inappropriate effort to force religion onto the nation; it is an attempt to return the country to its properly Christian roots.

The Greens' actions are intelligible and understandable, especially in light of the moral imperative they feel to spread the Gospel. They are not content merely to profess Christianity; they want to witness to the world and improve the moral character of the nation. Their controversial efforts, as people of faith, to influence politics do not constitute a deliberate attempt to trespass across the boundary between church and state. They are merely enacting their constitutional right to advocate for their view of how the country should be run, like any other individual, family, community, or lobbying group. The authenticity of their faith commitments is not in doubt; all of their actions are sincere and internally coherent, and to many people they are also commendable and even heroic. Their actions are not, however, consonant with the public persona they have projected in the media, as a family that had quietly gone about its private business before being morally obligated by oppressive government intervention to finally take a stand. Long before the HHS mandate was even a gleam in President Obama's eye, the Greens had been religiously motivated political activists. David Green may describe himself in almost libertarian terms as a businessman who likes to be left alone to simply run his company, but this self-description jars with his family's actions and activism.[40] The Greens' carefully crafted media image is inaccurate. If they are Christian heroes now, they were always Christian heroes. If they are culture warriors now, that has been the case for many years. They may not have sought the spotlight, but they always desired to convert the nation. They believe in the church-state divide but also, and absolutely coherently, in the rights of religion to try and influence public values and political choices.

In the last decade, the Greens have focused their efforts on a web of projects centered around the Bible. The prioritizing of the Bible is nothing new to them, of course; as evangelicals, the Scripture stands at the heart of their faith. In their recent ventures, however, they have gone far beyond funding Bible translations and distributing Bible tracts. Leadership in this initiative has also shifted, from David Green to his son Steve, the current CEO of Hobby Lobby. Although David was raised in the Pentecostal tradition, and raised his own children in that church, Steve and his family belong to a Baptist congregation in Oklahoma City. Such shifting allegiances are not uncommon among evangelicals.[41] Indeed, this change, according Steve Green, is more about comfort than it is about doctrine: his church adheres to most of the same faith claims as the Pentecostal community he grew up in, including the absolute centrality of the Bible: "We believe the Bible is God's Word and has ultimate authority in our beliefs and actions," says the statement of faith on the church's website.[42] There are a thousand flavors of evangelicalism, and theirs is just one.[43] As is the case with the prosperity gospel, many individuals and congregations have their own variation of these core beliefs.

In public speeches, as well as in conversation with us, Steve Green regularly invokes the term "biblical worldview." This phrase, which may seem opaque to the nonevangelical, has a specific resonance within Green's faith community. The term was popularized in the 1960s in the work of the influential evangelical

Francis Schaeffer, and it has since thoroughly permeated evangelical discourse.[44] Molly Worthen, in her book *Apostles of Reason*, lists a range of "worldview"-based projects: "Worldview Academy" camps in Texas; the "Worldview Initiative in Tennessee; a "Worldview Curriculum" at Whitefield College in Florida; a certificate in "Worldview Studies" from Boyce College in Louisville.[45] Though it uses the particular referent of the Bible, "biblical worldview" is in fact an all-encompassing concept: as the website for Focus on the Family puts it, "Someone with a biblical worldview believes his primary reason for existence is to love and serve God." In language that echoes that of Steve Green's church, it goes on: "A biblical worldview is based on the infallible Word of God. When you believe the Bible is entirely true, then you allow it to be the foundation of everything you say and do."[46] This is fully consonant with how the Greens, both Steve and David, and millions of other Americans describe their lives and their livelihoods. What it implies—and what runs through almost every aspect of the Greens' work, though they may not be fully aware of it—is a basic equation of the Bible with an identifiably conservative brand of Protestant Christianity.

What is unexpected about the Greens' current projects, therefore, is not that they should be interested in promoting the Bible. It is, rather, the very public nature of these ventures, which stands in stark contrast to the relatively low profile with which they have carried out most of their philanthropic work. In November 2009, the Green family began a sweeping project of collecting biblical manuscripts. In the eight years since then they have acquired tens of thousands of artifacts. Their rate of acquisition is unparalleled: until recently, when we published our 2016 article about it in *The Atlantic*, the publicity for what came to be known as the Green Collection called it the largest privately held collection of biblical antiquities in the world.[47] While there are more prestigious university collections in existence, none is positioned to have the same kind of impact as the Green Collection, which is destined for public consumption on a massive scale.

The eventual home of the collection will be the Museum of the Bible, a vast 430,000-square-foot facility slated to open in Washington, D.C., in the fall of 2017.[48] The museum will include numerous exhibits, many on loan from world-class universities and collections, but will be drawn predominantly from the Green Collection. The Museum of the Bible is owned and will be operated by Museum of the Bible, Inc. (hereafter MOTB, to help distinguish it from the identically named physical museum), a nonprofit organization established by the Green family in 2010. Steve Green is listed as the founder and chairman of the board. He dedicates approximately half of his time to MOTB.

Unlike the other charities to which Hobby Lobby is committed, the Museum of the Bible describes itself as having an explicitly nonsectarian orientation and mission. Time and time again representatives told us that the museum would not evangelize to its visitors or issue them invitations to be born again. Instead, it would showcase the agreement among Jews, Catholics, and Protestants about the centrality of the Bible and its impact in the world.

The Greens have sponsored two other major Bible-centered projects, directly tied to their collection of biblical antiquities and the accompanying museum, both in the realm of education. The antiquities collection has not merely been left to sit unexamined in the Hobby Lobby warehouses; almost since they began collecting, the Greens and MOTB have funded a small group of scholars, along with their undergraduate and graduate students, who are tasked with studying the collection's artifacts—a project known as the Green Scholars Initiative. This investment in higher education, involving some of the most prominent names in scholarship on religion, is unusual in the evangelical community, which has often shied away from direct engagement with the world of secular academia. As the museum project has been progressing, MOTB has, under Steve Green's leadership, also developed an elective Bible curriculum for use in public high schools both in the United States and, more recently, Israel and the United Kingdom. Like the museum itself, this curriculum aims to be explicitly nonsectarian, intending simply to educate participating students about the Bible's history and its cultural impact.

Given the strongly and openly evangelical bent of the Green family's charitable giving up to this point, the emphasis on the nonsectarian nature of these projects is new and noteworthy. The soft-spoken open-tent approach of the official statements provided by MOTB contrasts with the fiery passion of David Green's statements about the imperative to spread the Gospel. In 2009 he concluded an interview on his charitable giving saying, "I still believe you must be born again. I still believe the Bible says go and tell the world and preach the gospel. That's just the basic foundation of what I believe. . . . How can I just sit here and get comfortable when there are people that need to know Christ when I can do something about it?"[49] Many of those who have been involved from the beginning in building the museum share his priorities. Bob Hoskins, for example, the secretary of the board of MOTB and one of three individuals listed on every one of the nonprofit's filings, has made it his life's work to proselytize. The purpose of his own charity, One Hope, is "to affect destiny by providing God's Eternal Word to all children and youth of the World."[50] Rick Warren, the famous conservative megachurch pastor and best-selling author, also sits on the board. At first blush, it is strange to imagine that this group could be convinced to pour funds into an organization that is committed to avoiding explicit evangelization.

Some of this ostensible disconnect may be understood through the lens of the term that is used so frequently by Steve Green and MOTB: "nonsectarian." To the casual reader, "nonsectarian" can easily read as a synonym for nonreligious, impartial, or unbiased—and this may in fact be what Green and his affiliates hope to communicate by it. But the term has a history within Protestant circles that suggests a different frame of reference. This can be seen in part in the word "sectarian." Judaism, Catholicism, Islam, and even atheism are not "sects," but complete religious (or nonreligious) groups. Sects are subgroups within a given religion, and this was the way that the term "nonsectarian" was originally used in Protestant Christianity. It originated early in the mid-nineteenth century as a way of unifying Protestants of many varieties behind efforts to prescribe daily readings from the King James Bible in the nation's emerging public schools.[51]

In the mid-twentieth century, "nonsectarian" became code for "not fundamentalist," used by moderate evangelicals who were trying, especially in founding more ecumenical Christian colleges and universities, to distinguish themselves from conservative fundamentalist Protestantism. This is still the way that most Protestants employ the term: not to mean "nonreligious," but to mean "not denominationally specific"—though still within the broader world of Protestant Christianity. At times, it carries an even broader meaning: "nondoctrinal," or "generically religious," as in a public prayer that invokes God but without, for instance, closing with "in Jesus' name." Even this more general use, however, still implies a basic framework of Christian faith, although a more inclusive one.[52]

In this light, the constant invocation of "nonsectarianism" by Steve Green and MOTB makes somewhat more sense: while they speak of bringing the Bible to a wider public without attempting to evangelize, they may not be envisioning a purely academic, intellectual, historical, or cultural appreciation of the book. There is still an underlying religious commitment, which, given the personal beliefs of the Green family, should not be surprising. In fact, Green admits that his own understanding of the import of "nonsectarianism" has undergone a process of change over the past ten years: from something like "not fundamentalist," though still deeply evangelical, to something closer to "generically religious." It is not clear, however, that he has ever understood it to mean "nonreligious": whenever he touts the nonsectarian nature of the museum, he highlights the involvement of Catholic and Jewish groups (like the Vatican and the Israel Antiquities Authority) alongside his own Protestant tradition.

This book is an exploration of the unusual intersection of faith and business, biblical worldview and academic scholarship, religion and the public sphere—all of which are brought together in the Bible-focused initiatives of the Green family, Hobby Lobby, and MOTB. In the chapters that follow, we will look closely at these four major projects: the antiquities collection, the scholarly study of that collection, the Bible curriculum and related educational ventures, and the Museum of the Bible. Taken together, these make up a coherent attempt on the part of the Greens not only to promote the Bible, but to promote a particular conservative evangelical understanding of the Bible—even though they may not be entirely aware that this is in fact what they are doing. Indeed, part of what makes the Greens so compelling is that they are both transparent in their essential faith commitments and at the same time often unable to see the assumptions they bring with them to this project and the impact that those commitments have on the projects that they pursue.

This disconnect may be largely responsible for the fact that none of these projects has proceeded smoothly. Many of the issues that the Greens have faced in launching these ventures were reasonably predictable, yet the Greens were seemingly unprepared for them: questions surrounding the means by which they amassed their antiquities collection; scholarly pushback against their forays into academic research; legal challenges to their Bible curriculum; editorials and other forms of public skepticism about their Bible museum.

A charitable read on the bumps in the road is that the Greens were out of their depth, poorly informed, and a little naïve when it came to the worlds of antiquities collecting, academics, and museum governance. Certainly there is truth to this: the Greens are gifted retailers, but they lack experience in almost every area that they have waded into in recent years. They do not see this as a stumbling-block, however. On the contrary, this attitude also comes from the early nineteenth century, when common people relied on the nation's democratic ideology to assert their competence in every sphere of life.[53] The same confidence comes from the American tradition that treats success in one realm of affairs to license authority in other areas of life, including public office and influence.

In interviews, David Green has been ambivalent about the necessity of college for his grandchildren, urging them instead to discern and follow the path that God has chosen for them. David Green and his sons Mart and Steve have only a year of college among them, but they have faith and the conviction that they have succeeded with the assistance of God. It is this combination that gives them the audacity to attempt to reform the public school system, create a new model for the study of biblical artifacts, and build a museum to bring the Bible to the general public. If prosperity is a test of piety, then the relative success of the Green family speaks volumes. Their success is God-given, and, thus, the combination of faith and hard-nosed business practices that has brought them success is blessed with divine approval. The implementation of those practices in the pursuit of furthering God's plan for humanity is thus appropriate.

As academics, we are particularly attuned to the intersection of business and the academy, which in the past few decades has had its own troubled history. The sponsorship of scientific research by "big pharma" and food advocacy groups, the increasing view that academic work is just labor, and the ways in which wealthy donors can impact university operations have all elicited concern.[54] Academics have protested the privatization of their guilds and the ways that this adversely impacts research and academic freedom. The Greens are far from the only business owners to use money to command attention and status within the academy. Philanthropic educational initiatives like the Ford Foundation, the John Templeton Foundation, and ventures funded by the Koch Brothers are engaged in analogous practices. What makes the Green family's involvement remarkable is the ambiguous relationship their donations create among business, learning, and piety. The interventions in higher education of business-savvy self-made Christians without even college degrees creates an unstable hierarchy of values. For academics, qualifications and expertise are key, and for the past two centuries the humanities has, with some notable exceptions, remained relatively or at least conceptually isolated from entrepreneurial control. With the Greens, this is certainly changing, and it is no coincidence that these changes come at the behest of Protestant Americans looking to change the way the broader culture thinks about the Bible. In many ways, the democratizing, antielitist spirit of the Green family's efforts to shortcut academic expertise replicates the Protestant belief that people do not need intermediaries between themselves and God.

The task of this book is to describe, explain, and understand the ways in which the Green family is seeking to bring its biblical worldview to America. With their antiquities collection, their scholarly investments, their curriculum, their museum, and their iconic status in modern America, they are among the most influential and powerful Christians in the United States. The scope of their influence makes it tempting to draw comparison with the Vanderbilts and other industrialist robber barons, but in their sincerity, self-understanding, and business practices they are more like William Colgate. They are "the real deal": a sincere and well-intentioned family doing its best to improve the world in a manner consistent with their religious beliefs and cultural instincts. Even as we raise questions about their actions, we want to understand their motivations, explain their beliefs, and describe the ways that this small but powerful family is reshaping how the Bible is understood by the public.

1

THE COLLECTION

BY ALL ACCOUNTS, DONALD JONATHAN SHIPMAN DIDN'T HAVE THE appearance of a charitable activist. Known to his friends as Johnny, he was a man whose personal style was more mafia don than southern preacher: all pocket squares, chunky gold rings, and fur coats. Dallas born and bred, he dabbled in oil, jewelry, real estate, and movie production, but the heavy-set jaw concealed his deep Baptist roots. As a teenager, he had traveled the country spreading the gospel—even appearing on an NBC special and at Madison Square Garden—and for Shipman a savvy head for business and burning heart for God were complementary assets.

Shipman's interest didn't lie in the movies; he had a vision for something more arcane. His plan was to build a collection of biblical manuscripts and house it in a museum in Dallas. The idea had an aura of Indiana Jones flashiness to it, but Shipman couldn't do it alone: he needed a financial backer and someone with the expertise to identify and evaluate potential acquisitions.

For the latter he turned to Scott Carroll, a charismatic and well-educated New Testament scholar.[1] Carroll had solid experience building collections of manuscripts for wealthy private owners. In the 1990s, Carroll helped the investment banker Robert van Kampen build the eponymously named Van Kampen Collection of Bibles, one of the world's most significant private collections. Carroll had the academic chops to support Shipman's vision, and when Shipman contacted him he was in a difficult spot. The Van Kampen collection had been a dream assignment that endowed him with academic status and provided him access to original manuscripts and a remarkable library, but his world had collapsed a few years earlier. When van Kampen died, the collection was left in the hands of relatives who funneled its resources into an amusement park in Florida. Carroll said that scholars fled the project "like rats from a sinking ship," and he was no exception.[2] He ended up teaching a heavy course-load at Cornerstone University, a small nondenominational Christian liberal arts school in Grand Rapids, Michigan, a world away from the prestigious manuscript collection he had worked with before.

In 2000, Carroll received an out-of-the-blue call from Shipman recruiting him to his Dallas Bible museum project. To fund the idea, Shipman needed a donor with deep pockets, and he had one in mind. At the time, and in fact to this day, the Greens were the most generous Christian philanthropists in North America. But in the early 2000s they had yet to commit a substantial portion of their resources to a single cause. There was a lot of cash floating around the hallways of their Oklahoma City base, and the Green family attracted no shortage of pilgrims from religious charities, stumping for funds for their individual causes.

Shipman first met the Greens through his connections to the movie industry. Mart Green, brother of current Hobby Lobby CEO Steve Green, was interested in making Christian-themed films. At the time, Mart was deeply invested in telling the story of five Christian missionaries who were killed while attempting to bring the Gospel to the Huaroni natives of Ecuador, and Shipman was helping with fundraising. The film, which was released in 2005 as *End of the Spear*, turned out to be a public-relations disaster for the Greens when it became known that one of the lead actors, Chad Allen, was gay. Evangelicals questioned the film's Christian bona fides, and Mart Green gave an interview in which he stated that he would never have knowingly hired Allen to play the Christian hero if he had "known everything about him."[3] Evangelical scandal notwithstanding, the film gave Shipman his in.

In the early 2000s, Shipman and Carroll began to make annual trips to the vast hive of warehouses that make up Hobby Lobby's Oklahoma City headquarters to pitch the family on the idea of purchasing biblical manuscripts and donating them to Shipman's museum project. In the beginning, they weren't interested: "We went to this warehouse," Carroll said, "headquarters for their corporation, and met with Steve Green and maybe casually other people in the family, but basically had an hour to pitch them on an idea of collecting Bibles. . . . They were very cordial, [but] they were not interested at all and they showed us the door."

Shipman was not discouraged. They continued their visits, each time honing their pitch, emphasizing how investing in the project would make sense for the family. When the Greens describe the origins of their collection, they often mention one particular piece: a copy of the Gospel of Luke written on rare purple vellum that Carroll suggested they purchase for Shipman's museum. The manuscript, as they tell it, piqued their interest, and they bit on Carroll's offer. The sale eventually fell through, but in the course of negotiations the Greens found themselves hooked.

Carroll tells a slightly different version of events. The Greens warmed to the idea, he told us, as Shipman explained how financially profitable manuscripts could be. Shipman's insight was to marry the Green's financial acumen with his interest in antiquities. For years the Greens had been buying buildings in order to donate them to registered 501(c)(3) charities. Hobby Lobby had a dedicated staff who would tour potential properties looking for those that could be purchased below their appraised value. If such an opportunity presented itself, they would acquire the property, renovate it, and eventually donate it to a charity, after the IRS-required holding period of a year and a day. They would subsequently write off the donation for the entirety of the new appraised value. The magic ratio for the Greens was 1:3: for a given investment to be financially viable, they had to be able to write it off at three times the amount that they purchased it for.

Shipman took this real-estate model and applied it to manuscripts. At meetings with the Greens held between 2005 and 2008, Shipman began to show the Greens how antiquities could be acquired with almost no risk. The proposal, Carroll told us, was this: manuscripts would be acquired for a third or less of their projected eventual value. They would then be donated to a charitable organization—but this time the charitable organization would be their own, one that they control. "They liked that a lot," said Carroll, and with this the idea for the Green Collection and the National Bible Museum was born.

In November 2009, the Greens began to collect biblical manuscripts. In the subsequent four years, they amassed over forty thousand artifacts relating to the Bible. These artifacts are collectively known as "the Green Collection," but this is a misleading bit of nomenclature: "the Green Collection" doesn't exist as a legal entity. Everything in the Green Collection is owned by Hobby Lobby, Inc. As Hobby Lobby is legally defined as a closely held company, this means that the artifacts are effectively owned by the Green family, but the collection did not and does not have any separate status. It is legally the property of Hobby Lobby, and those who work for it receive payment for their services from the crafting store.

The Greens are not the first wealthy entrepreneurs to invest in biblical artifacts. John Pierpont Morgan, Robert Van Kampen, Martin Schøyen, and others have amassed large privately held collections in the past. And, like the Greens, they employed experts to help them do so. Others, like the investment mogul Frank Hanna, have acquired important artifacts and donated them to museums or libraries: in Hanna's case, the Vatican Library.

The financial incentive to donate items, and reap the substantial tax write-off, is commonplace among serious art and antiquities collectors; this is how many museums have traditionally acquired much of their holdings. Part of what sets the Greens apart from other collectors, however, is that when they donate pieces from their collection, they give them to their own nonprofit organization. When, in 2015, we asked Steve Green how the family decides what artifacts to donate to the Museum of the Bible, he candidly responded that the decision was financial: "I don't know that there's a lot of rhyme and reason to it. . . . We want to donate X amount and we can do it with this, and that's easy so we'll do it." Once donated to the Museum, however, the items never truly leave the Greens' control. The charitable organization known as Museum of the Bible, Inc. (MOTB) is also based at Hobby Lobby, Inc., in Oklahoma City. Once the bricks-and-mortar museum opens in D.C. the artifacts will be transferred there, but the museum, as we will see later in this book, effectively remains under Green control.

The Greens are also unusual for their hands-on approach to acquisitions. As the current Director of the Collection, David

Trobisch, told us, the Greens "aren't the Rockefellers"; they don't accumulate wealth for its own sake, but rather earn money in order to spend it.[4] There is, therefore, a budget. While purchases are negotiated through donor relations, major acquisitions are ultimately voted on by the family itself as part of a closed-door meeting involving David and Barbara Green, the founders of Hobby Lobby, and their children and children-in-law. For the present, the twenty-somethings that make up the next generation of the Green family are, according to Trobisch, only sitting in on the meetings. The fate of a particular purchase lies in the hands of David Green and his immediate family. The scholars involved in the acquisitions process, like Trobisch, find themselves on a tight leash.[5]

The family's judgment about which objects to acquire is based almost exclusively on financial value—mostly because, like many collectors, the Greens do not have the expertise in the field of antiquities to come to a decision regarding the historical value of any given object. Steve Green admitted, "That's not my world. . . . I have to rely on the experts that we have used to tell us, 'Here's a significant item.'" This business-minded focus on financial value sometimes seems at odds with the stated intention of the collection. Unlike many private collections, the Green Collection was always headed for a Bible museum. As Green has repeatedly stated, he and his family do not consider themselves pure collectors, but rather "storytellers": everything that they purchase is meant to contribute to the story they want to present about the Bible and its history and impact. Yet substantial portions of the Green Collection do not easily fit into that story. It would be reasonable enough for a Bible museum to display a handful of prebiblical ancient Mesopotamian cuneiform texts, or a few Torah scrolls from the seventeenth or eighteenth century—the Green Collection, however, holds thousands of each of these types of artifacts. The rationale is, again, a financial one: these are objects that can be bought relatively cheaply, but can be valued quite highly for tax purposes. In general, Torah scrolls could be purchased for $1500–$5000 in Europe and Syria, but were valued according to official appraisal guidelines set by the American Society of Appraisers. This value was determined from a combination of the replacement cost of a scroll (approximately

$75,000 per scroll) and its historical significance. After appraisal a restored Torah scroll could easily be valued between $80,000 and $500,000. From an economic standpoint, this is simply good business; but these acquisitions belie the purely "narrative" motivation for the existence and scope of the Green Collection. When the finances determine the purchases, many items that might not have been of interest suddenly become considerably more appealing.

At the end of 2009, Carroll resigned from his position at Cornerstone to assume full-time duties as director of the Green Collection. At first he understood himself to be building a collection that would be housed in Dallas. Along the way, however, the practicalities of the Dallas location and personality clashes—described to us by Cary Summers, the current president of MOTB, as "awkward, awkward, awkward"—led to Johnny Shipman's departure. His name was entirely effaced from every official description of the Green Collection's history—as if he had never been involved at all. (When we asked Steve Green about the beginnings of the collection, he referred only to "a group of guys that had this vision of putting in a Bible museum.") For the next two years, Carroll almost single-handedly shaped the formation of the collection, developed travelling exhibits, and oversaw the allocation of Green manuscripts to individual scholars for study.

In December 2009, only a few months after the purple manuscript sale fell through, the opportunity to purchase another flashy artifact came along. Produced around 1400, the manuscript known as the Rosebury Rolle preserves the earliest and most extensive English text and translation of the Bible—in this case the book of Psalms in Middle English. It predates by some forty years the edition attributed to John Wycliffe which is usually credited with being the first English biblical translation. Though Green had never heard of it—"I had no idea," he told us—the family was convinced by Carroll that the Rosebury Rolle had a "significant story to tell" and acquired it for £217,250. Other major acquisitions of this early period include a vast 20,000-item American history collection that had originally been assembled by Gene Albert, owner of Historical Reproductions, American Classic Limousines, and

Creative Home Builders, for his pet project the Christian Heritage Museum in Hagerstown, Maryland. The Greens purchased this particular collection, Carroll told us, because they were interested in the connection between Christianity and the founding of the American nation, and thus it "made sense to them"; it fit into the story they were trying to tell. The story told by their acquisitions, however, is an American Protestant one. Steve Green identified the Aitken Bible, the first complete English Bible printed in America, and authorized by the United States Congress in 1782, as his favorite artifact in the collection.[6]

The following years were something akin to a shopping spree. In the wake of the financial crisis in 2008, the global antiquities market was, like most everything else, depressed. People were cash-strapped, Carroll told us, and were willing to sell artifacts at well below their market price. In many cases, family collections had been the passionate projects of now-deceased relatives, whose descendants were looking to unload the dusty artifacts that had eaten up a portion of their inheritance. It was a buyer's market: Carroll energetically travelled the world utilizing his contacts with antiquities dealers in Jerusalem, Dubai, Istanbul, London, and elsewhere.

Among the major early purchases was the Codex Climaci Rescriptus, a vellum manuscript written in Aramaic and dated to between the fifth and ninth centuries CE. The text is a palimpsest: on the surface of the pages are two Syriac texts attributed to John Climacus, the seventh-century abbot of St. Catherine's Monastery in Sinai. But underneath the Syriac text lies another, earlier layer of writing that bears witness to the Greek version of the Hebrew Bible and portions of the New Testament Gospels. The first leaf of the manuscript was discovered in Cairo in 1895 (with more joining it from Berlin and elsewhere in Egypt), and it was housed in Westminster College at Cambridge until the decision was made by the college, out of financial need, to sell it. When the manuscript was originally offered at auction in July 2009, however, it failed to find a buyer. Recognizing an opportunity, the Greens swooped in a year later and negotiated a private sale through Sotheby's.

Many of the Green's acquisitions took place in this manner: out-of-auction and off-book, behind closed doors. In the case of the

Climaci Rescriptus, the Greens saw the opportunity to purchase the manuscript for a good price, within the parameters of their 1:3 model. But there were other reasons to be discrete. Those unburdening themselves of decades-old family heirlooms wanted the money but couldn't afford the publicity. Private sales, often arranged through auction houses, allow artifacts to exchange hands without too many questions being asked.

Within the world of the antiquities market, the sudden appearance of a new player with seemingly unlimited funds and a desire to acquire a lot of material in a hurry did not go unnoticed. Although the Greens and Carroll kept their eye on objects that were being sold through public auctions, they were also being directly approached by dealers looking to take advantage of the family's largesse. As the Greens bought more and more, they began to affect the market itself: prices across the board started to go up. While this potentially made their future purchases more expensive, acquisitions became more expensive for others, and disproportionately so for financially constrained universities and public collections. Artifacts that are displayed to the public have to be insured against damage and theft, and the cost of insurance is based, naturally, on the value of the items displayed. The value of those items is largely based on recent recorded sales. In 2016, Sofía Torallas-Tovar, curator of the papyrological collection at the Abadia de Montserrat, co-organized *Pharaoh's Reed*, a public exhibit of artifacts from Montserrat and Barcelona. She was asked by the sponsors of the exhibit to value the artifacts that would be displayed, and she quickly realized how valuable complete codices had become. In particular, she wanted to include a fifth-century Coptic Gospel book owned by a community of Jesuits in Catalunya.[7] Researching online for comparable artifacts, she discovered a fragment of Paul's Letter to the Romans (known as the Wyman fragment), which the Greens had purchased at auction at Sotheby's for more than three hundred thousand pounds in 2012.[8] If a scrap of an epistle had sold for so much money, she told us, how much would a beautiful complete edition of Coptic gospels be worth? And, more pressingly, how could they afford to insure it? In the end, the book was included only because the Jesuit superior general was willing to take a risk.

Without his generosity, the piece could never have been shown. Such issues are even more pressing when it comes to acquiring artifacts: universities can no longer afford to buy, and in some cases they may be unable to exhibit their holdings. For the Greens, however, the rising market in antiquities had the salutary effect of increasing the value of those items they had already acquired.

While the antiquities market was very much aware of the Greens' involvement, the public at large was not so well informed. Even for scholars, the existence of the Green Collection sometimes came to their attention only when they attempted to access a manuscript for academic study and discovered that it had been sold.

By the time public news of the existence of the Green Collection began to surface—the first report of it in the *New York Times* was published in June 2010—the Greens already owned more than 30,000 artifacts. With so many pieces being acquired in such a short period of time, questions began to surface: What, exactly, did the Greens own? Where were these artifacts coming from? How were these pieces being vetted and authenticated? Were these purchases above-board?

In the nineteenth century, European and American archaeologists and collectors would regularly uncover items of historical and artistic interest in their excavations. They thought nothing of appropriating and exporting those artifacts to their home countries and institutions. In some cases, those items became part of public exhibits at museums or publicly available university collections; in others the artifacts disappeared into private collections, where they became *objets d'art* or curiosities. In the latter cases, the importance of the object for academic inquiry, for its contribution to our cumulative knowledge about the past, was never a factor.

Over the course of the second half of the twentieth century, cultural watchdogs and governments became increasingly worried about these practices.[9] In the first place, it smacked of colonialism. The idea that foreign individuals and institutions could play a game of archaeological "finders keepers" in the Middle East, Egypt, and Latin America was reminiscent of the economic exploitation of the eighteenth and nineteenth centuries. Additionally, and in the wake of war, political unrest, and looting, there was a growing awareness that items that appeared on the market may have been stolen. The issue wasn't one merely of cultural destruction; it was also about financing theft and even terrorism. In many cases, those who stole items from museums did so violently and in order to finance political unrest. The same dangers can be seen even today in the looting that followed the the invasion of Iraq and the Arab Spring and in ISIS's well-documented theft, destruction, and sale of antiquities from Syria and Iraq.[10] In 1970, UNESCO created a set of guidelines regarding the preservation of cultural heritage, specifically targeted at preventing artifacts from leaving their countries of origin without government permission. This was a watershed moment for global consciousness regarding the problem of the illicit antiquities market. Since then, it has been understood by sellers, dealers, buyers, and scholars that provenance is of the utmost importance. Antiquities dealers around the world are aware that they must produce proof of provenance—that is, the trail of ownership going back, if possible, to the item's initial discovery—if they want to sell across international borders. In legal terms, the importance of the UNESCO agreement is more complicated. The United States ratified the guidelines only in 1983, and even since then the law is effective only when the United States has a bilateral agreement with another signatory regarding the protection of cultural property. (At the moment, such bilateral agreements exist only with sixteen countries, ranging from major sources of antiquities such as Italy and Greece to smaller nations like Belize and Mali.) Exceptions have been made for emergency situations, as is the case currently for Iraq and Syria.

More often, the rules that govern cultural artifacts are national cultural patrimony laws, many of which were instituted well before the 1970 date associated with the UNESCO convention. Egypt, for instance, has restricted the unauthorized removal of antiquities from within its borders since 1835, with regular updates to the law since then. If an artifact can be shown to have been removed from its country of origin while such laws were in place, it can be seized by the United States government not because of the UNESCO agreement, but under the National Stolen Property Act.

The UNESCO convention remains fundamental to the antiquities market, however, because it publicized the centrality of provenance in the sale and purchase of all cultural artifacts. In practical terms, what this means for anyone who wants to buy such items is that there needs to be demonstration of provenance: evidence that the item has a documented chain of discovery and custody within the temporal limitations called for by law. For countries that have cultural heritage laws—and most countries do—it needs to be demonstrated that the item left its country of origin before those laws went into effect. If the origins of the piece are unknown, or if it is impossible to prove that it was legally acquired, then it lacks provenance and runs the risk of being declared stolen property.

Such proof can be difficult to come by. Until recently, antiquities sales tended to be poorly documented. Private collectors often had no idea of precisely what they owned. Many items lack proper provenance, especially those that were bought before 1970, and the legislation governing their sale can be complicated. For collectors, dealers, curators, and academics alike this can be a frustrating business. There are doubtless thousands of artifacts that were legally sold that simply lack the proper documentation. If an aristocratic family purchased a papyrus fragment in the nineteenth century, for example, they are unlikely to be in possession of a receipt documenting the sale. For those invested in the religious and intellectual value of these documents, the prospect that unprovenanced artifacts might simply be ignored is especially painful.

This situation grows more complicated when partial records are available. In September 2005, the Akron, Ohio, art dealer and collector Bruce Ferrini declared bankruptcy. Ferrini, who had previously helped recover stolen artifacts from the Vatican and had appeared in a *National Geographic* documentary, had been sued by a former partner for embezzling funds and was suspected of having illegally imported Egyptian artifacts. In the wake of the lawsuit, many of his holdings were auctioned on eBay. A number of scholars, including University of Pennsylvania professor Robert Kraft, purchased papyri from Michael J. Farr, Ferrini's representative.[11] The provenance of these documents was difficult to pin down. When Kraft made inquiries about the origins of the papyri, he received a list of collections out of which the papyri had come, but no specific details about individual manuscripts. None of the purchasers could be certain of the legal status of their acquisitions. Ferrini had been accused of stealing pages from the only copy of the valuable and well-known Coptic text the *Gospel of Judas*.[12] According to Kraft, the knowledge that excerpts from this manuscript might be included in the eBay auctions drove up the price of the Coptic fragments.[13] The potential presence of stolen goods only generated more, rather than less, interest in auctions.

Some academics, like the Coptic scholar Hany Takla, who regularly purchases Coptic fragments on eBay, see themselves as rescuing documents from destruction.[14] There is little doubt that without his intervention, some important texts would have been physically broken up in order to accrue maximum profits. The fear that texts might be lost or destroyed drives those who argue that artifacts should be published, regardless of provenance: the knowledge of the past that can be gleaned from these ancient materials overrides concerns about legality. Others, like Christine Thomas, a scholar of early Christianity at the University of California, Santa Barbara, have suggested that if a text is authentic it should be published whether or not it has documented provenance.[15] There is an ongoing debate among academics about the ethics of acquiring and working with unprovenanced artifacts, and while a growing number of academic societies are prohibiting the presentation or publication of work that is based on unprovenanced texts, this is a recent development in the field.[16] Some have argued that, when they are brought to Europe or the United States, even looted artifacts are rescued from potential destruction. Others might counter that the idea of Western scholars as saviors of cultural heritage is both deeply colonialist and, historically speaking, inaccurate: many artifacts brought to Europe in the nineteenth and early twentieth centuries were subsequently destroyed or looted in the chaos of World War II. The actions of those working on behalf of the Green Collection, therefore, should be viewed within this larger context of academic debate. This does not mean, of course, that the problem can be ignored.

This issue is exemplified in the case of the handful of Dead Sea Scrolls purchased by Steve Green between 2009 and 2014. Since 2002, a wave of scrolls has made its way to the antiquities market—approximately seventy in total to date. For collectors such as Green and Martin Schøyen, this has meant an opportunity to own some of the most desirable biblical artifacts in existence.[17] But not a single one of these newly "discovered" scrolls has any reasonable provenance; unlike the original Dead Sea Scrolls, it is not known which cave at the site of Qumran they came from, much less where they have been since then. The total lack of provenance is a universal issue with the scrolls; in other words, there is effectively no due diligence to be done here, as there is no hope of clarifying the chain of ownership.

Given the centrality of the Dead Sea Scrolls for biblical scholarship in the seventy years since their discovery, many scholars feel that even without provenance pieces of the Dead Sea Scrolls should always be published. But the sheer number of Dead Sea Scrolls fragments that have hit the market in the last fifteen years or so has also raised eyebrows. Eibert Tigchelaar, a highly respected expert on the scrolls, has expressed his doubts about the authenticity of some of these texts. He points not only to the number of fragments, but also to some unexpected scribal features, and, perhaps most suggestively, to the fact that while there are around nine hundred known Dead Sea Scroll manuscripts, virtually none of the newly available fragments seem to match up with any previously known. Moreover, while the manuscripts of the Dead Sea Scrolls contain a variety of texts, many of which have to do with the internal organization of the Qumran sect, the vast majority of the new fragments are biblical.[18]

What this points to, for Tigchelaar and others, is the high probability that some, if not all, of the recently available Dead Sea Scrolls fragments are modern-day forgeries. The high percentage of biblical texts represented reflects the higher value that such manuscripts fetch on the open market—and one can certainly see that tendency at work in the Green Collection. More sharply, the Norwegian scholar Arstein Justnes points to the fact that one fragment, purchased by Southwest Baptist Theological Seminary, just happens to contain both of the passages from Leviticus in which homosexuality is designated as an abomination. For Justnes, this remarkable coincidence is in fact evidence that these fragments are being forged with the specific purpose of luring wealthy evangelical individuals and institutions.[19] Whether or not Justnes is right, the Dead Sea Scrolls fragments illustrate the risks that are entailed when dealing with unprovenanced artifacts: not just that they may be illicit, but that they may, in fact, not be authentic at all.[20]

Provenance may seem like a technicality, but it is of crucial importance. The illicit antiquities trade is a booming business, especially in the last twenty-five years. Since the disruption of strong central governments in the Middle East—from the first Gulf War to the Arab Spring to the rise of the Taliban, al Qaeda, and now ISIS—the looting of archaeological sites in search of valuable artifacts to sell on the black market has increased dramatically. Aerial photography of the region shows a landscape pockmarked by illicit digging. Multiple reports confirm that ISIS uses money gained through the sale of antiquities to fund its activities. Every sale and purchase of unprovenanced antiquities sustains the market for illegal artifacts.

The scholarly response to the news about the existence of the Green Collection and its massive holdings was deeply colored by the lack of information that surrounded it. At first, the only real clues about its contents were to be found through Scott Carroll's social media presence. In many ways, this is where the trouble started for the Green Collection: Scott Carroll's flamboyant style did not sit well with academics for whom "careful" is a synonym for "excellent." Carroll was open about his methods and activities, describing himself hunting for texts in the desert, in the backstreets of Istanbul, and in shadier parts of London. But Carroll's well-crafted Indiana Jones persona drew attention and criticism from scholarly watchers.[21] Many hypothesized that the collection had been amassed too quickly for the authenticity, importance, and legality of the artifacts to have been properly verified.[22]

In particular, Carroll's methods of acquiring artifacts were highly scrutinized by academic bloggers Roberta Mazza, Paul Barford, Brice Jones, and Dorothy King.[23] On Facebook Carroll described working through desks stacked high with disorganized texts in Istanbul and entering Turkish-run apartments in London that housed Egyptian sarcophagi, golden mummy masks, and thousands of manuscripts. Even his Facebook friends asked whether he could be sure about the legality of these texts. Moreover, Carroll's methods of handling those papyri he had acquired were, to put it delicately, unorthodox. On social media the man who claims to have been responsible for selecting and training curatorial staff and overseeing the preservation of the Green Collection describes transporting a tenth-century gold-lettered psalter into the United States in his carry-on luggage.[24]

When questioned online by friends about the provenance and legality of his acquisitions, Carroll produced the same stock response: that all of his activities are done in accordance with national and international law and U.S. Customs regulations. Yet even Cary Summers, the president of MOTB, agrees that much of the material purchased during the Carroll years was worthless and poorly vetted. This period, described by Summers as a time when Carroll would return "with a big plastic bag here or there," saw Carroll acquire a substantial number of fragments, the origins and even contents of which were often unclear.[25] Carroll's papyrological scavenger hunt in the back alleys of Istanbul and clandestine apartments of London was seemingly propelled forward by his excitement about what these texts might contain, rather than by careful study of what was actually being acquired. While on social media Carroll claims to have discovered the earliest copies of Greek plays, Gospel fragments, and letters from Paul, Summers admits that most of what Carroll discovered is "junk" and that "even the dealers" didn't know where it was from.

One particular aspect of Carroll's behavior garnered scrutiny and condemnation: his treatment of Egyptian mummy masks. In the course of building the Green Collection, Carroll acquired numerous funerary masks used in the burial rituals of ancient Roman Egyptians. The majority of mummy masks from this era were constructed from cartonnage—a kind of ancient papier-mache in which scraps of linen and, temptingly, papyrus were glued together.

Dismantling these masks, therefore, might potentially yield a trove of hitherto unknown texts. And starting in 2010, Carroll began advertising his retrieval of fragments of papyrus that had long been hidden inside these masks. Videos posted to YouTube show Carroll using Palmolive to dissolve the ancient Egyptian artifacts. Publicly, Carroll and others claimed that the mummy masks were undamaged. A press release for an exhibit at Gordon-Conwell Theological Seminary in 2012, sponsored by the Museum of the Bible, stated, "Carroll [had] developed a method to extract writings reused in the infrastructure of mummy coverings while preserving the decorative external features." But only two years earlier the preservation of those decorative features was not Carroll's priority: in a status update to his Facebook followers in 2010, he describes dissolving two-thousand-year-old masks in a pot on the kitchen stove—while watching college football.

This might, quite understandably, seem like a peculiar side venture for a collection of artifacts so keenly focused on the Bible. The practice of destroying ancient Egyptian mummy masks in order to retrieve fragments of ancient writing was already well known to classicists and papyrologists. While the majority of cartonnage is composed of relatively banal texts, often ancient tax receipts, there is always the possibility (albeit very slim) of making a major discovery. The chance that one of these masks might contain Christian papyri raises the stakes further. For evangelicals, the prospect that a mummy mask may contain what is potentially the oldest fragment of the Jesus story makes the contents more valuable than the container.

Scott Carroll's Facebook posts had already tipped off the academy to the fact that the Green Collection was dissolving masks, but, in 2012, a scholar associated with the collection announced a remarkable discovery. In a debate with the well-known agnostic scholar Bart Ehrman at Chapel Hill, North Carolina, Dan Wallace, founder of the Center for the Study of New Testament Manuscripts at Dallas Theological Seminary, declared that a first-century papyrus fragment of the Gospel of Mark had been discovered in the cartonnage of an Egyptian funerary mask and that it would shortly be published. It wasn't published then, and still hasn't been. But two years later the same announcement was made by Craig

Evans, Professor of New Testament at Acadia Divinity College in Nova Scotia, in a speech presented at the 2014 Apologetics Canada conference. Like Wallace, Evans claimed that it was the earliest known fragment of the Gospels and added that carbon dating (as well as handwriting analysis) had dated it to the first century.

Within evangelical Protestant circles, the potential value of mummy masks as archaeological sites from which scripture can be retrieved has created a buzz. In 2014, the Christian apologist Josh McDowell, an associate of both Scott Carroll and Dan Wallace, claimed to have harvested a cache of five New Testament fragments from a mummy mask, three of which he declared to be the "earliest ever" examples of those passages.[26]

The destruction of mummy masks was part of a broader evangelical project in which Carroll was participating. But he was working under the aegis of the Green Collection. Masks were dissolved in front of undergraduate and graduate students at multiple Green-sponsored events. In 2011, Carroll, in his role as director of the Green Collection, dissolved mummy masks with students at Baylor University. "I never knew dish soap could lead to new discoveries in literature!" one student exclaimed.[27] Carroll wasn't the only Green associate to be engaged in the search for Christian texts hidden in Egyptian artifacts. At an annual Green-sponsored student conference at Oxford called LOGOS (to be further discussed in the next chapter), three scholars affiliated with the Green Collection—Jerry Pattengale, from Indiana Wesleyan University; Jeffrey Fish, from Baylor University, and Dirk Obbink, from Oxford—dissolved masks in a sequence of chemical baths in order to retrieve scraps of material. Students participated in a limited fashion: they handed the principal investigators tools for the extraction of papyri and sheets of art paper. One student told us that he will "never forget the atmosphere of excitement" and "the thrill of being in uncharted territory." Another was more succinct: "It was awesome."[28]

The goal, these students were told, was to retrieve fragments of the Bible. The Scott Carroll years produced regular claims that valuable New Testament fragments had been reclaimed from mummy mask cartonnage. Two previously unpublished and remarkable papyri on display in Green Collection exhibitions, at the Vatican and at Baylor University, were initially claimed to have been uncovered in this way. Even though the Green Collection has since distanced itself from these claims, the supposed discovery of early fragments of Galatians and Hebrews in funerary masks supplied the rationale for the continued acquisition and destruction of mummy masks.

It is only fair to acknowledge that Green Collection employees have repeatedly asserted to us that the era of destroying mummy masks is in the past. Both Josephine Dru, then the curator of the Green Collection papyri, and Christian Askeland, one of the Green Collection's "Distinguished Scholars" and a well-known papyrologist, told us that this would never happen under Green Collection supervision anymore. Yet the MOTB website for their traveling exhibit, *Passages*, still proudly proclaims that the exhibit includes "an archaeological tent site revealing how biblical texts are recovered from ancient Egyptian mummy masks."[29]

Scott Carroll's methods for dismantling the masks earned him widespread censure. The lack of concern for the fate of the Egyptian artwork that the destruction of mummy masks demonstrates is grounded in two rather subjective criteria, both of which warrant additional scrutiny. The first is the quality of the artifacts: Green Collection representatives and scholars claim that the objects destroyed are not, as Craig Evans remarked, of "museum quality." This is a sentiment shared by some other classicists: if the masks are low quality, the argument goes, why not try to uncover what is inside? It is unclear, however, who is responsible for deciding which masks are destroyed. When we interviewed Craig Evans in January 2015, he told us that such decisions "are based on expert opinion," but as to who exactly those experts might be, he said, "I do not know specifically." When the issue at hand is the destruction of 2,000-year-old Egyptian antiquities, it seems important that the task be authorized, documented, and performed by experts.[30]

The second criterion might be described as the colonialist impulse: the sense that even a minute chance of discovering a rare Christian fragment outweighs the value of preserving a relatively common burial mask. To put this in the words of Scott Carroll:

"What's inside is much more precious than what's on the outside."[31] Cultural colonialism and curatorial carelessness aside, however, there is a more serious problem. The breathless destruction of mummy masks performed at Green-sponsored events is predicated on the assumption that mummy masks at least have the potential to contain fragments of the New Testament. But it is scholarly consensus that cartonnage was used in Egyptian funerary art only during a particular and precisely datable period, a period that concluded with the end of the reign of the emperor Augustus in 14 CE. As the renowned papyrologist Roger Bagnall wrote in his book *Everyday Writing in the Graeco-Roman East*, "cartonnage . . . is a specialty of the Ptolemaic period. I know of no certain example before the reign of Ptolemy II [283–246 BCE] or after that of Augustus [27 BCE–14 CE]."[32] Every scholar with whom we spoke agreed: by the time Jesus died, papyri ceased to play a role in the creation of mummy masks. There is, therefore, no possibility of discovering fragments of the New Testament in ancient Egyptian mummy masks. If this is so, then "digging into the faces" of Egyptian masks, as Evans put it, is nothing more than cultural vandalism.

What, then, of the purportedly first-century fragment of the Gospel of Mark that both Dan Wallace and Craig Evans announced had been recovered from a mummy mask? Wallace initially claimed to have seen it, but both Wallace and Evans retreated from the discovery when talking to media outlets. They were, they said, legally prevented from discussing it further. When nonevangelical papyrologists requested to see the fragment so that they could evaluate it for themselves, they were told to wait for publication—a wait that is still ongoing.[33] The only remaining clue to its location is an interview at the National Conference on Christian Apologetics, shot on a cellphone and posted to YouTube, in which Scott Carroll told Josh McDowell that he first saw the fragment on the pool table that papyrologist Dirk Obbink keeps in his office at Christ Church College, Oxford.[34] Despite appearing in Green Collection publicity materials, promising graduate students positions at Oxford partially funded by the Green family, and consulting with the Greens on acquisitions, Dirk Obbink refused to comment on the subject, claiming that he is "not involved in the study of [the Green] collection."

Though it had first been publicly revealed by Green Collection affiliates, official representatives of the Green Collection denied knowing anything about the Mark fragment. When we first asked David Trobisch and Michael Holmes, respectively the current directors of the Green Collection and the Green Scholars Initiative, about the papyrus they implied that it was all a misunderstanding. Holmes said he did not know to which papyrus Evans was referring.[35] Trobisch said that he "had not seen it" but that some in the organization imagined that it must have been mistakenly dated. When we asked Steve Green himself, however, we got a very different response. Green was clearly familiar with the Mark fragment: "At some point it was like, this is an item I want to pursue." When we returned to Holmes with Green's comments, he conceded that, in fact, he did know about the existence of the papyrus and believed it to be located in the UK. Holmes assured us that he intends to clear up the confusion and share everything he knows. Until such a time, however—and that time has not yet come—he appears to be complicit in obscuring information about at least one of the Greens' more sensational holdings.

If it were merely the case that some Green Collection materials are of unknown origin, it might be possible to give them the benefit of the doubt when it comes to the question of provenance. After all, the standards of evidence required for antiquities acquisitions today are much stricter than they were in the past. But the papyri said to have been extracted from mummy masks, and particularly the purported first-century Mark fragment, seem to be examples of not just a lack of provenance but a deliberate obfuscation of it. And to these problems can be added the fact that on at least one occasion the Greens engaged in acquisition practices that drew the attention of law enforcement.

In 2011, a shipment destined for Hobby Lobby of somewhere between 200 and 300 small clay tablets inscribed with cuneiform, the writing of ancient Mesopotamia, was seized by United States Customs agents in Memphis. When we broke the story of this seizure for *The Daily Beast*, a senior law-enforcement source confirmed to us that these artifacts had been purchased and were being imported by the Green family of Oklahoma City.[36] Since that seizure the Greens had been under investigation by the federal government for the illicit importation of antiquities from Iraq.

When we asked Cary Summers about the investigation, he told us that it was simply the result of a logistical problem. "There was a shipment and it had improper paperwork—incomplete paperwork that was attached to it." That innocuous phrase—"incomplete paperwork"—makes it sound as if some forms were simply missing a date or a signature. That is rarely the case with questionably acquired ancient artifacts—and were the problem merely logistical, the chances are slim that it would take years to resolve.

While making it sound like a situation that might end amicably—"Hopefully we'll get this resolved one way or the other"—Summers also suggested that this is the sort of thing that just happens when it comes to antiquities collecting, and that the Museum of the Bible is not unlike other major institutions that have had similar experiences with problematic provenance. He used Yale University's cuneiform collection, known as the Babylonian Collection, as an example: "How many tablets does Yale have?" (Answer: approximately forty-five thousand.) "How many have been sent back, how many returned to various people? I don't know, half of them?"

The answer, in fact, is none, because the analogy Summers used is a bad one. The Babylonian Collection at Yale was created in 1909 and all but completed by 1925. No new acquisitions have been made in the post-1970 UNESCO convention era. This is quite different from a purchase made in 2011, when issues of cultural heritage were well known and international laws were in place. There are, of course, institutions that have had to return objects because of problems with provenance or demands for cultural repatriation. In 2012, the Princeton University Art Museum returned nearly 200 items to Italy, where the dealer who had sold them to Princeton was under investigation. In 2013, Cornell University returned to Iraq approximately 10,000 cuneiform tablets that had been donated by a private collector, under the suspicion that they had been looted in the wake of the Gulf War.

Yet Summers did not concede that the seized cuneiform tablets were illegal. He suggested that the tablets were merely "held up in customs," as if this was merely a case of bureaucratic delays. "Sometimes this stuff just sits, and nobody does anything with it." But an individual close to the investigation told us that investigators have accumulated hundreds of hours of interviews, which doesn't sound like bureaucratic delay—and which also suggests that there is more at stake here than merely a logistical oversight.

An attorney familiar with customs investigations explained that cases like this often center on improperly filled-out paperwork. There are two types of customs declarations: informal entry and formal entry. Informal entry is generally for shipments that have a collective monetary value of under $2,500; formal entry is for anything above that. In cases where people are trying to bring something into the country that they shouldn't, one of the common ways to do so is to undervalue whatever the item is, often by misidentifying it, so that it goes through the expedited informal-entry process rather than the more closely scrutinized formal entry.

If someone looking to bring antiquities into the United States knows that the artifacts should never have left their country of origin, or lack proper provenance, the only way to get them through customs is to lie: about the country of origin, about the country of export, about the value, about the identity. (This happened recently in the 2015 case of a Picasso worth $15 million, which was listed on the customs declaration as a "handicraft" worth $37.[37]) When such lies are detected, neither UNESCO regulations nor national cultural patrimony laws need to be invoked: these are simple cases of smuggling, and the items in question immediately fit the standard definition of contraband. One source familiar with the Hobby Lobby investigation told us that this is precisely what happened in this case: the tablets were described on their FedEx shipping label as samples—bound for a crafts store—of "hand-crafted clay tiles." This description may have been technically accurate, but the monetary value assigned to them—around $300—vastly underestimates their true worth, and, just as important, obscures their identification as the cultural heritage of Iraq.

It cannot be said that the Greens were totally ignorant of the world in which they were engaging. In the summer of 2010, Patty Gerstenblith, a law professor at DePaul University working in the area of cultural heritage, met privately with the Greens in order to explain to them precisely these issues: how to do due diligence with regard to provenance and how to watch out for legal complications with regard to antiquities sales. In her own words, she "read them the riot act."[38] And a year later, the Greens imported the tablets that have now become the subject of the federal investigation. When we spoke to Steve Green and asked him, in general, if it was possible that there were illicit artifacts in his collection, he responded, "That's possible." He neglected to mention was that they were under investigation for precisely that.

This episode is illustrative particularly of the way that the family has imported its business practices into a different arena, with ensuing complications. Green is aware that provenance can sometimes be an issue—"that is a risk within this world," he told us—but seems to underestimate the degree to which provenance matters, and the real-world ramifications of the illicit antiquities trade. He compared it to an experience he had with Hobby Lobby: the stores were selling Christmas tins with a design that turned out to be copyrighted by another vendor, and Hobby Lobby had to negotiate a settlement. "That's just part of business," he said. "There's millions of pieces of artwork out there, and you just don't know. It's the same kind of thing in the antiquities world."

To a businessman unfamiliar with the ethics of cultural heritage, perhaps these situations are parallel. But what looks like a mere business risk by the time it gets to Steve Green's desk has a far more complicated and unpleasant history. "The actual really bad violence seems to be happening really close to the source," Neil Brodie, an expert on the criminal antiquities trade at the Scottish Centre for Crime and Justice Research at the University of Glasgow, told us. "And the more up the chain you get the more you're going from really violent organized crime to more kind of white-collar type crime. You're going from violence to fraud."

In 2012, the Museum of the Bible, Inc.—the nonprofit organization that the Greens created as an umbrella for their various Bible-related activities, and to which their collection of artifacts is being donated—underwent a significant change in mission and direction. In their first federal nonprofit filing, in 2010, the purpose of the organization was described in starkly evangelical terms: "To bring to life the living word of God, to tell its compelling story of preservation, and to inspire confidence in the absolute authority and reliability of the Bible." Two years later, however, the form read quite differently: "We exist to invite people to engage with the Bible through our four primary activities: traveling exhibits, scholarship, building of a permanent museum, and developing elective high school curriculum."

This shift coincided with other significant changes to the public face of the organization, including the hiring of a public relations firm, DeMoss. Changes were afoot within the Green Collection as well: in August 2012 Scott Carroll announced on his Facebook feed that he and the Green family had parted ways. The circumstances of his departure are difficult to decipher. According to Carroll, it was a difference of vision that led to the split, although those differences do not seem to align with the broader institutional changes at MOTB. Carroll wrote to his followers, "Regrettably, [the Green family and I do] not share the same vision regarding the future of the museum. I have an unswerving belief that a successful museum of the Bible must be nonsectarian and that scholars and scholarship should not be used to promote a narrow religious agenda—right or not."[39] Carroll seems to have been accusing the Greens of hewing closer to an evangelical agenda at precisely the moment that they were ostensibly drifting toward greater inclusivity.

Representatives from the Green Collection are more opaque, citing personality conflicts as the rationale for the split. Several people suggested that Carroll was too publicity hungry for the Greens' taste, and that his desire to be the face of the collection was poorly received by his employers. Certainly there seemed to have been a clash over intellectual property—Carroll told us that when he asked for royalties for the guide book he produced to accompany the Green Collection's traveling exhibit, *Passages*, he received a steely response. To the Greens his work was bought and paid for; he was something akin to a factory worker.

It would be sensible enough to assume that Carroll had been fired because of his role in acquiring illicit antiquities. This explanation, however, is demonstrably false. In the first place, Carroll was never empowered to make purchases on his own authority. The Green family approved every purchase themselves—tellingly, Carroll was not a subject of the federal investigation. Moreover, the timeline is off: Carroll continued to work for the Green family for nearly a year after the seizure of the cuneiform tablets. None of the MOTB executives we spoke to in the course of our investigation suggested that lack of professionalism, or legal or ethical mistakes, was the impetus for Carroll's departure.

The departure of Carroll, whatever the real reason, was a watershed moment for the Green Collection, which, at least by Carroll's account, existed largely due to his efforts: he considers himself responsible for amassing the vast majority of the 40,000 artifacts that form the Green Collection and underwrite the Museum of the Bible. Then again, some in the organization—at least after Carroll was gone—have downplayed his importance. Cary Summers suggested to us that Carroll stayed on after Shipman's departure only because he had experience with manuscript acquisitions. What is clear, however, is that once Carroll left, the Greens began to rewrite the story of his contributions. They both scrubbed the internet of references to Carroll's involvement and subtly created a public narrative in which Carroll was responsible for any mishandling of acquisitions and artifacts. After years of representing the Green Collection in the press and in events around the world, Carroll had effectively become a scapegoat.

In February 2014, some sixteen months after Carroll's departure, the Green family hired David Trobisch to be the new director of the Green Collection. In many ways Trobisch was an unusual pick for the Greens: trained as a text-critical scholar in his native Germany, Trobisch studied under the liberal Protestant scholar Gerd Theissen. Many in the academy viewed his arrival as a step in the right direction for the Greens: while he was not especially qualified to appraise or work with papyri, he had real scholarly credentials and did not seem to have a conservative religious bias. A great deal of positive news coverage of the Museum of the Bible, buying into the post-Carroll narrative promoted by the Greens and MOTB, has suggested that Trobisch was hired to correct past mistakes and to move the organization in a more academically minded direction.

Much of this is true. But in 2014, when Trobisch was recruited to the organization, he was, like Scott Carroll before him, in a professional rut. Trobisch was a published scholar who had previously taught as a visiting professor at Yale Divinity School and as a regular faculty member of the Bangor Theological Seminary in Maine. In 2010, with the seminary on the verge of collapse (it would close for good in 2013), he left the academy and moved to Springfield, Missouri, working as a self-described "independent scholar."[40] The Greens didn't hire him based on his reputation as a scholar. They encountered him through his work with the American Bible Society, an organization devoted to translating and distributing the Bible throughout the world, "so all people may experience its life-changing message." It was actually Mart Green who met Trobisch first. Mart was working on a venture called E10, an evangelical missionary project that takes its rise from the biblical command to spread the gospel to the whole world and that was finalizing a translation of the Bible into every living language. After a single meeting at the Dallas airport, Mart suggested to his brother and Summers that they meet with Trobisch. When they learned that Trobisch lived "only a few miles away" from Cary Summers in Springfield, the coincidence seemed "crazy," and they brought him over to the organization.

For Trobisch the assignment was a dream come true. A stocky man, who sports the standard academic uniform of slightly ill-fitting suits and goatee, he wears a welcoming smile and greets even potentially hostile colleagues with an open demeanor. He is, in his own way, quite charming. Like Carroll before him, Trobisch enjoys the power and prestige of heading what is currently one of the wealthiest organizations in the world of religion. The Green Collection has given him the status that previously eluded him, and he wears it ostentatiously.

Even as he enjoys his new status, Trobisch is eager to curry favor with fellow academics and struggles with the culture clash between his own liberal German Protestant background and the American evangelicalism of the Greens. In November 2014, at a conference panel on antiquities, Trobisch responded to accusations that the Green Collection was tainted by the conservative values of its patrons by awkwardly proclaiming, "Some of my friends are lesbians." It was a bizarre statement in any context, but it was designed to set him apart from his evangelical employers. Over the course of several interviews with us, he called the process of working with the Green family "frustrating," and told us that he did not admire the way they run their business. He respects Steve Green, he told us, but labeled his perspective, in essence, unscholarly.[41] He further described the motivations of the conservative Christian donors he meets at MOTB fundraisers as "unbearable."

Like his predecessor, Trobisch is not a trained papyrologist or curator. Carroll had experience working for Van Kampen, but Trobisch was a text critic: a scholar who studies the variations and consistencies found in the textual record of the Bible, in its various papyri and codices, and tries to understand the transmission of the text through time and space. Strangely, and perhaps because the discipline of papyrology does not have strong ideological or religious underpinnings, those concerned with the history of the material documents are rarely hired by the Green Collection or Museum of the Bible. The same mismatch of expertise and position in the Green empire can be seen in the 2014 hire of Michael Holmes—a text critic like Trobisch, though arguably more renowned in the field—as the director of the Green Scholars Initiative. Like Trobisch, Holmes replaced an early Green associate—in this case, Jerry Pattengale—who had few substantial academic credentials in this area. And, as was the case with Trobisch, the hire of Holmes gave the organization an added veneer of scholarly credibility.

Everyone from Summers to Trobisch to Holmes made sure to insist that, since the new guard took over, the acquisitions process has been much more careful than it was before. This is undoubtedly true: regardless of his lack of experience in the antiquities trade, Trobisch is sure to be more professional than Carroll. At the same time, however, the difference should not be overstated, if for no other reason than that since Carroll left the organization the rate of acquisition has declined sharply. No longer are thousands of items being acquired in huge gulps. Steve Green explained that this was a conscious choice, though not one that had anything to do with the new leadership: "At first we had nothing, we had no artifacts, so we needed everything, so we were buying everything that was presented, practically. . . . We are now at a point where it's not like we need everything . . . so we've become much more selective now." In that sense, little can be said about whether Trobisch has truly ushered in a new style of acquisition. Michael Holmes told us that no new papyri had entered the collection since he took over in 2014.

In the larger narrative of the Museum of the Bible, the dismissal of Scott Carroll and subsequent hiring of David Trobisch marked a turning point in the history of the Green Collection and MOTB. They had made mistakes in the past, they told us, but those were largely a result of having hired the wrong people and naively relying on their advice. The changes they made, however, though billed as a fresh start, were largely cosmetic. Closer examination reveals that improprieties, especially in regard to acquisitions, continued even after Carroll's departure.

In 2014, an exhibit of biblical artifacts was displayed with great fanfare at the Vatican. Called "Verbum Domini," or "The Word of the Lord," it featured items from the Green Collection. Along with rare fragments of the Dead Sea Scrolls and a first edition of the King James Bible were lesser-known items, including some never-before-seen ancient biblical manuscripts.

Among the two hundred artifacts was a papyrus fragment of the New Testament. Its edges are frayed, but it is clearly decipherable: the text is from the second chapter of the book of Galatians. It is written in Coptic, the language of Egyptian Christianity for much of the first millennium. While visually it looks like Greek, because it uses many Greek letters, the script hints at the papyrus's origins in the arid climate of late antique Egypt. Given its small size—about four inches by four inches—most visitors probably gave it little more than a passing glance. But it immediately caught the eye of Roberta Mazza, a papyrologist from the University of Manchester. Although this was the first public display of the papyrus,

Mazza had seen it before: it had been offered for sale on eBay less than two years earlier.

In October 2012, a Turkish dealer operating under the name MixAntik had listed an unidentified Coptic papyrus on the online auction site, one of many such pieces that this dealer had been offering over the previous year.[42] Although MixAntik did not name it as being a biblical text, he seems to have known that it was more valuable than most of his offerings, which often sold for as little as $20: this one had a price tag of $14,000. Brice Jones, an American papyrologist, quickly identified the text as being from Galatians, and, when he asked MixAntik for more details, was told that the papyrus came from Egypt.[43] This was already a legal red flag: as both Turkey and Egypt have strict laws governing the export of cultural artifacts, MixAntik's sale seems to have been self-incriminatingly illegal. Shortly thereafter, MixAntik changed his eBay handle to ebuyerrrr—and eventually disappeared from the site entirely. The Galatians papyrus, however, made its way from an anonymous corner of eBay to an exhibition in the heart of the Roman Catholic Church and, to this day, remains part of the Green Collection. As we began looking into the Green Collection for our article in *The Atlantic*, the Galatians fragment seemed like an obvious test case for the question of provenance: how did the Greens go about ascertaining the provenance of the items they were purchasing, and how much of that information might they be willing to share with other interested parties? Our initial inquiries into the papyrus were handled by Josephine Dru, then curator of papyri for the Green Collection. She told us that the Greens had not bought it on eBay, but that it had been legally purchased from a trusted London dealer in 2013. That dealer, she said, traced the papyrus back to a large lot of papyri that had been sold at Christie's in November 2011. And that lot, in turn, had a clear provenance, having originally been part of a collection known as the Robinson Collection, a segment of which had been donated to the University of Mississippi back in 1955—well before the UNESCO regulations went into effect. Though the appearance of the papyrus on eBay was difficult to explain, there seemed to be no legal problem with the provenance of the fragment—at least, everyone at the Green Collection declared themselves to be satisfied.

Behind the veil of public confidence, however, representatives for the Green Collection exhibited signs of concern. The eBay sale created doubts about the fragment's connection to the Robinson Collection. How was it that, between the Christie's auction in London in 2011 and the Green Collection's acquisition from their dealer in 2013, the papyrus came to be offered for sale online, in Turkey, by a dealer known to trade in illicit artifacts? And why—if indeed it had been part of a perfectly legal sale at Christie's—would the online vendor MixAntik obscure the established provenance of the fragment, claiming that it had come out of Egypt, when illicit antiquities sell for far less than those with a clean provenance? The eBay sale, both generally and in its details, complicated the Green Collection's straightforward narrative more than they were willing to admit.

Some people involved in the Green Collection attempted to eliminate the eBay listing from the history of the papyrus altogether. When we asked Christian Askeland, the main papyrologist employed by the Greens to study their Coptic manuscripts, about the provenance of this particular Coptic text, he denied that MixAntik had ever authentically had the manuscript in hand to sell, suggesting instead that he had simply had a picture of it, presumably in order to scam a potential buyer. This story, however, raises even more questions than it answers. How did MixAntik come into possession of photographs of the papyrus? They had never appeared online before, and it seems unlikely that an honest dealer would have passed photographs around to unscrupulous online traders. Why would MixAntik go to such lengths to fake a sale? Although he was known to sell illegal artifacts, he did not seem to have made a habit of swindling his customers. If he had acquired the photographs from a legitimate dealer, it seems likely that the fragment would have been identified and that MixAntik would have incorporated that information into his listing.

Askeland's theory suffers a serious blow when the images of the papyrus put on eBay by MixAntik are closely examined. The piece is set against a slate gray background, perhaps a table top, with a transparent ruler set to the side to show the size of the papyrus. The same background, and the same ruler, appear in another listing by the same seller.[44] There seems to be little doubt that MixAntik did, in fact, have the papyrus in his possession when he offered it for sale. It does not help the credibility of his argument that, before becoming a full-time employee of the Greens, Askeland himself raised the possibility in a blog post that they may have purchased the fragment directly from MixAntik.[45]

Askeland, at least, acknowledged that the eBay sale was a problem that needed to be reckoned with. This was not the case with David Trobisch, the director of the Green Collection, who in our interactions with him seemed mostly annoyed that anyone would even bother to ask such basic questions. He described the eBay sale as "a curiosity," but one irrelevant to the question of provenance. He even tried shaming us into dropping the line of inquiry, suggesting that it was "something Fox New [sic] would like to spin," but that it was beneath higher journalistic standards.

Even while Trobisch was telling us that this was a question hardly worth asking, he was trying to track down some of the answers for himself. In May 2015—after we first asked about the provenance of the Galatians fragment—Trobisch and Dru made their way to the University of Mississippi, where they spoke to the curators of the Robinson Collection about whether there were any photographs of the Galatians piece to be found there.

This visit to the Robinson Collection in Mississippi is curious on a number of levels. Most simply, there is the question of why they would have felt the need to ask for images of the Galatians fragment in the first place. They had declared the provenance of the piece to be perfectly fine—yet the fact that they were doing further research suggests that they were not as confident as they publicly proclaimed. This disconnect was only compounded by the manner in which Trobisch disclosed the trip to Mississippi. In all of our conversations with him, and with Josephine Dru, in the summer and fall of 2015, neither of them told us that they had gone to visit the Robinson Collection, even when we asked directly about the Galatians fragment. Trobisch first mentioned the excursion not to us, but to the fact checkers at *The Atlantic*, when they asked him about the papyrus. He told them that the provenance was good—that he had even been to the University of Mississippi to look at photographs, and that there was no problem.

But there was a problem. What Trobisch didn't tell the fact checkers—what he told us only when we asked to see whatever he had found down in Mississippi—was that when he and Dru went searching for evidence that the Galatians papyrus had once been in the Robinson Collection, they came away empty-handed. There were no photographs to be had.

In the decades that elapsed between the donation of the Robinson Collection to the University of Mississippi and its journey to the floor of Christie's, other scholars would have had the opportunity to survey the materials. And yet there is no mention of a New Testament papyrus, either in a brief overview of the Robinson Collection published in 1961 or in the Christie's listing from 2011. The lot description from the auction mentions "a receipt for a wheat transaction," and describes the contents of the lot as "documentary, petitionary and literary excerpts, receipts, contracts and accounts." Had they known that the Galatians papyrus was in the lot, they would have been certain to mention it: the entire lot sold at Christie's for $11,610—the Galatians fragment alone was listed on eBay for $14,000.

No one from the University of Mississippi, nor anyone from Christie's, who as a matter of course bring in experts to help assess the value of their auction items, noticed this singular papyrus. And while it is certainly true that in a large collection individual pieces might be overlooked, this one—an important New Testament manuscript, with enough text preserved to have been quickly recognized by Brice Jones as being from Galatians—is a remarkable oversight.

Without any record of the Galatians fragment, either at Mississippi or at the Christie's auction, how could the Green Collection be certain that the fragment was actually ever part of the Robinson Collection, which was the basis for their claim of clean provenance? When we put this question directly to David Trobisch, he threw it back at us: "Do you have any evidence that it is not from the Robinson Collection?" Aggressive tone aside, this is to mistake where the burden of proof lies. It is, of course, impossible to prove a negative—but that is not how provenance works. It must be shown that an artifact has a clean provenance, despite Trobisch's statement that "lack of evidence does not prove anything." The fact that Trobisch and Dru looked for evidence at the University of Mississippi, however, suggests that his attitude was, at best, disingenuous.

As it turned out, the University of Mississippi may have been a false lead in any case: the Robinson Collection, we learned, was larger and more widely dispersed than Trobisch seemed to know. The papyrologist Brent Nongbri alerted us to an article by William Willis, the scholar at the University of Mississippi to whom the Robinson Collection had originally been bequeathed in 1958. Willis had donated a portion of the collection to the University of Mississippi, but when he left there for Duke in 1963 he took with him the remainder of the collection, and proceeded to donate the rest of the papyri to the Duke library. In a 1985 article describing the history of the Duke Collection, Willis wrote that only a portion of the papyri in the Robinson Collection had been identified.[46] Though no one at MOTB had ever raised the possibility, it was not impossible to imagine that the Galatians fragment was one of these unidentified Duke manuscripts. In the years since Willis wrote his summary, however, Duke has photographed and digitally cataloged its holdings from the Robinson Collection; if the Galatians fragment had been among them, it would have become public knowledge. More crucially, papyrologists at Duke confirmed to us that their library has not sold or otherwise deaccessioned their holdings from the Robinson Collection.[47] Thus the riddle of the eBay sale in 2012 remains unexplained. The earliest documentation of the Galatians fragment's existence is still the photographs included in the eBay auction, in which it is not identified.

When pressed, Trobisch said that when he "went through the correspondence again" he found that the provenance letter filed with the purchase identified the Galatians fragment as being from the "U.S. Collection of Bill Noah, and D M Robinson." At this point, however, the real issue was not whether documentation connecting the papyrus to the Robinson Collection existed, but whether there was any evidence that such documentation was believable. Considering cultural heritage laws and UN resolutions, any reasonably intelligent seller would have strong grounds for ensuring the clean provenance of the artifact. And, indeed, forged letters of provenance are not unknown. The "Gospel of Jesus's Wife" was burst onto the public stage in 2012, when the Harvard professor Karen King announced its discovery at the International Congress of Coptic Studies.[48] Almost from the beginning, scholars questioned its authenticity—MOTB's own Bible curriculum refers to it as a forgery—but it was a 2016 investigation by the journalist Ariel Sabar into the provenance of the text that unraveled the authenticity of the fragment. A well-educated German named Walter Fritz likely had fabricated not only the writing on the fragment, but also the provenance documents that accompanied it.[49] The affair of the "Gospel of Jesus's Wife" makes the question about the provenance of the Galatians fragment more than merely academic: was there any proof, beyond the mere statement of a deeply interested party, to back up the link to the Robinson Collection, the link on which the entire provenance of the Galatians fragment hinged?

There is no such proof. Trobisch confirmed that this was the entirety of the Green Collection's evidence for the provenance of the piece: the statement of the seller, unsupported by any documentation demonstrating the basis for such a claim—no identifying marks of the Robinson Collection, no photographs, no sales history.

As we continued to puzzle over this Galatians manuscript, our interest was increasingly drawn back to that provenance letter quoted to us by Trobisch. He had intended this to be proof that the fragment was from the Robinson Collection; as the evidence for that link faded away, we became more curious about the other name in the letter. This was the first time Bill Noah had ever been mentioned in connection with this document, and the connection was not obvious: he was neither a contemporary of Robinson nor an academic.

Dr. William H. Noah is, rather, a respected physician and amateur biblical historian who, with the book dealer Lee Biondi and the disgraced manuscript collector Bruce C. Ferrini, was one of three co-founders of a touring Bible exhibit in the early 2000s. In 2004, Noah split from Ferrini and Biondi, and sued them for his share of the profits from their venture. Biondi and Noah spun off their former collaboration into competing exhibits, with missions that were eerily similar both to one another and to that of Museum of the Bible. Biondi's exhibit was named *Dead Sea Scrolls to the Bible in America*; Noah's was called *Ink and Blood: Dead Sea Scrolls to the Gutenberg*. Noah's exhibition toured the United States in various incarnations from 2006 until 2012. The display cases and other accoutrements from the exhibit are now in storage; the artifacts were returned to the collections from which they were borrowed.[50]

Bill Noah has some ties to the Green Collection. He sold a couple of pieces to Johnny Shipman (including a Coptic receipt that previously belonged to Ferrini) that have since found their way into the Green Collection. It seemed plausible that he may have sold other Coptic papyri. But when we asked Noah whether he had ever owned a Coptic fragment of Galatians or anything from the Robinson collection, he said no. This makes sense: in 2011, when the Robinson Collection was on the auction block at Christie's, the *Ink and Blood* exhibit was winding down. As the Christie's lot was not advertised as containing any biblical material, there was no reason for Noah to have been interested in it anyway. And in 2012, when the picture of the fragment appeared on eBay, his exhibit was on the verge of closing. It is difficult to believe that he was in the market for antiquities, but if he had been, one would expect that the fragment would have joined his touring collection. Had he owned the fragment before its sale as part of the Robinson collection, one would, likewise, have expected some of the materials to be incorporated into his exhibit. At no point in his career has Noah had the technical training, facilities, or staff necessary for handling dozens of packets of fragmentary papyri.

When we asked Noah if anyone from MOTB or the Green Collection had ever called him to verify that he had owned the manuscript, he said that he had never been asked about it.[51] Eugenio

Donadoni, director of the Christie's manuscript department, confirmed that Noah was "neither the buyer nor consignor" of the lot in which the Robinson papyri were sold. Perhaps the fact that Noah had sold the Green family a different Coptic piece led to the misattribution, but this does not explain why the Galatians fragment would also have been connected to the Robinson collection. Nor does it explain how it was that a trusted dealer would have made this mistake if, as Trobisch told us, this information was included in the letter that accompanied the fragment's sale. It appears that the provenance documentation for the Galatians fragment has been compromised, although it is difficult to say whether or not it was deliberately falsified. This leaves us with an unprovenanced artifact, the origins of which, prior to its appearance on eBay, are completely unknown.

It is perhaps revealing that, at the moment that he finally admitted just how little evidence the Green Collection has about the provenance of this artifact, Trobisch also made sure to say, "The purchase happened before I joined the collection." This was not the first time he had said this to us; nor was he the only person to throw that fact into conversation. Josephine Dru: "I was not involved in the acquisition process." Christian Askeland: "This is before I worked for the Green Collection." Given the purchase date of 2013, it seemed likely that the purchase had been negotiated by Cary Summers. In the months that elapsed between Carroll's departure in 2012 and Trobisch's arrival in 2014, Cary Summers told us, he had acted as de facto head of the collection, presenting potential acquisitions to the family and negotiating the terms of sales. But with regard to the Galatians papyrus, Summers told us he didn't quite remember: "I think that was something that Scott had started way back." Carroll, for his part, denies ever having seen the Galatians papyrus. This seems believable: the item appeared on eBay only a few weeks before he left the Green Collection, and certainly not "way back." Thus even if MOTB and Green Collection administrators claim that the Galatians fragment is perfectly legitimate, they also seem to want as much distance as possible from it. Nobody wants to take responsibility for the papyrus, and, given the many unanswered questions that surround it, it is easy to see why. It disrupts their narrative that, with Carroll's departure, the collection turned over a new leaf.

In 2016, and in the wake of our articles in *The Daily Beast* and *The Atlantic*, the Green Collection went offline. Statements by MOTB served to distance it from the Green family and the Green Collection: despite Cary Summers, the president of MOTB, having been the one to confirm the existence of the federal investigation to us, MOTB quickly clarified to inquiring members of the press that it was the Greens and Hobby Lobby that were under investigation, and that MOTB had nothing to do with it. Not long thereafter, the website for the Green Collection effectively disappeared. Without looking at the cached internet pages, the only hints of the collection's existence are in brief, tersely worded summaries on the MOTB website. The Green Collection—which never had any legal status to begin with—retreated into the shadows.

Of course, the artifacts themselves are still in the Hobby Lobby warehouses in Oklahoma City or on loan to other exhibitions, and the Museum of the Bible still touts the massive collection that will eventually find its home in Washington, D.C. What has happened is not a change in the collection, but a change of its name: the Green Collection is now known as the Museum Collection. This nomenclature serves to obscure more than to clarify: the designation is given not only to those artifacts that have been donated by the Greens to MOTB, but also to those not yet donated. And changing the name of the collection does not alleviate any of the problems of provenance; in a sense, by obscuring even the current owners, it only heightens awareness of the issue.

The examples that we have discussed here are just those that have bobbed to the surface of academic consciousness. But there is good reason to think that these are merely the tip of the iceberg. Michael Holmes, the current director of the Green Scholars Initiative, told us that there are crates of papyri in the collection that no one can match to documentation of purchases. This suggests that there is potentially a substantial trove of unprovenanced papyri in the holdings of the Green Collection, the origins of which are documented even more poorly than the Galatians fragment. Despite the widespread institutional acknowledgment that the acquisitions of the Scott Carroll years were riddled with potential problems of legality and, it has been mooted, even authenticity, no one associated with the Greens or MOTB has ever suggested that they would consider returning or removing from the collection even a single item to its previous owners or country of origin. Repatriation is a complicated issue, but the fact remains: even as they disavow the earlier era of acquisitions and administration, the collection and museum continue to claim the artifacts from that period, continue to boast of their 40,000-piece holdings. It is as if simply admitting that mistakes were made relieves them of the obligation to take responsibility for those mistakes or correct them.

Nor does there appear to be much effort to research or document the provenance of the artifacts in the collection. When we inquired about the provenance and authenticity of a cuneiform-inscribed brick from Larsa (in modern-day Iraq), a photograph of which appeared on the MOTB Facebook feed, we were told by Lance Allred, the curator responsible for cuneiform objects, that the acquisition happened before his time and that he could not assist us in determining its provenance. "To research it," he said, "would require quite a lot of work on my part."

David Trobisch echoed Allred's sense that provenance was secondary and something that lay beyond the bounds of his personal responsibility. When we pressed him on the provenance of the Galatians fragment that appeared on eBay, he suggested that we go to Mississippi ourselves to "try to solve the riddle." Even without making a trip to the South, within the space of a morning and two phone calls we were able to ascertain that the provenance of the Galatians fragment provided by Trobisch is inaccurate. This is not to suggest that Green Collection employees are perpetrating a deception; but for all of the extensive research they claimed to have conducted, they never took the most basic steps in trying to track down the origins of this piece. There is a sense among some curators and directors that they are in no way obligated to solve these problems themselves. Cyrus Vance, the Manhattan District Attorney, recently cautioned against just this sort of attitude: "The process of establishing an item's provenance may not be easy, and it's often not straightforward, but the alternative is the implicit endorsement of an unacceptable practice through willful ignorance."[52] What is lacking among the members of the Green organization is any sense of due diligence.

Moreover, it is not clear that those employed by the Greens fully understood what provenance actually is. And, whatever they may say, this appears to be a problem not confined to the Scott Carroll era. In late October 2015, before our piece in *The Atlantic* was published, we received an email from David Trobisch berating us for discussing issues of provenance in it. Among his arguments was the statement that they have between 10,000 and 15,000 printed books, and that it is "hard not to have provenance when the year and place of publication is on the title page." This is a fundamental misapprehension of how provenance works. Provenance is about the ability to document the legal chain of ownership. If a printed book manufactured in the eighteenth century was stolen during wartime and later sold for profit, its provenance would be corrupted. (This is why, for example, artwork stolen by the Nazis during the Holocaust is not considered to have a clean provenance.) Merely knowing when and where a book was printed does not mean that it was acquired legally or ethically. By training, David Trobisch is a New Testament scholar, and New Testament scholars sometimes use the term *provenance*, as Trobisch did, to refer to the circumstances of a text's composition. But to use the term in that way in the world of the antiquities trade is an error, and one that is troubling.

It is unclear if anyone associated with the Green Collection is addressing, in depth or with transparency, the legal and ethical issues surrounding provenance. In 2016, Josephine Dru contacted some prominent papyrologists asking for their assistance in identifying the provenance of papyri in the collection. The flow of information does not go both ways. Emails we sent to various Green Collection curators requesting the details of the provenance of items in the collection that had already been displayed or advertised went unanswered for weeks, if they were ever answered at all. The scholarly guild has repeatedly been promised that the artifacts would be published, but they are years overdue. Delays, of various lengths, are not uncommon in the academic world; but when a collection is as prominent as this one, when its size and scope are so publicly touted, and when it is known to be destined for a major museum, the degree of accountability is necessarily higher.

2

THE GREEN SCHOLARS INITIATIVE

IN EARLY 2011, JENNIFER LARSON, A PROFESSOR OF CLASSICS AT Kent State University, was grading papers in her office when the phone rang. On the other end of the line was Scott Carroll, and he had an offer for her: would she be interested in studying a Greek papyrus with a group of her undergraduate students? Larson thought she might be talking to a con artist—in part, perhaps, because she had never worked with actual ancient papyrus before. "That sounds lovely, but I'm not a papyrologist," she told Carroll. He was unfazed—and, indeed, had he looked at her resume in advance, he would have known this already. "No worries," he replied. "You'll see, it's going to be fantastic."

Not long thereafter, Carroll arrived on the campus of Kent State for preliminary discussions with the library about housing the papyrus. Carroll put on a show, opening his backpack and pulling out papyri in front of the dean of the school. The special collection librarians were less impressed than they were unnerved, both by Carroll's demeanor and by the requirements of having an ancient manuscript in their possession. Like Larson, the Kent State library had no experience with papyri. Moreover, this particular papyrus came with certain strings attached: both Larson and Kent State were required to sign an agreement limiting access to the text only to Larson and her students, including digital images of the papyrus. As a public institution, this went against usual standards and practices.

Despite her reservations, Larson agreed to take on the project once she learned that the Oxford papyrologist Dirk Obbink would be involved in a supervisory position, and in August of that same year Carroll returned, bearing the papyrus in question. The document was a well-preserved first-century CE dowry text from

Egypt, the Greek writing covering nearly a full page. Carroll met with the students Larson had assembled, energizing them with his enthusiasm for ancient artifacts. Carroll was not shy about physically interacting with the materials: he encouraged the students to remove the papyrus from its protective glass case. He told the students that he could identify the origins and date of a papyrus, not by the usual scholarly methods—carbon dating, handwriting analysis, linguistic markers—but by smelling and even tasting it. (Larson, knowing that the manuscript was insured for $200,000, declined to remove the papyrus, thereby also forestalling any attempts to sample it directly.)

Once the papyrus was in Kent State's possession, Larson and her students set to work on it. The students involved were not advanced classics majors; their first step was to enroll in Elementary Greek I. It seems, however, that once they learned the alphabet they were ready to contribute, at least to the process of transcribing the text. (As it turned out, recognizing letter forms in the papyrus became the impetus for some of them to actually go on and learn the Greek language.) Understanding the content of the papyrus required still more expertise, which again the students lacked: upon finding a date in the document, the students struggled, albeit temporarily, to identify which emperor must have been ruling at the time—a struggle that was resolved, as is so often the case, by turning to Wikipedia.

Two years later, Larson, with the help of her students, had done the work necessary to produce a published edition of the manuscript, and in 2014 Larson and Kent State gave the papyrus back to the Green Collection. By this time Scott Carroll was no longer working for the Green family, but the larger project lived on, and still does. Jennifer Larson and her students were among the first to participate in what is known as the Green Scholars Initiative (GSI).[1]

Almost from the beginning of the Green Collection, in the summer of 2010, Steve Green made clear that there were two extensions of the collection that he wanted to see implemented: the first was a traveling exhibit, what would eventually become *Passages* (see chapter 4). The second was a process by which the artifacts in the collection would be subject to academic study: this became the GSI.

The program, in its broad strokes—distributing artifacts to faculty who would then bring their students on board, thereby intentionally combining study and pedagogy in order to inspire the next generation of scholars—was the brainchild of Carroll, who had been doing similar work with students in his previous positions. For the administration of the program, however, Carroll turned to an old friend and graduate school classmate, Jerry Pattengale. Pattengale was, at the time, assistant provost at Indiana Wesleyan University, a small evangelical Christian school in Marion, Indiana. He had made his name by developing what he called "Purpose-Guided Education," a pedagogical philosophy aimed at maintaining student interest and involvement in their studies by concentrating on the student's own core values, morals, and beliefs. The majority of Pattengale's book-length publications, whether authored or edited, are in the realm of pedagogy (e.g., *Why I Teach: And Why It Matters to My Students*, 2009); some are explicitly Christian (*Straight Talk: Clear Answers about Today's Christianity*, 2004); and some are a combination of both (*Consider the Source: Young Scholars and the Timeless Truths of Christianity*, 2000).[2]

At the University of Miami in the late 1980s, Pattengale, like Carroll, had studied under Edwin Yamauchi, a conservative evangelical Christian apologist/historian. Yamauchi and Pattengale would go on, in 1996, to co-found The Scriptorium, a private Bible-oriented foundation that would eventually become part of The Holy Land Experience, a Christian theme park, in Orlando.[3] Pattengale was not hired because of his expertise in ancient manuscripts, even though that is the field in which he had been trained. Carroll told us that by the time he reached out to Pattengale, his old classmate had "lost the skills for languages and things of that nature." He was, however, capable in ways that Carroll, perhaps, was not: "He's a great administrator, in contact with people, sorting things out and doing what he's doing."

This is the task Pattengale set to: using his contacts to identify academics that could join the GSI. He approached two groups: those who could serve as senior scholars, in what would be effectively an advisory and editorial role, and those who would be working with the materials firsthand. The senior level was the first priority, and it was not long before a brace of authoritative scholars had joined the GSI ranks: Emanuel Tov, from Hebrew University in Jerusalem, for Hebrew manuscripts; Dirk Obbink, from Oxford, for papyrology; Ralph Hanna and Christopher de Hamel, from Oxford and Cambridge, respectively, for medieval texts; Alister McGrath and Gordon Campbell, from Oxford and the University of Leicester, for the King James Bible; and others.[4]

These scholars, all supremely qualified to work on those parts of the Green Collection with which their interests overlapped, were not, however, asked to actually engage in the scholarly analysis of any artifacts directly. They were there primarily, as Pattengale told us, to be "available for mentoring." What they seem to have mainly been used for is name recognition. Jennifer Larson's doubts about Scott Carroll and the entire enterprise were alleviated when she learned that Dirk Obbink was involved. Other GSI scholars have also pointed to Obbink's name, and Emanuel Tov's, as a reason that they felt comfortable joining the project.

When it came to the "scholar-mentors," as the main body of the GSI faculty participants were called, there were considerably fewer qualifications necessary to be selected. Pattengale distinguished between "top scholars as the main consultants over projects, and capable scholars working on items." Jennifer Larson was not chosen because she was an expert papyrologist, as she admitted and as Carroll (and Pattengale) knew. Though she was never told how she ended up on their list—indeed, first on their list—according to Pattengale it was essentially by chance: "I happened to be speaking [at Kent State] on another book." This sort of casual, almost accidental, relationship seems to account for much, if not in fact most, of the GSI's initial membership. Scholars were identified by chance encounter (Larson at Kent State), by geographical proximity (Lisa Wolfe at Oklahoma City University), or, seemingly most often, through the extensive network of evangelically oriented schools to which Pattengale, in his position at Indiana Wesleyan, was well connected. Early assignments went to Renate Hood at Mary Hardin-Baylor University, a Baptist school in Texas; Mike

Holmes at Bethel University, an evangelical school in St. Paul; Stephen Andrews at Midwestern Baptist Theological Seminary, in Kansas City.

The original intention had been to draw on scholars from a range of institutions: public and private, large and small, secular and seminary. It did not turn out that way. Christian Askeland, who along with his other roles serves as the GSI's Regional Director for the central United States, described the initial organization of the GSI as primarily "relational . . . sometimes it would just be Jerry moving around and talking to people and going to different universities."[5] This "relational" nature went in both directions: according to both Pattengale and Askeland, once word got out about the GSI, they were inundated with requests to work with Green Collection material, thereby throwing off any attempt to create a balanced roster of institutions. Thus, despite plans to involve major research universities alongside smaller private institutions—to, as Carroll said, "select schools that were not merely in their wheelhouse, were not merely evangelical, but that were broader than that"—there was soon, as Askeland put it, a "pretty heavy slant toward CCCU schools"—that is, the Council for Christian Colleges and Universities, an association of colleges and universities whose mission is "to advance the cause of Christ-centered higher education and to help our institutions transform lives by faithfully relating scholarship and service to biblical truth"[6]—"and it just had to do with the people who were rubbing shoulders."

The schools and individuals to whom Pattengale and the GSI turned were both similar in nature and, at the same time, diffuse: a single scholar at one school, a single scholar at another. With the exception perhaps only of Baylor University, which proudly hosts "the initiative's main undergraduate program," there is no concentration of scholars working on GSI material.[7] This might be explained as a conscious attempt to spread the wealth around, as it were; it may, however, have to do with the nature of evangelical scholarship in the United States. As the historian Mark Noll points out, there is no centralized evangelical institution in the United States to coordinate scholars and their projects as Britain has, for instance, with Tyndale House at Cambridge (with which the GSI has a relationship).[8] In a sense, the GSI is providing something of a similar service, linking disparate institutions and scholars together under a single project.

The University of Mary Hardin-Baylor; Midwestern Baptist Theological Seminary; Azusa Pacific University; Wheaton College; Southern Nazarene University; Multnomah University; Gordon-Conwell Seminary; Shepherds Theological Seminary; Gordon College; Pepperdine University; Dallas Theological Seminary—almost every school selected by the GSI has been explicitly Christian, and often explicitly conservative. (Shepherds Theological Seminary may top that particular category, as it proclaims that the Bible is "trust without any mixture of error" and affirms "the biblical view of men and women and their relationship to each other in the home and church . . . believing that God has appointed men and men only to the Elder/Pastor position."[9]) The paucity of major American research universities on the list of schools hosting a GSI project is striking. Again, however, the nature of the American educational landscape may be relevant: Noll notes that, again in contrast to the situation in Britain, in America "evangelicals who conduct research in Scripture usually teach at seminaries or Christian colleges."[10] It can become difficult to disentangle cause from effect when it comes to the makeup of the GSI: did a focus on recruiting evangelical scholars lead to a reliance on the evangelical network of schools with which Pattengale and the Greens were familiar, or did reliance on that network result in the natural choice of evangelical scholars?

People affiliated with the GSI state repeatedly and categorically that there is no litmus test for participation. In November 2013, Jerry Pattengale said explicitly, "There is no religious requirement for involvement." He then went on, however, to qualify that somewhat: "We attempt not to recruit scholars that are predisposed critically against a view."[11]

More significant, and certainly clearer, is Steve Green's stated position on who is eligible to be selected as a GSI scholar. In a speech given before the conservative Council for National Policy in 2013, Green echoed Pattengale's words, saying that they would look for scholars who "are just going to present the evidence without being adversarial." He was more forthcoming, however, on the question of "adversarial against what?" He continued: "If you want to say that this piece of papyrus says that Jesus had a wife, then I don't have use for you because you are making that up. It is not what it says. But if you are going to give me the facts, I don't care what stripe you are from, but if you are a good scholar we have use for you."[12] Green is alluding here to the controversial "Gospel of Jesus's Wife." The text itself does not exactly say that Jesus had a wife, though it does seem to have Jesus referring to someone, perhaps Mary Magdalene, as "my wife." More important, however, none of the scholars who worked on that papyrus made the claim that Jesus actually had a wife. What they claimed was that the papyrus was evidence—and only one piece of evidence among many—of an ongoing discussion in early Christianity regarding the question of Jesus's marital status.

As it turned out, the papyrus is a forgery. But that determination was conclusively made only in 2014—that is, after Green's speech. Moreover, the scholars who published and worked on the Gospel of Jesus's Wife were, indeed, "good scholars." They were, in fact, some of the very best papyrologists and scholars of early Christianity in the world: Karen King from Harvard, Anne-Marie Luijendjik from Princeton, and Roger Bagnall from NYU. And the authenticity of the "Gospel of Jesus's Wife" notwithstanding, the existence in early Christianity of disparate views regarding Jesus's marital status is a matter of scholarly conversation. Green accuses them of "making that up," because, in his view, "it is not what it says." The "it" here would, it appears, be the Bible, or the traditional Christian stance regarding Jesus's bachelorhood.

What Green's statement reveals is a bias against any scholarship that might challenge the traditional Christian understanding of the Bible and the biblical story. By describing some scholars as "adversarial," Green creates a false distinction between scholars who adhere to biblical tradition and those who are, somehow, against the Bible. From this perspective—that is, the perspective of the person who is funding the GSI—it is perhaps less coincidental that so many scholars and institutions associated with the program are explicitly Christian. And it may explain why so many of the leading papyrologists in the academy have not been involved in the GSI.

Papyrology is a highly specialized field. Proper analysis of ancient manuscripts requires a remarkable range of expertise: multiple dead languages, often with numerous dialectical variations on each; orthography and handwriting; historical context; genre and literary conventions; material concerns, including the nature of the papyrus and ink used; scribal habits; codicology, the study of how ancient books were physically made; and more. The rigorous training required of graduate students in papyrology is not for the faint of heart, and it is no coincidence that there are relatively few truly competent papyrologists in the world.

Compounding the difficulty of the field is the relative scarcity of new materials to be studied, especially for the oldest texts. Papyrus survives only in very particular conditions: moisture is especially dangerous, which is why the largest troves are found in desert contexts—the Dead Sea Scrolls, for example, or the Oxyrhynchus papyri from Egypt. Many manuscripts are now in collections at major institutions, at university libraries such as the Bodleian at Oxford or the Beinecke at Yale, or at the Vatican Library in Rome. While these collections, including the Vatican's, are generally accessible to trained scholars, they are often not particularly well archived, such that there is an element of chance involved even in locating unpublished papyri. The other major source for unstudied manuscripts is private collections, which are less easily accessible, and often less well publicized.

The Green Collection straddles the line between the two: it is a private collection, but it is also at least nominally part of a major project for the public, the Museum of the Bible. The existence of the GSI effectively announced to the academic world that there was a new and substantial body of material to be studied. Those scholars who had trained for much of their lives to work on papyri were understandably eager to gain access, or, at the very least, to know what sorts of materials were in the Green Collection that might add to our collective knowledge about early Christianity and the world from which it emerged.

Yet entry into the Green Collection was not always so straightforward, at least not for everyone. One papyrologist, who asked not to be named for fear of professional retribution, told us that back in 2012 he had contacted the then-head of papyri for the GSI, Mariam Ayad at the University of Memphis, following the normal procedures for inquiring about access to a collection: he asked about the nature of the collection, where the materials came from, and whether they were available either digitally or in person. Given his experience with other collections, he expected at least to be given access, especially as he was not asking for any publication rights, which are a more complicated matter. Yet he, and some who inquired along with him, were simply ignored.

This was cause for frustration—a feeling that was compounded when it became clear that unpublished papyri were being assigned, and for publication, to scholars with no papyrological training or experience whatsoever. A fragment of the Dead Sea Scrolls was given to Lisa Wolfe of Oklahoma City University, a Bible scholar and pastor who had never done any work with material artifacts, but who is rather, in her own words, "more of a narrative critic," someone who focuses mostly on hermeneutics, on modes of biblical interpretation.[13] Perhaps most startlingly, one of the first scholars selected by the GSI was Renate Hood of the University of Mary Hardin-Baylor, a professor of Christian Studies with, again, no papyrological experience—and she was given not a marriage contract or a small scrap of Hebrew, but rather one of the most famous and important biblical papyri in the world: one of the earliest surviving witnesses of the Gospel of John, known as P39, worth hundreds of thousands of dollars.

The lack of papyrological expertise among those scholars assigned to work directly with the papyri was a feature of the GSI, not a bug: Pattengale told us, "There was the understanding that very few scholars would have the ability to do the papyrology side of it or the text studies side." Yet the GSI structure is such that even when untrained scholars take on a project for publication, their inexperience does not come through in the edited volume. The senior scholars are there to protect the GSI rank and file from themselves. Emanuel Tov, for instance, who oversees the publication of the

Hebrew texts from the Green Collection, and who is perhaps the most important textual critic of the Hebrew Bible alive today, was perfectly willing to admit that many of the GSI scholars lack the training appropriate to the task they are doing. He considers it his responsibility as overseer and editor to make sure that what they turn in to him becomes publishable according to the usual scholarly standards.[14] The lack of training among GSI scholars is, as Pattengale put it, "taken care of by the senior scholars when it goes to the publishing level."

In this way, the GSI is a mentoring program not only for up-and-coming students, but also for faculty. But it is a strange one. Faculty who long ago decided on their chosen area of study are suddenly wading into the vast sea of papyrology. Yet they are not really allowed to learn to swim on their own: they are always dependent on the life raft of the senior scholars. Without the GSI support structure, almost none of the GSI scholars will be equipped to analyze another ancient manuscript on their own; nor, given their positions and career choices, is there any indication that they would want to.

If there were enough ancient manuscripts to keep every trained scholar busy for the foreseeable future, the distribution of Green Collection artifacts to inexperienced papyrologists might be seen as more acceptable. But this is not the case. For professional papyrologists, for whom the ability to work on new material is career-defining, the GSI was an insult. When we told one scholar about the dowry contract that Jennifer Larson had been given, he could barely contain himself: "You've got to be kidding me!" That her students were in Elementary Greek and using Wikipedia did not ameliorate his unhappiness.

Whether because of preexisting personal relationships or because of a more concerted effort to employ only scholars with certain religious or otherwise ideological predispositions, a marked dichotomy in treatment quickly became apparent. While some who craved access were denied it, others were actively recruited to join the GSI. Pattengale has been reported to make generous offers to those he wants involved: meals, hotels, scholarships for faculty and students. At the 2012 Society of Biblical Literature conference in Chicago, the participants in a blog called Evangelical Textual

Criticism gathered for their annual dinner together. Near the end of the meal, Peter Williams, a GSI scholar from Tyndale House at Cambridge, announced to the group that Pattengale was on his way, and encouraged them all to give him a good welcome. When Pattengale arrived, he proceeded to pay for the meal—for everyone's meal—on behalf of the GSI.

To graduate students, and for many faculty members as well, the Greens appear to be offering access to otherwise unreachable materials, as well as some financial support. The GSI gives monetary prizes—$5,000, plus funds for attending conferences (the checks for which, at least at first, came directly from Hobby Lobby, Inc.)—to its most accomplished graduate students, and has paid scholars hundreds of dollars simply to participate in GSI-sponsored panels. In a field in which people work largely for their love of ideas, even a little money can make a big splash. But the Greens are getting a terrific bargain, especially when it comes to the more established scholars: for what to them is a paltry sum, they get the prestige of having important names, both of individuals and of their home institutions, associated with their product. Some of our colleagues have told us that they were asked to speak on Green-sponsored panels, or to travel to Washington, D.C. for a day of consulting on the museum. Such opportunities may bring small financial reward for the scholar in question, a few hundred dollars plus travel expenses, but for the Greens it permits them to say that their projects have received input from leading academic minds, even though there is no guarantee that that input will be listened to. Indeed, one scholar we spoke to had been in negotiations to display some of his research on the textual history of the Bible at the museum, but withdrew from the project when it became clear that the museum staff were unwilling to accept any guidance regarding the broader presentation of biblical scholarship.

Pattengale told us that he "can't personally think of ever not accommodating someone in some way . . . I don't know personally of ever denying someone that had a reason to see something to be allowed to see it." He admitted that there were probably some individual examples of a scholar not being allowed to see Green Collection materials, but he chalked up such situations to surplus demand: "There's an entitlement, sometimes, that creates a wave of requests . . . there's simply too many people to assist, just too many requests." It seems clear, however, that access to the Green Collection, and participation in the GSI, has largely been a one-way street. The same papyrologist who had been ignored in 2012 was, as it turns out, approached by Pattengale a year later and invited to become involved. By this time, however, there were already too many red flags surrounding the GSI. Among those cautionary warnings was a requirement that was at odds with most common standards and practices in humanities scholarship: signing up with the GSI also meant signing a non-disclosure agreement.

> This confidentiality and nondisclosure agreement dated and effective as of ______ (date) by and between Hobby Lobby Stores, Inc. d.b.a. "The Green Collection" and ______ ("Scholar"). . . . Confidential and proprietary information shall include any information or communications which is provided to Scholar by the Green Collection. . . . Scholar shall safeguard and keep confidential the Information; and shall not disclose the Information to any party, without the prior written consent of The Green Collection, in any manner whatsoever, in whole or in part. Scholar shall disclose the Information only to those of The Green Collection's Representative who have a need to know such Information. . . . Upon written request by The Green Collection, all Information and copies thereof, including that portion of the Information which consists of any and all documents or anything else internally prepared or obtained by Scholar, shall be returned to The Green Collection immediately or destroyed by Scholar or its Representatives. . . . In the event of a breach or threatened breach of any provision of this Agreement, The Green Collection shall be entitled to injunctive relief restraining and enjoining Scholar. . . . All Information shall remain the exclusive property of The Green Collection.[15]

In the business world, nondisclosure agreements are commonplace. They are used to protect company secrets and plans, and to ensure that competing interests cannot gain any undue advantages. Hobby Lobby is, first and foremost, a business, with a corporate structure and corporate lawyers. The nondisclosure agreements that GSI scholars were required to sign in order to participate emerge from that world. Such a document is, however, virtually unheard-of in the academy, and especially in the humanities.[16]

Papyrologists who request access to collections for the purpose of studying and, it is hoped, publishing a given text often come to either oral or written agreements with the host institution. Such agreements often entail no more than a limitation on the number of items a scholar may work on at one time, a time frame within which the research can be conducted, and a request that the institution be notified about any resulting publications for the purposes of keeping accurate bibliographic records. Because ancient papyri are not subject to copyright, images are often freely available on institutional websites, and few if any restrictions are placed on their reproduction.[17]

The nondisclosure agreements produced and required by the GSI go well beyond the generally accepted practice for institutional collections. Indeed, in their thorough stringency, they effectively impair the basic modes of scholarly discourse in the humanities, where no patents are at stake, but where dialogue and information-sharing are fundamental. Unlike the sciences, in which replicability is a defining feature, in the humanities the question is not whether one's ideas can be reproduced, but how well they stand up to the challenges of both evidence and logic. Having a wide range of interlocutors is not only desirable; the back and forth among scholars from differing perspectives is the very essence of the work.

Especially in this age of the internet, where data and ideas can be shared instantaneously, restrictions on information distribution are increasingly anathema. Yet the most obvious examples of how the GSI's nondisclosure agreements constrain the usual scholarly discourse are from the relatively old-fashioned world of the academic conference. The GSI recognizes that presenting work in progress at conferences is an established practice, and one that can enhance a scholar's reputation. Thus there have been a few times when a scholar has spoken publicly about work being done under the auspices of the GSI. Often, however, the public speech has come into conflict with the private nondisclosure agreement, creating awkward situations for all involved.

At a conference in the summer of 2015, a GSI scholar spoke about an unpublished manuscript of potential significance. When asked about the plans for its publication, he indicated that he was not allowed to answer. When asked about the details of the manuscript's provenance, he also refused to say—despite claiming in his talk that it was the "oldest ever" of its kind. In 2012, at the annual conference of the Society of Biblical Literature, the main professional society for biblical scholars, two graduate students from Baylor University and Pepperdine University presented a paper entitled "Initial Findings on a Newly Discovered Early Fragment of Romans." The abstract for the paper said that the papyrus "may be one of the earliest witnesses to the Pauline corpus."[18] Yet the presenters were hamstrung by their inability to share crucial information with the audience. Despite the claim of the abstract, they were unable or unwilling to speak about the dating and provenance of the papyrus. They could not, or at least would not, show images of the reverse side of the fragment. And they refused to allow anyone to take pictures during their presentation. As one scholar who attended the talk said, "It was like the Secret Service had shown up at SBL."

What is perhaps most disturbing about the last example is that it involved graduate students, who are as firmly bound by the nondisclosure agreements as are the established scholars who serve as their mentors. Indeed, it is not only graduate students, but even undergraduates who feel the effects of these restrictions. At Multnomah University, a nondenominational Christian school in Portland, Oregon, Karl Kutz, Professor of Bible and Biblical Languages, was selected by the GSI to work on an unpublished fragment of the Dead Sea Scrolls. (Like so many GSI scholars, Kutz was well trained in the primary language—in this case, Hebrew—but had no expertise in working directly with the material evidence.) He incorporated the study of his GSI fragment into an advanced Hebrew course; yet there was something unique about this particular class. The undergraduates who worked on the Scrolls fragment with him had to sign a nondisclosure agreement. As a result, they were required to leave all their class notes with Kutz at the end of each session and were prohibited from discussing their work in the course with their fellow students at Multnomah.[19]

There is a significant ethical dilemma entailed in this sort of situation, one that is present in every classroom, graduate or undergraduate, working with GSI materials. Students end up taking courses, for credit, in which they are intellectually constrained. The work that they are doing is no doubt educational, but they are not working solely for their own educational benefit. In signing the nondisclosure agreement, and indeed in being involved with a GSI project at all, they are also working for a private company—Hobby Lobby. The inherent power imbalance between faculty and students renders this situation unavoidably exploitative.

The involvement of students in the GSI has been central to the program from its very inception. Investments made in college often form the basis of lifelong commitments, as educators and recruiters of various stripes have long known. The value of influencing students has been recognized in the evangelical community as well (on which see more in the following chapter). In the late 1980s, the retail giant Walmart began generously funding a program called "Students in Free Enterprise," or SIFE. As Bethany Moreton describes it in her profile of the company, SIFE was "an explicitly ideological organization that trained young activists . . . for the elaboration and dissemination of Christian free enterprise." The program was wildly successful, now active across the globe. Its relationship with Walmart remains central to its existence and purpose: according to Moreton, "by 2003, the company hired 35 percent of its management trainees out of SIFE." SIFE was at once a mechanism for promoting a particular (free-market) worldview and also a farm system for Walmart, ensuring that the next generation of managers had already bought into the company's overarching philosophy.[20]

The GSI, though not nearly as extensive or influential, serves a similar purpose for the Greens. "It looked like we were heading to a place where we . . . could raise up a new generation of text scholars, or at least expedite the process," Pattengale told us. So too, for Carroll, the GSI was founded on a "vision of placing items in university campuses and then using those as a way to inspire students" to pursue more advanced study. Such goals are laudable: the experience of working hands-on with ancient materials is indisputably special, and does often lead to a strong desire to press further in such academic pursuits.

Yet the system established by the GSI is, for the most part, purely inspirational. Due in large part to the lack of expertise among the faculty mentors selected, students are often not given any substantial training in the actual applied work of papyrology. When asked to describe the kind of work they did, and the tools they acquired, GSI students told us stories about learning to identify letter forms—sometimes without even knowing the language itself—and about using online databases to search for strings of letters and words, hoping to match what they were seeing with a known text. These are tasks that could be done by anyone, and often in fact by a decent computer program. The students were, in effect, temps—doing data-entry-level work, albeit on rare and, at times, very valuable texts.

In fact, a substantial amount of the work done on GSI materials, by both students and scholars alike, is done digitally. Very few of the scholars analyzing and publishing these texts have actually been given direct physical access to the materials. In part, this is a technical or financial issue: transporting a highly valuable artifact from one part of the country to another requires great expense and care. Storing it properly upon arrival is also necessary, and not every academic institution has such facilities in place or the financial means to install them. (One early GSI project, the study at Midwestern Baptist Theological Seminary of an important manuscript of Psalms known as P24, was abandoned because of financial constraints: in order to house the manuscript, the school was asked to renovate one of its rooms to ensure secure storage, a demand that could not be met.[21]) As Carroll said, "There were insurance issues, how things were transported, and how they were placed, and who bore the responsibility for that, and how you vet institutions' capability of having things." As a result, the majority of GSI scholars and their students interact with their texts only on a computer screen; the actual papyri remain in storage in Oklahoma City. (Everyone we have spoken to confirms that the Greens have excellent storage facilities for their artifacts—better, often, than those found at many major universities.)

To be fair, new developments in digital imaging technology mean that often more can be done with a digital image now than could previously be done even in person. The GSI has used the services of Bruce Zuckerman, who runs an operation out of the University of Southern California called the West Semitic Research Project, which provides remarkably high-resolution images of ancient texts along with a variety of high-tech ways to manipulate those images. And this digital manipulation was at the center of much GSI work, especially on the handful of papyri that had already been previously published. As one student said, "I spent every day staring at a computer screen zoomed in to an image of a manuscript [in which] I had to try and find 'invisible' letters." And a substantial part of the training that GSI scholars are given is in the use of the digital imaging technology.

This type of analysis can result in useful discoveries. A GSI team at Pepperdine University, in southern California, led by two well-respected scholars of New Testament and early Christianity, Ronald Cox and Randall Chesnutt, was assigned a well-known fourth-century manuscript of Romans 4–5 known officially as MS 0220, and colloquially as the Wyman Fragment, named for its original purchaser in 1950. The manuscript was famous and already extensively published when the Greens purchased it at auction at Sotheby's in July 2012 for just over £300,000.[22] Any new investigation would therefore depend on using new technology—without ever actually handling the physical object, which never left its secure storage in Oklahoma City. And, indeed, Zuckerman's technology did allow the team to more conclusively establish some of the readings in the text, including one that had been considered uncertain until a Pepperdine student, Natalie Lewis, used her skills with Photoshop to render a definitive judgment.[23]

It is not the case that such digital efforts are unimportant. Rather, they are only a small part of the process of analyzing ancient manuscripts. For most trained papyrologists, the most valuable and closest work on a given piece must be done in person. The ability to physically handle and manipulate a papyrus is crucial for evaluating it in almost every aspect. Even Carroll lamented the necessity of working only digitally: "You work with wonderful digital images, but then you're not inspiring by touching and tasting and handling things."

That depends, however, on what kind of inspiration is hoped for. A reasonable number of students told us that they intend to go on in various academic fields related to their GSI experience, though this is a self-selecting group: those students with an interest in taking classes or working on ancient manuscripts are probably already predisposed to such a career path. It is impossible to know whether more students would join the scholarly ranks if they had more direct access to the physical objects, rather than to the digital images alone. But whether they worked first-hand or via computer screen, almost every student told us that they were, indeed, inspired by their work with the GSI.

We asked a number of GSI students what they had learned from the experience of working so closely with ancient texts, and what about it they found rewarding. Their answers were illuminating. While one or two did mention having received better training in languages, most did not, or could not, provide any specific new knowledge or skill that they had acquired. Some, rather, talked about how they had not previously appreciated how much effort it took to do this sort of work: "The thing I came away with . . . was a great respect for those academics who work on biblical translations." And some talked more openly about how working with the GSI impacted their faith: "The Green Foundation is remarkable in the way that they procure these texts from worlds away and remind young students like myself of the materiality of the heritage I identify with." "It was fulfilling to see my personal faith attested in centuries-old documents."

GSI students are, indeed, being inspired. The question is whether this faith-based inspiration is a by-product of the scholarly pursuit or, as it were, vice versa. It is difficult not to connect the GSI student involvement and experience with Pattengale's "purpose-guided education" philosophy. In Pattengale's model, the way to get students involved and excited about their education is to give them a personal hook: a cause that they might care about that could drive their studies. It is possible to see in the GSI that same concept in reverse: the study is the hook—the ability to work with materials and feel that one is accomplishing something novel, or exploring a new world. One student put it in terms of feeling like

Indiana Jones. If the study is the hook, though, then the hoped-for outcome is the attachment to a cause: in this case, a deeper appreciation of biblical and textual study, even a deeper commitment to Christianity. The pedagogical approach of the GSI can, viewed from a certain angle, look an awful lot like evangelization. Steve Green seems to understand it that way: "We are wanting to engage students so that we can raise up a whole new generation that has a love and a passion for God's work."[24]

For students who do take their involvement with GSI as a stepping stone toward further academic pursuits, the experience of working with material artifacts is understood as giving them a leg up, making them both better prepared and more desirable as graduate students and early-career scholars. "It just helps set them apart," Pattengale said. "I assume it's a positive, when you're looking at a student who's applying, . . . to have worked on some original material." This is certainly true—in theory. The problem, however, is that these same students are effectively prohibited from talking in any depth about the work that they did. One of the most forthcoming students was able to tell us only that "what has been made public about our piece is that it is a manuscript fragment on papyrus of one of the canonical gospels"—he cannot even say which one—"very small in size, dating to the third or fourth century." Another shared that he was working on a fragment of the Dead Sea Scrolls, but that he had "agreed not to disclose sensitive materials or information about the fragment I was studying until it is published," and that he "only disclosed the project to members of the GSI and those who were supervising my graduate work." A third said, along the same lines, "Once all the details are published, I'll be glad to share more."

The professional advantages gained from working closely with material artifacts are rendered moot when that work cannot be described or discussed. The nondisclosure agreements that permitted these students to participate in the GSI are prohibiting them from benefiting from that participation. This conflict seems unavoidable: if student involvement is a fundamental principle of the GSI, then secrecy is even more so. Whether it is due to this secrecy, or merely to a growing awareness of the ethical problems surrounding the Green Collection and the GSI, the professional rewards that might be hoped for from students may be more idealized than realized: we have heard of more than one highly respected graduate program that has turned down applicants specifically because they had worked for the GSI.

Perhaps the most famous discovery in the history of biblical studies was that in 1947 of the Dead Sea Scrolls, in the caves overlooking the ancient site of Qumran. The scrolls upended many long-held assumptions about early Judaism, biblical interpretation, and the very text of the Bible itself. Reams of scholarship have been produced, with no end in sight. Yet for the first forty-plus years after their discovery, the Dead Sea Scrolls were unavailable to the majority of scholars, and only a handful of them were published.

In the first few years after their discovery, a few major Dead Sea Scroll texts were quickly made available in facsimile, including perhaps the most famous, the Great Isaiah Scroll (a facsimile copy of which is owned by the Greens). In 1954, a team of scholars was assembled in Jerusalem to dedicate themselves to the reassembly and publication of the scrolls. The first volume appeared in 1955; four more were published in the 1960s. Given the vast amount of material, and its obvious importance, there was great demand for a faster pace of publication. Yet up to and throughout the 1980s, access to the unpublished Dead Sea Scrolls was limited exclusively to those scholars who were officially part of the project. Any work they did, any knowledge that they accumulated, was held back from the rest of the scholarly community. As Yale professor John Collins has written, "By the end of the 1980s there was a furious clamor for the publication of the remaining scrolls."[25]

The analogy between the Green Collection and the Dead Sea Scrolls is easy to see. Indeed, it was made by Emanuel Tov in conversation with us. "They have many things in common," he said. "The publication of the Dead Sea Scrolls was . . . equally secretive as this project." The GSI, in its insularity, is effectively mimicking the original Dead Sea Scrolls team of scholars. "It has an element of not distributing information," Tov said; "that was true of the Scrolls also." And Tov should know: it is no small irony that the eventual opening of the Dead Sea Scrolls to the entire scholarly community, a significant moment in the field of biblical studies that occurred only in 1991, nearly forty-five years after the scrolls were first discovered, was spearheaded by the newly-appointed editor-in-chief of the project—Emanuel Tov.

Despite knowing well how problematic it is to withhold material and information that is of broad academic interest, and how much resentment in the scholarly community such secrecy causes, Tov and others continue to participate in the GSI at the highest ranks. The rise of digital information sharing has only exacerbated the perception that something is fundamentally not right with the GSI's secretive procedures. Even before the internet, it was usual for scholars to share prepublication work with their peers; it is now almost *de rigeur* for newly discovered material to be distributed for feedback and assistance. As Tov admits, GSI policy is "against—it's different from scholarly procedures today." Few involved with the GSI, however, seem to recognize this. Forty years ago, the renowned Dead Sea Scrolls scholar Geza Vermes declared that "unless drastic measures are taken at once," the ongoing secrecy surrounding the scrolls "is likely to become the academic scandal *par excellence* of the twentieth century."[26] In the field of biblical studies, at least, it is safe to say that the Green Collection and the GSI have already achieved that status for the twenty-first century.

There is an important difference between the GSI and the scholarly team that worked on the Dead Sea Scrolls, however—aside from the universally recognized world-class caliber of the scholars who worked on the scrolls. Unlike the scrolls team, which was assembled by the archaeologist who excavated the site where they were found, and which was funded largely by the Rockefeller Foundation, the GSI is funded and administered by a privately held company, by a family, that holds very particular religious beliefs regarding the material under investigation. As we have already seen, this directly affects the types of scholars that are selected to work on the Green Collection artifacts. While any religious litmus test for participation in the GSI is vigorously denied, it cannot be ignored that just such a test is imposed by the Green family and

Hobby Lobby in their other philanthropic ventures, and that this is a family business that has labored for decades to promote a specific faith-based understanding of the Bible. As with laboratory testing that is funded by pharmaceutical companies, claims of objectivity must be weighed against the inherent bias of the source of financing. It matters where the money is coming from.

There are a number of related ways that this bias presents itself in the case of the GSI. Foremost among them relates to the central question of what the purpose of this type of scholarship is. For the majority of its existence, text criticism has been interested in trying to understand how textual variations came into being, how changes were introduced into the written record, and thereby to ascertain which of these fragments preserve the earliest version of the biblical text. The goal of text criticism, for much of its history, has been to peel back the layers of accumulated variants and to uncover a pristine version of the Bible. Given this agenda, it is unsurprising that the majority of text critics are evangelical Christians, for it is here, as perhaps nowhere else, that the critical aims of scholarship intersect with the faith claims of evangelicalism, which is invested both in the infallibility of scripture—as it was first written down—and in rediscovering the authentic words of Jesus himself. As Noll has pointed out, "the relationship between research and biblical infallibility provides considerable motivation for scholarship. Research can . . . demonstrate that supposed errors in Scripture lack certain support from scholarly evidence."[27] Moreover, the technical nature of text criticism allows evangelicals to participate in scholarship while avoiding the complications entailed by modern critical trends toward postpositivism (the recognition that researchers are influenced by their own background and values) that inevitably surface in more philosophically oriented areas such as history. Like grammar, another area where evangelical scholars tend to cluster and excel, text criticism seems—or at least seemed—like a safe area of research.

In the 1960s, however, the Harvard scholar Eldon Epp argued that the "original text" of the New Testament was essentially beyond our reach: that the random and fragmentary nature of the evidence makes it impossible for scholars to discover what the authors of the books of the Bible had originally written down. Epp's ideas opened the doors to a new direction in text criticism, one that emphasizes, rather than attempts to eliminate, the diversity and complexity of the manuscript evidence. In its mass-market form, this approach has been presented as a threat to cherished Christian notions about the authentic witness of the Bible. In the hands of the popular scholar Bart Ehrman, author of books like *Misquoting Jesus: The Story Behind Who Changed the Bible and Why*, the mere existence of thousands of fragments of contradictory material becomes a faith-killer. How can scripture be inerrant when we can't even know what scripture originally said?

The GSI can seem at times like a conscious push-back against contemporary trends in text criticism. It is the position of the Green family that, as Steve Green has said, the Bible "was accurately transmitted." This is, to Green's mind, one of the main purposes of the Green Collection and the Museum of the Bible. "You want to say that there was a telephone game and it was passed down and it changed over time, you're free to believe that. But let me show you the evidence." He then proceeded to integrate the Jewish people into his evangelical narrative of perfect biblical transmission: "God gave those people a job, and they did that job well. They took it seriously, and they do to this day take it seriously. We have a debt of gratitude to the Jewish people, because they provided us with the Hebrew text and they did it well."

Even the Dead Sea Scrolls, which, in academia, overturned many long-held notions of textual authority and biblical canon, are understood by Green to be part of this narrative. "It's an incredible story to be told that really dispels a lot of the critics. Let's look at it honestly—yeah, there's some variations, we don't want to say that there's not, yeah, there is—but let's focus. Let's spend ninety percent [of our time] on the ninety percent [of the scrolls that are consistent with modern Bibles] and realize that's incredible." Green's dismissal of the variants in the Dead Sea Scrolls—variants that include a very different book of Samuel from the traditional Hebrew text, a book of Jeremiah that is approximately one eighth shorter than the traditional text, and a number of Psalms that are not part of our Bibles today, along with innumerable small additions and other changes—borders on willful ignorance.

With Green and his resources standing behind the GSI, it is perhaps unsurprising that his understanding of the perfection of the Bible's transmission should trickle down through the project. GSI student participants have come away from their experiences with a similar impression. "The consistency of biblical writings is incredible," one told us. Another said, "It's impressive how well the biblical message has been preserved."

The use of scholars and students who lack the proper training to analyze ancient papyri may be described as a pedagogical exercise, but it dovetails closely with a broader classic evangelical trope: the dismissal of "expert" opinion in favor of the "knowledge" of the layperson, Richard Hofstadter's famous "anti-intellectualism," or what Noll describes as "an evangelical suspicion of the magisterial expert." Noll quotes a pithy version of this stance: "Have we to await a communication from Tübingen, or a telegram from Oxford, before we can read the Bible?"[28] This attitude goes back to the Reformation notion of *sola scriptura*, "the Bible alone," and the rejection of papal authority over biblical interpretation. It has found its modern evangelical counterpart in, for example, the rejection of scientific discoveries regarding evolution in favor of a creationist biblical model of human origins. (In Texas, during the controversy over the new public school curriculum a few years ago, one of the leaders of the antievolution group said, "Somebody's gotta stand up to the experts!"[29])

The GSI is, in its way, proving an analogous case: one need not be part of the small cabal of "experts" in papyrology in order to recognize the import of these ancient biblical texts. Randall Stephens and Karl Giberson note that credentialing, a centerpiece of the secular academy, is generally less respected among evangelicals.[30] The great historian of Christian fundamentalism George Marsden described the perspective this way: "The Bible in the hands of the common person was of greater value than any amount of education."[31] The Bible—even its manuscript history—belongs to everyone, not just to the few. Anyone, in the GSI model, can be a text critic, and even work with previously unpublished materials, and even get published in a major press. No advanced degrees or lengthy training are required, just a few reference volumes and some good digital images. Even an undergraduate with no knowledge of ancient languages can do most of the work. And once the experts have had their hold on the physical material loosened, so too their interpretation of it need be given no greater weight.

As Steve Green and other members of the Museum of the Bible team repeatedly state, the principle behind the Green Collection is not collecting for collecting's sake. They are, they insist, storytellers first and foremost, and everything that they acquire is for the purpose of telling that story. What this means in practice is that there is an inherent selection bias at work. It is easier to maintain the claim that the Bible has been flawlessly transmitted when any evidence to the contrary has been excluded—because it does not fit the story.

This selection bias manifests itself in a number of ways. Some of the most famous early Christian papyri are those known as the Gnostic Gospels—a catchall phrase for the wide variety of ancient Christian writings that were eventually deemed heretical. For scholars, these texts are an invaluable resource for recognizing and understanding the diversity of thought in early Christianity; they problematize in important ways traditional notions of a direct line of pure faith from Jesus to the present.[32] As Christian Askeland put it to us, such texts "probably do more to tell us about the diversity of orthodoxy"; they are "representatives of how weird Christians were in the first few centuries—as weird as they are today."

It is therefore notable that the Green Collection does not—to our knowledge, and that of Askeland as well—contain any texts of this nature. This is not, however, for lack of opportunity. In 2010, Scott Carroll brought Steve Green to see the famous Gospel of Judas, initiating an almost year-long process of negotiations for its potential acquisition. The family eventually passed. Both Carroll and Cary Summers told us that the reason the Greens declined to purchase the Gospel of Judas was that its provenance was too much in doubt. Though it is true that the provenance of the Gospel of Judas is highly questionable, it is hard to believe that this was the motivating factor for turning it down—after all, the Greens have a well-established record of purchasing artifacts with questionable provenance. In fact, the initial discussion about the Gospel of Judas took place very soon after the purchase of the cuneiform tablets for which Hobby Lobby was under federal investigation.[33] It is more likely, therefore, that the Gospel of Judas falls under a different category, one articulated by Steve Green: "We're buyers of items to tell the story. We pass on more than we buy because it doesn't fit what we are trying to tell."[34]

Along similar lines, none of the papyri on display at *Passages*, the traveling exhibition, or that have been promoted on the organization's various social media outlets, contains any meaningful discrepancies vis-à-vis the traditional biblical text. This may be simply a matter of chance: there are only so many manuscripts in the world, and only so many that could have been purchased for the Green Collection; it is possible that they have never had the opportunity to acquire one with an important textual variant. (They do, however, proudly display famously misprinted Bibles, including the Great "He" King James Bible, the first edition of the translation, in which the word "he" was mistakenly printed in place of "she" in the book of Ruth, an error corrected in the second edition.) At the same time, however, there is reason to suspect that the avoidance of particularly challenging artifacts may have an element of intention to it.

Relatively early in the history of the Green Collection, the famous evangelical pastor (and current MOTB board member) Rick Warren came to visit the Hobby Lobby headquarters in Oklahoma City and was given a tour of their acquisitions. Scott Carroll, who was then in charge of the collection, brought out a manuscript of the Gospel of John. He pointed out that this papyrus—like a number of ancient manuscripts of John—did not include the passage known as "Jesus and the woman taken in adultery," a passage famous for being the source of the phrase, "He who is without sin among you, let him first cast a stone at her." Carroll asked Warren what he thought it meant that this episode was missing from the manuscript; Warren correctly answered that it implied that the passage was a later addition to the gospel.[35] David Green, the family patriarch, then pulled Carroll aside and tore into him: "You will not use this collection to undermine the King James Bible!"

This episode is illustrative on several levels. It serves as a stark reminder that, whether explicit or not, there is a faith-based agenda at work at the wellspring of the Green Collection, at the source from which all the funding, and therefore the entire project, flows. David Green's concern with the authenticity of the King James Version is grounded in the common evangelical belief, especially among Pentecostals and Baptists, that the King James Bible is the only valid English translation; sometimes it is even considered to have been divinely inspired, putting it on par with the original biblical writings in Hebrew and Greek.[36] From this perspective, the King James is not really a translation of the Bible at all; it is simply the Bible.

Green's outburst also points to the potential for censorship of not only voices, but of material evidence, that speaks against that agenda—even in a private encounter with a friendly audience (Rick Warren is on the board of the Museum of the Bible, and promotes it widely). And it raises another worrisome possibility: that the Green Collection owns items that its founders find theologically problematic, but is intentionally keeping them out of circulation. The manuscript of John that Carroll showed Warren has never been displayed or otherwise advertised as being part of the Green Collection. As far as we are aware, no GSI team is studying it. Thus if it is in fact owned by Hobby Lobby, it has effectively disappeared—which means that it is unavailable for study by any scholar, whether from the GSI or otherwise. This is the danger of keeping the collection and its research secret: while those artifacts that promote the story the Greens want to tell are slowly being processed, no one may ever know what important manuscripts exist in the vast Hobby Lobby storage facility.

The artifacts that are actually publicized and promoted by the Green Collection and the GSI have a tendency to be described in consistent terms: quite often, though there is little other information provided, it is announced that a given manuscript is "the earliest" of its kind. This is especially the case when it comes to fragments of the Bible. The most prominent of these is certainly the mysterious Mark papyrus discussed in the previous chapter, but it is not alone. As we have already seen, GSI students presented a fragment of Romans that received a similar designation; Scott Carroll, as noted earlier, repeatedly claimed to have found the earliest version of various New Testament texts.

The search for "the earliest" example of a biblical text holds a universal appeal, though not an undifferentiated one. For most scholars, the benefit of early texts comes mostly from their scarcity: the farther back in time we go, the fewer texts we have. Thus earlier artifacts fill in gaps in our knowledge: they might change our understanding of the date of a book's composition, or provide evidence about the circulation of Christian literature in the Roman Empire. In evangelical circles, however, more is at stake: new discoveries of ancient New Testament papyri allow us to inch ever closer to the earliest proclamations of the Messiah and his faithful followers. When the aim is not to reconstruct the diversity of ancient Christianity, but to get back to the original words of the Bible, it is no wonder that many of the most important manuscript discoveries have been billed as the "first" or the "earliest" fragment of this or that biblical text. The earlier a fragment can be dated, so it is thought, the more likely it is to preserve the original words of the (divinely inspired) biblical authors, and the more significant it becomes for lay Christians: from God's lips to our ears, skipping the two thousand years of history and human error in between.

It is unsurprising, then, that the Green Collection seems to have a particular affinity for the idea of the "earliest" biblical manuscripts. In some cases, this may be no more than an acquisitions strategy: targeting early texts in particular. In other cases, however, this may be a function of a top-down directive to the GSI. We were told that at conferences for GSI participants, in which GSI leadership and senior scholars provided guidance and advice to the faculty working directly with the material, those faculty were instructed to date their texts as early as possible. Dating ancient texts is an inexact science at best, especially in the hands of untrained papyrologists. And on statistical grounds, early papyri are simply unexpected. Askeland roughly estimates that from the first to the fourth centuries CE we should expect there to have been fifteen times as many manuscripts written in each successive century, and that our modern discoveries of ancient texts should therefore follow the same pattern. To put it the other way: however many manuscripts we have recovered from the fourth century, we should expect fifteen times fewer in the third, and another fifteen times fewer in the second. "If we have fifty manuscripts from the fourth century, how many should we have from the first century?" Askeland asked.[37] In other words, dating manuscripts as early as possible is not only overstating our ability to date texts in the first place; it is also pushing the limits of statistical likelihood. When in doubt, exaggerated claims about the early dating of manuscripts should be avoided. The GSI—whether to increase publicity or for faith-based reasons—does exactly the opposite.

The individual scholars who work on Green Collection materials, and their students, may well be entirely unaware of the overarching agenda of the GSI. But the project is ultimately shaped by its source of funding, and Steve Green has repeatedly made clear that there is an ulterior motive at work in having academics working with his artifacts. It is not that the GSI scholarship, whatever its results may be, will shape the story that Green wants to tell. It is the reverse: Green and the Museum of the Bible want to tell a particular story, and the GSI is there to give that story a veneer of authority. "We needed to have scholarly credibility with what we have, with what we were saying," Green told us. "We wanted to pretty much undergird all that we did . . . so it's not me, it's what the biblical scholarly community is saying about these things that brings credibility to it."

The GSI, however, is not "the biblical scholarly community." It is, rather, a private academy, paid for, directed, and controlled by Hobby Lobby. It is a group of hand-picked scholars who are provided with a vetted selection of artifacts, the study of which is intended to play into a faith-based narrative of the Bible and its transmission. How Green understands the payoff of the GSI's work is illuminating: "I think the more that we learn about this book, the better off we are. If this book is not what it is, I want to know about it—but what we keep finding is that, boy, it validates what the book says. So the more we study, the more we know, the better off I think the world is—the faith community is." This well-intentioned statement is not critical scholarship: it is faith masquerading as impartial scholarship; academic study employed—literally—for evangelical purposes.

Despite its ostensibly limited scope, the GSI is an important component of the Green family's overall mission even beyond its function as the scholarly backing for the evangelical vision of the Bible that they want to promote. Although even the most senior scholars in the GSI may well not be aware of it, the GSI plays a central role in the internal mechanisms of the Green Collection and, in fact, of the greater Hobby Lobby corporation.

The Green Collection, as described in the previous chapter, contains a certain percentage of artifacts with less-than-pristine provenance, and a far greater percentage of artifacts with a provenance that the Green Collection refuses to make public. Although there is an ongoing debate, many scholars today have come to the conclusion that, in order to help dampen the trade in illicit antiquities, unprovenanced artifacts should not be published. This is a stance that requires broad participation in order to be effective. When a scholar does choose to publish an unprovenanced artifact, it quickly becomes impossible for even those who strongly oppose such publication to ignore the existence of the item in question. If some scholars are working with more data, even if some of it is of questionable origins, those who choose to limit their data set based on ethical considerations place themselves at a competitive disadvantage. Once an unprovenanced item enters the scholarly conversation by being published, it is nearly impossible to remove it.[38]

What this means in practice is that publication effectively erases the stigma that comes with bad provenance. The artifact in question gets absorbed into the scholarly bloodstream, and is, eventually, indistinguishable from the unblemished material. (This is the case in large part because so much of the standard material evidence in the field was collected before anyone began paying any attention to the notion of provenance—the Dead Sea Scrolls, for example, would struggle to pass scholarly muster today on this front. Thus adding one or two more unprovenanced artifacts into the broader academic world is easier than it would be had provenance been a concern from the beginning.)

The scholars of the GSI, as the ones charged with the study and publication of the Green Collection materials, are the only people with the capacity to prevent unprovenanced Green Collection items from being published. Unfortunately, it is clear that no such efforts are being made.

Jennifer Larson made sure that her students understood the importance of provenance; they ensured the valid provenance of their Greek papyrus as part of their research. Yet this case is an exception, rather than the rule. Larson and her students were not provided with any information about the provenance of their artifact when it was given to them, as seems to be typical for the GSI.

The current director of the GSI, Mike Holmes, has suggested that it is premature to ask such questions before publication. In a blog post, he raises three competing interests when it comes to revealing this kind of information: "the need: (1) to acknowledge the privacy and ownership rights of the owner of the artifact; (2) to minimize distractions for the researcher investigating the artifact; and (3) to satisfy the legitimate curiosity of the scholarly community and other public audiences."[39] Given the order of presentation, and the fact that the first two entries seem to speak against publicizing provenance, it is clear where Holmes's interests lie, and troubling that he categorizes an ethical and legal issue as a distraction.

While his list is *prima facie* reasonable, there are some complicating factors when it comes to the GSI. He says with regard to the first item that owners "may have good reasons for not wanting to publicize their ownership of an artifact." Yet the Green family clearly wants to publicize their ownership: they are publishing volumes devoted to their possessions, they are putting their artifacts on display all over the world, and they mention with great frequency the large number of items that they own. As for the second item, it is true that scholars may "prefer not to be distracted by a seemingly endless series of e-mail questions and statements." But the best way to preclude such distraction is simply to openly provide information about provenance. Furthermore, presenting an artifact at a conference, or discussing it with the media, is effectively inviting inquiry, especially with regard to provenance, which—particularly when it comes to the Green Collection—is the first question that every scholar asks about a new artifact.

Holmes says that "for every item published under the auspices of the GSI, the goal will be to give, as part of the initial publication, as much detail as necessary regarding (a) provenance, both ancient and modern (subject, of course, to any legal restrictions attached to the terms of purchase); (b) authenticity; and (c) date." Two phrases here are key. First, "as much detail as necessary"—to which most scholars would reply, "All of the detail is necessary." The judgment as to what amount of detail is required to pass scholarly muster is one that is determined by the inquiring scholarly community, not by the owners. If information is being withheld, that only raises further suspicions—especially as there is no obvious reason that any available information about provenance should not be shared. The second phrase is "subject . . . to any legal restrictions attached to the terms of purchase." While it is true that such restrictions are sometimes attached, so that, in this case, the Greens would not be allowed to reveal from whom they bought an item, these legal niceties do not play well in the scholarly world. Indeed, a text that has a restricted provenance is functionally the same as a text that lacks provenance altogether. It is a mockery of the ethical considerations when the only people who can vouch for the legal provenance or authenticity of a text are those who own it, and who therefore have a clear financial interest in clearing any potential hurdles. The Green family, or the GSI, announcing that an artifact has a clean provenance is effectively meaningless to the scholarly community at large, as well it should be.

Yet this seems to be precisely what it happening. One GSI scholar that we spoke to, Karl Kutz, told us that he was provided with no information regarding the provenance of the Dead Sea Scroll fragment he was given to work with, nor did he bother to look into it. It was his understanding, he said, that the question of provenance would be handled in the introduction to the published volume of Dead Sea Scrolls in the Green Collection, written in this case by

Emanuel Tov. In 2016, this volume was finally published—to date, the only publication of any Green Collection materials.[40] And, as Kutz correctly understood, the issue of provenance is taken up exclusively by Tov in his opening remarks; there is no discussion of provenance in any of the treatments of the individual scrolls. Yet the introduction itself provides no useful information whatsoever about the sales history of a single scroll in the collection. The reader is told the dates on which the Greens purchased the scroll fragments, but no more than that. The entire discussion takes up only one page.[41]

More remarkably, the question of the authenticity of the fragments, raised by multiple scholars, receives only a paragraph of discussion in another introductory essay, by Kipp Davis; yet the potential problems he notes there are not reflected in the analyses of the individual fragments. (One Dead Sea Scroll fragment was highlighted on the Museum of the Bible's Instagram account as recently as April 2017, despite having been flagged in print by Davis as having problems that "raise suspicion about [its] authenticity." There is a striking disconnect between the scholarship on the fragments—even that scholarship produced by the GSI itself—and the promotional purposes to which they are put by MOTB.) Michael Holmes has announced that tests are being undertaken to determine whether any of the fragments are forgeries—but this only after they have been published.[42] The GSI, in other words, knowingly published Green Collection artifacts without having even attempted to assess their authenticity, much less their provenance. There is no acknowledgment that any of this is problematic; when, at a conference session dedicated to the volume, we asked how the organization could defend purchasing, studying, and publishing unprovenanced and likely forged items, given that such activities only provide further incentive for looters and forgers, Jerry Pattengale responded that he believed that they had taken "the high road" by being open about such problems.

What seems to be taking place is an enormous game of passing the buck. One scholar who inquired about the issue of provenance in the forthcoming GSI publications was told that all such concerns were being vetted by the publishing house, Brill; when the same question was put to Brill, the reply came back that such concerns were being handled by the GSI. In the end, however, all the pushing off of responsibility is for naught. Participation in the illicit antiquities trade attaches whenever unprovenanced antiquities are purchased, studied, or published. Everyone in the scholarly food chain is implicated: the billionaire who purchases the artifact, the press that publishes the artifact, the senior scholar who edits the volume, the scholar who does the initial work on the item, and even—and this has its own ethical implications—the student who studies the artifact in class. The purchase of unprovenanced antiquities is against the law—and ignorance of the law, especially willful ignorance, and especially among scholars, who can hardly claim to be unaware of the importance of provenance, is no excuse. (Remarkably enough, even Mike Holmes himself told us that when he received his first artifact from the GSI, the question of its provenance "never occurred to me.") By studying and publishing Green Collection artifacts that do not come with a rock-solid provenance, the GSI effectively launders potentially illicit antiquities.

Of even more direct benefit to the Green family is the raw financial advantage that comes from its artifacts being subject to scholarly analysis. According to Scott Carroll, Steve Green understood the GSI to exist in order to "tell us what [the artifacts] are." This sounds banal, but the mere ability to identify a text makes an enormous difference in its value—and this is especially so when a text can be identified as Christian or especially early. Academic study, and especially publication, further increases the value of an artifact. This is certainly the case for unprovenanced items, as publication gives them a veneer of legitimacy, but it is true across the board. When Christie's or Sotheby's puts an artifact up for auction, it is accompanied by a list of all the publications that treat the item in question. The more often an artifact is cited, the more important it seems to be, and therefore the more it can fetch on the auction block. Additionally, when an artifact is chosen for study by the GSI, it may require steps to be taken for its preservation—cleaning, framing, et cetera—all of which also increases the value of the item.

The monetary value of items in the Green Collection is not merely an abstract calculation of the Greens' net worth. The Green

Collection plays an important role in the financial calculus of the Green family and Hobby Lobby. Every artifact that the Greens purchase is intended eventually to be donated, either to the Museum of the Bible or to some other institution. And every donation comes with a tax write-off of the item's appraised value. Thus whenever an artifact's value can be increased after purchase, the amount that the Greens receive in tax benefits from donating it also increases.

This is not a fringe benefit of the Green Collection, or even of the GSI: it is a substantial part of their reason for existing in the first place. As Scott Carroll told us, the GSI "is absolutely necessary . . . to the whole gifting process." He related a story of David Green, the founder of Hobby Lobby, coming to him in late 2011 and proclaiming that, by tax day on April 15, the company needed what Carroll described as an "astronomical" figure, somewhere in the tens of millions, in tax write-offs, in gifts from the Green Collection to the Museum of the Bible. Yet the value of almost nothing in the collection had been finally determined, precisely because the GSI scholars had not yet finished their analyses, much less published anything. With only a few rare exceptions, such as already well-known, valuable items, it makes no sense for the Greens to donate an artifact to the museum before it has been published. It would be like throwing money away.

Everyone who participates in the GSI, from Mike Holmes to a freshman undergraduate, is contributing to the Green family's bottom line. Every item that is studied and published is now worth more—sometimes substantially more—than it was when the Greens acquired it. And that added value comes back directly to the Greens, and to Hobby Lobby, through the tax benefits they receive for donating their artifacts (and donating them, it should be remembered, to a nonprofit that they also control). Scholars may believe in the intellectual merit of the narrow academic questions that they are asking of the Green Collection materials. But they are, knowingly or not, also supporting every other venture that Hobby Lobby and the Green family prioritize: all of the legal pursuits, all of the missionary projects, and the entire social agenda that is so beloved of the evangelical right. The GSI is not insulated from any of this: it is, rather, a closely interwoven part of it.

Like the Green Collection, the Green Scholars Initiative has undergone a change in nomenclature. It is now known simply as the Scholars Initiative. The attempt to dissociate the projects under the MOTB umbrella from the Green name remains, however, at odds with the underlying reality, especially in this case. Just as the majority of the items in the Museum Collection are still owned by the Greens, so too the members of the Scholars Initiative are tasked largely with studying items that formally belong to Hobby Lobby.

In some ways, the issues that haunt the Scholars Initiative are identical to those that surround corporate sponsorship of academia in general. External investments, both financial and ideological, can come to govern the production of research. We need only look, for example, at the detrimental effects of the sugar lobby's funding of research into the health effects of consuming fat to see how corporate interests play into the production of human knowledge. The same phenomenon exists with philanthropic organizations: grant recipients always play by the rules of the funding body. In the case of the Green Scholars, the collection of material available was driven by a desire to tell an overarching narrative about the Bible. It is a story in which the scholars themselves have limited say. A social network that, accidentally or not, is marked by shared religious commitments governed the selection of participants in the Scholars Initiative. This is not to say that members of the Scholars Initiative are unqualified. There are, for example, brilliant evangelical text critics out there, many of whom do not subscribe to Steve Green's view that God "saved" the Dead Sea Scrolls or that the original text of the New Testament is in our possession. But that is not what they were hired for. The Greens have employed members of the Scholars Initiative to "tell them what [manuscripts] they have." They were not employed as dialogue partners or tutors; they were commissioned to do work that would help catalogue the collection and raise the value of the Green family's holdings.

It is here that the Scholars Initiative differs from other charitable organizations like the Ford Foundation, the John Templeton Foundation, and the Bill & Melinda Gates Foundation. The Green Family will profit from the research of those in their organization, and they are able to control the way information about their holdings is published and disseminated. The nondisclosure agreements signed by students and scholars tie the hands of those participants in ways that agreements between scholars and public collections usually do not. The Scholars Initiative is in this respect more akin to industry-funded scientific research. It is part of a religio-industrial complex that is privatized, industrialized, and controlled.

3

EDUCATION

IN THE FALL OF 2013, WHEN THE HOBBY LOBBY LAWSUIT AGAINST THE Department of Health and Human Services was still making its way up the ladder to the Supreme Court, Steve Green took on a new project much closer to home. He paid a visit to the board of the Mustang School District, a suburb of Oklahoma City, to present them with an opportunity. Green was offering Mustang a chance to be the first public school district in the United States to use a new four-year Bible curriculum in the classroom—a curriculum funded by Hobby Lobby and designed by Jerry Pattengale, then the director of the Green Scholars Initiative. Mustang was the first school district to consider the curriculum, but they were not to be the last: Pattengale intended to have the course in at least 100 schools by the start of the school year in 2016, and in thousands by 2017.[1]

The promotion of Bible curricula in public schools is not new, of course, and especially coming from the evangelical movement. The National Council on Bible Curriculum in Public Schools (NCBCPS), endorsed by groups like the Southern Baptist Convention and the Family Research Council, has created and distributed an elective Bible curriculum for public schools that, by its own reckoning, has reached 650,000 students in 39 states. Despite its widespread adoption, the curriculum is not without its critics, who allege that it ignores current scholarship in favor of promoting religious perspectives such as creationism. The NCBCPS consciously pushes back against the secular standards current in public education: "There has been a great social regression since the Bible was removed from our schools," their website reads.[2] Some of the same people involved in the NCBCPS were also part of the successful effort to reform the Texas state high school curriculum in 2009 and 2010, a movement that drew widespread condemnation for, among other causes dear to conservatives, downplaying the separation of church and state.

While the NCBCPS is open about treating the Bible as a religious text first and foremost, Green promised the Mustang school board that his curriculum would not be "about a denomination, or a religion," but would merely tell the story of the Bible as a book.[3] In April 2014, the board voted—four members in favor, one abstaining—to adopt the course for a single year on a trial basis, starting in the fall of 2014.[4] In mid-July, however, Pattengale announced that the project would have to be postponed, due to "unforeseen delays"; it would now launch in January 2015.[5] On November 25, the Mustang Public Schools reversed their initial decision: "The topic of a Bible course in the Mustang School District is no longer a discussion item nor is there a plan to provide such a course in the foreseeable future," wrote the superintendent, Sean McDaniel.[6] What led to this abrupt change of plans?

First, there were some procedural hiccups. At the initial meeting with Green in 2013, McDaniel assured the school board that the entire curriculum would be available for review before any final decision was made. Yet when the vote was taken six months later to approve the course, this was not the case. The sole abstention, in fact, was based on the lack of opportunity to review the materials. Of the planned 800-page textbook, only the first quarter was made available—and that only on the day of the vote.[7]

In addition, it seemed as if McDaniel had gone out of his way to avoid any public scrutiny of the curriculum. Oklahoma law requires that meetings of school boards and any other official groups be open to the public. Yet the very same day that the board voted to approve the curriculum its members split into two groups—thereby dropping their numbers below the quorum needed to constitute an official meeting—and traveled to the Hobby Lobby headquarters in Oklahoma City to meet privately with Green. This unusual procedure was demanded by Hobby Lobby, or at least by their public relations firm, which was involved in making the meetings happen. It was at these meetings that the school board saw a portion of the curriculum for the first time.[8]

McDaniel suggested that this was merely an opportunity for the board to get a better look at the materials, without the bother of dealing with the media. "My thought," he said, "was, 'Hey, let's hold off on having a public meeting until we see a little more.' "[9] As the vote was taken later that day, however, there was never an opportunity for any legitimate public engagement with the curriculum. As Andrew Seidel, a lawyer with the Freedom from Religion Foundation, said at the time, "They've been a bit disingenuous about it."[10] There was also some misleading information regarding how deeply Steve Green himself was involved in the project. Pattengale had said that Green was involved only insofar as he was on the board of the Museum of the Bible. But the meetings were held at the Hobby Lobby headquarters, and McDaniel described the program as being designed by "Hobby Lobby and its president." At the very least, the attempt to circumvent the law drew the attention of the Oklahoma County prosecutor's office, though no charges were ever brought.

The more important motivating factor for dropping the curriculum, however, had to do with the content of the curriculum itself, the manner in which it presented the Bible. Teaching the Bible in public schools is not against the law; in 1963, the Supreme Court ruled that the Bible was an acceptable topic, but only "when presented objectively as part of a secular program of education."[11] A lower federal court ruled that "if that which is taught seeks either to disparage or to encourage a commitment to a set of religious beliefs, it is constitutionally impermissible."[12] These crucial qualifications were the focus of watchdogs such as the Freedom from Religion Foundation and the ACLU, whose alarms were raised when news spread of Green's Bible course. While any Bible curriculum will draw the attention of these groups, Green's involvement was a red flag, and not only because of his family's very public evangelical beliefs.

In April 2013, Steve Green gave a speech in which he described the plan to develop the curriculum. "This nation is in danger because of its ignorance of what God has taught. There are lessons from the past that we can learn from the dangers of ignorance of this book. We need to know it. And if we don't know it, our future is going to be very scary. So we need to be able to teach and educate students."[13] The curriculum, he explained, would be designed to follow the three-part scheme that was already planned for the eventual Museum of the Bible: the story the Bible tells; the historical evidence for the biblical account; and the cultural impact of the Bible. The curriculum would, Green stated, be "nonsectarian." Yet his description of the course belied that stance. When it comes to the historical evidence, Green proclaimed, "The book that we have is a reliable historical document . . . and when we present the evidence, the evidence is overwhelming." As for the cultural impact, "the goal in this section is to show that this book, when we apply it to our lives, in all aspects of life, it has been good. Because it has. In every area of our life, when we as man live according to its precepts, it has been good for us. So it's true, it's good." And although the Mustang school district would consider the curriculum only as an elective, this was not Green's ultimate goal: "Some day, I would argue, it should be mandated."[14]

The legalities of what they were attempting could not be lost on the Greens themselves. From 2006 through 2014, Hobby Lobby's annual Independence Day message, published in newspapers around the country, regularly criticized the 1963 Supreme Court ruling opposing the mandatory teaching of the Bible in public schools and, instead, cited an 1844 opinion encouraging it, along with an 1892 opinion declaring America to be "a Christian nation."[15] It is not surprising, then, that the ACLU might think that this particular curriculum deserved closer attention, vowing to examine it closely.[16] From Green's perspective, this was not merely a matter of attempting to ensure compliance with the Supreme Court's ruling. It was an attack, a salvo in a global war against the Bible. "There is this battle, you know this, on this earth," he told us. Whether consciously or not, Green was echoing the words of Ken Ham, perhaps America's most public biblical literalist and young-earth creationist, and the founder of the Creation Museum: "It's an incredible spiritual battle in this nation between Christianity and secular humanism."[17]

Green went on: "There are those that love and hate this book, and there are those that want to eradicate it. We were getting these threatening lawsuits about the Bible curriculum—before they even saw the curriculum they were threatening," an apparent reference to the ACLU and its partners. "What they're proposing is ignorance," he continued. "They don't want people to know about this book." He then put the conflict in nearly eschatological terms: "That in itself is a worldview: they're proposing their worldview over a biblical worldview, and that's where the conflict is." Similar language is used by James Dobson, the former head of Focus on the Family: "Nothing short of a great Civil War of Values rages today throughout North America. Two sides with vastly differing and incompatible worldviews are locked in a bitter conflict that permeates every level of society."[18] As Green put it, "Wars are created because of a conflict of worldviews. . . . If you want to embrace a secular worldview, well, let's look at other secular worldviews and see what that has created: it's created the greatest tragedies in the world, the atheistic communistic worldview has been the most destructive. . . . In essence that's what they're proposing, is one without religion, in essence an atheistic communistic worldview."

As he spoke, Green effectively equated a concern for secular teaching of the Bible with atheism and communism—which seem to be interchangeable, or perhaps even identical, in his mind. But he also proved the ACLU right in a way, as he also equated learning about the Bible through his curriculum with adopting a "biblical worldview." "What is wrong with understanding that our government was built on biblical principles?" he asked us (echoing, consciously or not, the language of the NCBCPS: "We need to refer to the original documents that inspired Americanism and our religious heritage"). "What are they afraid of? That's the question." In fact, Green went on to reveal that he was aware of their concerns: "If they're concerned about it being taught in a proselytizing way, that's one thing," he said. This was, of course, precisely what they were concerned about. But, Green insisted, their objections were leveled even before they had seen the curriculum: "They had no clue."

As it turned out, however, the worries of the ACLU and its partners were well founded. Just a few days after the Mustang school district approved the course, the ACLU acquired a draft of the first

220 pages of the curriculum, which they turned over to the Associated Press. The AP, in turn, passed it to Mark Chancey, a professor at Southern Methodist University who specializes in the church-state divide and the question of religion in public education and who works with the Texas Freedom Network Education Fund, a watchdog group for the constitutionality of religion courses in public schools.[19]

Chancey's fifteen-page report on the Hobby Lobby curriculum was clear: "Concerns about the curriculum's constitutionality and academic quality are well placed." The details Chancey highlighted matched all too closely the program that Green had laid out in his speech. The characters in the Bible were presented as historical figures—including Adam and Eve. The traditional Mosaic authorship of the Torah, or Pentateuch, was upheld. The six-day creation story of Genesis 1 was reconciled with modern science. The Bible's essential historicity was confirmed from the outset, with a section titled "How Do We Know that the Bible's Historical Narratives are Reliable?" and with conclusions to individual discussions that stated, "We can conclude that the Bible, especially when viewed alongside other historical information, is a reliable historical source." The textbook highlighted seven themes through which the Bible would be read—themes that were indisputably theological in orientation: "Love, God's presence, God's justice, God's plan, trust, and human choice." Chancey went on to point out the curriculum's regular appeal to theological language and ideas, its promotion of the notion that God's promises have been fulfilled in our day, its use, without comment, of the Protestant canon, its suggestion that the Bible is the origin of all good in modern culture but none of the bad, and its tone of "religious triumphalism." The curriculum, despite Green's claims, was far from being nonsectarian.[20]

Chancey also noted that the press release for the curriculum stated that "more than 70 scholars have written and overseen" its development, a claim that Green had made to the Mustang school board as well: "We want to find the leading scholars to help us and we will be pulling from this group to help write this curriculum," referring to the members of the Green Scholars Initiative.[21] Yet Chancey suspected that the scholarly input into the curriculum was far less than was claimed. Indeed, none of the people from the GSI that we spoke to said that they had any hand in creating or consulting on the Bible curriculum; it seems to have been almost entirely the work of Jerry Pattengale alone.

With the draft of the curriculum in hand, the ACLU raised the level of its rhetoric. "The deeper we get into it," the legal director of the ACLU of Oklahoma said, "the more red flags we see."[22] In the end, it was the threat of a lawsuit that moved the Mustang school board to pull the plug. According to McDaniel, the superintendent, there had been two "non-negotiables": review of the final curriculum—which seemed not to have been a problem when the board accepted the course earlier in the year—and the lack of a "commitment to provide legal coverage to the district" (though there is some dispute over where that commitment was expected to come from: the district's insurance policy, a nonprofit legal group, or Hobby Lobby itself).[23] McDaniel claimed that these were the only reasons for scrapping the course, and that the school district was not responding to pressure from any outside groups.[24] In light of Chancey's review, a third reason might have been in play as well: in April 2014, when the board voted to approve the curriculum, McDaniel had said, "This is a purely academic endeavor. If it turns into something beyond that, either we will correct it or we will get rid of it."[25] The academic problems might not have been apparent when the curriculum was presented to the board in private meetings at Hobby Lobby headquarters, but they would have been impossible to ignore after Chancey's report.

In the wake of the failure of the Mustang district Bible curriculum, Pattengale vowed to press on: "Museum of the Bible remains committed to providing an elective high school Bible curriculum. . . . We look forward to working with other school districts interested in such an offering."[26] When we spoke with Pattengale in the summer of 2015, he told us that he hoped a revamped curriculum might be used in some schools the following year. Cary Summers, however, the president of MOTB, denied this possibility. As of now, there are no plans to relaunch the Bible curriculum in public schools in the United States—though, as we will see below, the curriculum project continues.

The Museum of the Bible curriculum was designed specifically for high school students, with the explicit intention of reaching as many young minds as possible. But the Green family had already long established itself as a major force in higher education.

The last half-century has seen an enormous flow of money to support evangelical scholarship in colleges and universities across the country. Hundreds of millions of dollars have been provided by organizations such as the Lilly Endowment, the Pew Charitable Trust, the DeMoss foundation, and Christian Union. They have created programs such as the Rhodes Consultation on the Future of the Church-Related College, the Evangelical Scholars Program, and the Christian College Coalition, which aim to provide Christian scholars and schools with resources for closer cooperation and alignment.[27] Evangelical interventions in higher education, in turn, are part of a broader trend toward private donations to educational institutions supporting a variety of specific, often conservative, causes: the banking giant BB&T funding programs devoted to Ayn Rand at twenty-five colleges and universities;[28] the Koch brothers giving almost $20 million to support their libertarian economic philosophy;[29] the John Templeton Foundation financing the "Religious Freedom Project" at Baylor University, to name but a few of the most prominent.[30]

Unlike most of these larger grant-giving organizations, the Green family has concentrated its efforts on supporting specifically evangelical institutions. Some of their earliest contributions to evangelical higher education came in the form of land. Borrowing from Hobby Lobby's business practices, the Greens would purchase failing properties at undermarket cost, then donate those properties to schools in search of a new home—garnering a tidy tax write-off for themselves in the process. In 2004, they spent $10 million to purchase a former Ericsson plant in Lynchburg, VA, and gave it to Liberty University (after leasing it to them for a year for a nominal $1).[31] In 2007, the former site of Bradford College in Haverhill, MA, was purchased and donated to Zion Bible College (now known as Northpoint Bible College). In 2009, the Greens acquired the Northfield, MA, campus of the Northfield Mount Hermon prep school, and sunk $9 million worth of renovations into the property, with the intention of donating the land to whichever Christian university best made its case.

Liberty University is fairly well known: founded by Jerry Falwell, it has played host to numerous conservative speakers, and is a regular site for Republican candidates to demonstrate their evangelical credentials. It is currently led by Jerry Falwell, Jr., who recently made headlines by encouraging his students to carry concealed handguns, especially to guard against Muslims.[32] The university is unapologetically evangelical: in a 2006 job listing, it explicitly sought faculty who would "demonstrate a personal faith commitment to its evangelical Christian purpose," which includes teaching young-earth creationism as preferable to evolution.[33]

Northpoint Bible College is a Pentecostal school (the same faith tradition as David Green) and exists for the purpose of training Pentecostal ministers, with degrees offered only in Bible and Theology. According to their website, their "history is rich with stories of the miraculous hand of God"—including the gift from Hobby Lobby: "In 2008, the college was miraculously blessed with its current beautiful and historic 18 acre residential campus."[34] It is accredited only by the Association for Biblical Higher Education, a Christian organization that requires its member schools to sign on to a statement of faith that includes a commitment to affirm that the Bible is "the inspired, the only infallible, authoritative Word of God."[35]

The Northfield Mount Hermon campus remains unoccupied, though not for lack of effort. In 2012, it appeared that the Greens were ready to donate the property to Grand Canyon University, a self-described "Christian college with a biblically rooted mission."[36] Originally a Baptist school (Steve Green's denomination), Grand Canyon University's doctrinal statement, like those of the other institutions with which the Greens have been linked, affirms that the Bible is "inspired, the only infallible, true and authoritative Word of God." It also states that marriage is between one man and one woman, and that sex before marriage is against the divine will.[37]

The deal to donate the Northfield property to Grand Canyon University fell through, however, because the residents of Northfield expressed discomfort with the size of the expected incoming student body, and because there was some consternation about the explicitly evangelical nature of the school and how it would affect the established culture of the town and surrounding area. This seemed to puzzle Jerry Pattengale: "While most communities nationwide are offering amazing abatements and have teams that roll out the red carpets for new businesses, . . . many in Northfield basically shut doors or tried to."[38] Faced with the failure of the Grand Canyon University agreement, and acknowledging how much time and effort the family had put into finding even a single suitable suitor for the campus, the Greens decided to donate the land to the National Christian Foundation, who would then manage the process of identifying a new occupant. The National Christian Foundation's website promoting the campus gives special consideration to "organizations that have at the center of their mission advancing the Gospel of Jesus Christ."[39]

Many evangelical organizations—like, of course, many organizations of all kinds—promote their educational agendas in a more direct way: by providing funding for endowed chairs, often in the study of evangelicalism. D. Michael Lindsay points to the establishment of the McDonald Family Professorship in Evangelical Theological Studies at Harvard Divinity School, and quotes the donor, Alonzo McDonald, as saying that his aim was "to create more space for evangelicals in places like Emory and Harvard."[40] The Greens, to our knowledge, have not taken this route, with one exception—and it is an unusual one. The evangelical text critic Christian Askeland holds a faculty position at Indiana Wesleyan University (the same school where Jerry Pattengale serves as assistant provost). Askeland is listed on the IWU website as "Assistant Research Professor of Christian Origins" as well as "Central Region Director and Distinguished Scholar of Coptic Texts, Green Scholars Initiative."[41] What the website does not reveal, but Askeland told us, is that he is not paid by IWU at all; he is, rather, a full-time employee of the GSI. It is not unusual for independent scholars to take research positions at universities; these usually consist of little more than institutional affiliation and access to libraries and other resources. Askeland, by contrast, has full voting rights as a faculty member—despite the fact that the university is not actually employing him. This may be less an example of how the Greens are attempting to influence evangelical higher education, and more an illustration of how evangelical networks work.

Philanthropy is a cornerstone of the Greens' family and business philosophy, and in this they are part of a growing trend across evangelical Christianity over the past decades. Among the wealthy in this community it is seen as a strategic investment, a way to ensure that their financial power is harnessed toward the furthering of evangelical interests in society. It is a form of stewardship. And, as is the case with the Greens, much evangelical philanthropy is directed to "parachurch" groups, rather than directly to their own local churches.[42] Money is given to organizations that conform to the standards of the faith; this is why the National Christian Foundation, which collects gifts and distributes them to Christian nonprofits—and whose vision statement reads, "Every person reached and restored through the love of Christ"—has become a $1 billion per year grant agency.[43]

In this light, the common thread running through each of the institutions to which the Greens have donated land (or a faculty position) is easy enough to spot. In their charitable giving, across the board, the Green family requires its potential recipients to pass a doctrinal test, founded on a literalist understanding of the inerrancy of the Bible.[44] By far their largest contribution to evangelical higher education, however, was not a donation of land, but rather a full-scale financial rescue of one of evangelical Christianity's central educational powerhouses: Oral Roberts University.

In 2007, the university was wracked by scandal, with allegations of gross financial impropriety leveled against the president, Richard Roberts. The school reported over $50 million in debt. ORU had long been one of the flagship Christian institutions in the country, and—perhaps swayed also by its relative proximity, being located in Tulsa, Oklahoma—the Green family felt compelled to save it from going under. At the time, the Greens had no connection with ORU: in an interview, David Green said, "You have to understand that I didn't go to college and I didn't know anybody over there, not a soul at ORU." From his perspective, this was not a financial decision—in fact, he lamented the notion of becoming involved with an institution that was running a substantial deficit, around $16 million per year. It was, rather, a calling of faith: "I just knew it was a Christian school and God caused me to grieve."[45]

After a meeting with Oral Roberts himself at which the terms of the deal were put on the table, the Greens gave an initial gift of $62 million in January 2008, with a further $8 million coming later that year. In exchange for their financial support, the Greens demanded that the university's entire board of regents voluntarily resign, to be replaced by twenty-three members entirely of the Greens' choosing. The board would be chaired by Mart Green, David's son and Steve's brother.

Part of the change implemented with the new board of regents was a move away from the prosperity gospel that had become popular among the school's leaders and back toward the more traditional form of Pentecostal faith on which it was founded. The school's website proclaims that the school was "founded in the fires of evangelism and upon the unchanging precepts of the Bible."[46] On the spiritual front, the Greens were a strong fit to take leadership of the school. But while they had previously given considerable money to higher education, they had no experience in actually running a university. Indeed, neither David Green nor either of his sons had attended college at all.

This was not a stumbling block: the Greens could look to their peers for examples of other evangelical leaders with no formal education who nevertheless founded Christian universities: Oral Roberts (Oral Roberts University), Jerry Falwell (Liberty University), and Pat Robertson (Regent University). As Stephens and Giberson note, "Within much of the parallel culture of evangelicalism, academic credibility has very little to do with the ability to create and even run universities. Nor are academic credibility and academic credentials very closely related."[47]

The Greens relied on their business savvy to guide them, and it seems to have paid off: Oral Roberts University is now financially solvent again, and Mart Green has stepped down from the board. The new chair is Robert Hoskins, the president of OneHope, a Christian mission that receives substantial financial support from the Greens. He is also a member of the board of the Museum of the Bible.

In April 2015, the Museum of the Bible publicized a new initiative, called Covenant Journey. Modeled on the highly successful Birthright program for Jewish young adults, Covenant Journey is an eleven-day trip to Israel for Christian college students, deeply underwritten by Museum of the Bible (the students pay only $500 for the experience, considerably less than the cost of the airfare alone). One of the aims of the program is to strengthen participants' ties to Israel, advocacy for which has been a longstanding aspect of evangelical Christianity. Another explicit aim, however, is to enhance the Christian faith of the participants.[48] "As young adults experience Israel firsthand, their faith is strengthened," Steve Green proclaimed at the program launch event.[49]

The Museum of the Bible is financing the program, according to their press release, "because it furthers the Museum's goal of inviting people from across the world, from all backgrounds and religious affiliations, to engage with the Bible."[50] Needless to say, this particular program is focused on people from one particular part of the world, and from one religious affiliation. And the definition of "engage with the Bible" employed here is relatively broad. The program is designed to encourage support for the modern state of Israel and the growth of individual Christian faith; it is unclear how much participants will actually learn about the Bible in the process. In his statement, Steve Green described Israel as the place "where Abraham journeyed and gave birth to the nation of Israel, David conquered Goliath, and the Prophets and Apostles wrote and lived." If this sort of literalist understanding of the biblical narrative is what students will encounter on the trip, then they will be receiving a strong theological education in evangelical Christianity, but not a particularly good education in the Bible and its historicity.

The program's itinerary hits many of the usual highlights for an Israel trip: the Western Wall and Yad Vashem, the Holocaust memorial in Jerusalem; a visit to Masada and Qumran, the site where the Dead Sea Scrolls were discovered; a buoyant swim in the Dead Sea. It also unsurprisingly focuses on Christian sites: the Mount of

Beatitudes, the Sea of Galilee, Gethsemane, Caiaphas's house, the Antonio Fortress, the Via Dolorosa, and more.[51] Two elements of the trip stand out in particular, however. At the end of the first day, after visiting the Sea of Galilee, the students descend to the Jordan River, where they are baptized. Adult baptism by immersion is a significant aspect of evangelical Christianity (as opposed to the infant baptism perhaps more familiar from Catholicism and some mainline Protestant traditions), and is a central doctrine of Pentecostalism specifically.

The second noteworthy aspect of the Covenant Journey trip is the visit on the final day to the site of Jesus's final resting-place: not the Church of the Holy Sepulchre, traditionally identified since the fourth century CE as the burial-place of Jesus, but the Garden Tomb, discovered in the mid-nineteenth century and considered by many evangelicals to be the more authentic site. Although there are reasons to doubt that the Church of the Holy Sepulchre is the historical location of Jesus's crucifixion and burial, many scholars, including Dan Bahat, one of Israel's leading archaeologists of Jerusalem, believe that the site (if not the physical tomb itself) may well be accurate.[52] The Garden Tomb, on the other hand, has no strong archaeological support; another authority on Jerusalem's archaeology, Gabriel Barkay, has argued that the tomb is almost a millennium earlier than the time of Jesus.[53] Again here we can see the theological dimensions of Covenant Journey at play, overshadowing history and archaeology—and the Bible itself.

Given the explicitly Christian character of the program, many of these features may not be unexpected—including the line on the application form in which aspiring participants are asked to provide the name of their church. The application form, it might be noted, is more direct about the program's purposes than the press release and launch event might suggest: "It is designed specifically to motivate its participants to discover and affirm their Christian identity," the form says, "providing participants with the ability to advocate for Israel upon their return." Engagement with the Bible may be the aim of MOTB, but it is only a means to an end for Covenant Journey. As a self-identified "nonsectarian" nonprofit, MOTB's involvement raises questions: Covenant Journey seems to be quite openly a faith-building activity for evangelical Protestants. It conforms quite closely to the beliefs of Steve Green and his family, but perhaps runs somewhat afoul of the broader mission statement of the MOTB organization.

Perhaps the most salient evidence for the sectarian nature of the Covenant Journey program is one that was strikingly absent from MOTB's official press release. Although the statement made clear that the program is funded by MOTB, in conjunction with the Philos Project (an organization devoted to promoting "positive Christian engagement in the Middle East" and funded by Paul Singer, a prominent neoconservative), there was no mention of who actually designed and would be running the trip. As it turns out, Covenant Journey is a project of Liberty Counsel Action—the most recent name for The Liberty Alliance, the organization founded by Jerry Falwell to promote the vision of his Moral Majority. Its name changed when it came under the umbrella authority of Liberty Counsel, the evangelical legal nonprofit that was most recently in the news for representing Kim Davis, the Kentucky clerk who refused to issue same-sex marriage licenses. In addition to its strong support for the state of Israel, Liberty Counsel is one of the most prominent groups in the socially conservative movement, especially in the fight against gay rights: in 2015, the Southern Poverty Law Center designated them as a hate group.[54]

Covenant Journey is promoted by Museum of the Bible as just another means of supporting engagement with the Bible. But from its itinerary to its application to its organizers, it is abundantly clear that the program is less about engaging with the Bible and far more about promoting and supporting a particular form of evangelical Christianity.

Paracurricular evangelical programs in higher education are a long-time staple of the evangelical movement.[55] Beyond merely promoting evangelical positions and serving as campus ministries, these types of programs create and sustain evangelical communities by providing spaces, often in secular contexts, for common beliefs and ideas. They are generally understood as a response to a sense of exclusion from the broader academy on the part of evangelicals.[56] Such ventures began largely in the first third of the twentieth century, but have expanded dramatically since. One may think of programs such as Campus Crusade for Christ (now known as "Cru"), the Veritas Forum, InterVarsity Christian Fellowship, the Navigators, and others. These programs, especially when they serve as meeting grounds for students (and faculty) from disparate institutions, have become a venue for evangelicals to see how their individual and localized community groups are participating in the wider project of garnering intellectual credibility for evangelical scholarship. In his study of the evangelical movement in the academy, Lindsay notes InterVarsity's "Following Christ" conferences, which "allow evangelical academics to meet and discuss ongoing research interests," and The Ivy League Congress on Faith and Action, which brings in industry leaders and faculty members to "speak about their faith commitments and their professional lives."[57]

The Green Scholars Initiative is an example of how the Green family and Museum of the Bible have taken up the advancement of programmatic initiatives in higher education. As noted in the previous chapter, this program is ostensibly a purely scholarly venture; yet the schools, and therefore the students, chosen to participate are very often those with explicitly Christian leanings. Students come away from their GSI projects with a strengthened Christian faith and with affirmation of the traditional evangelical view of biblical transmission.

The GSI is very much akin to Walmart's SIFE project: a program that provides students with specific training in an academic field, one that is close to the heart of its funders—free markets in the case of SIFE, and the Bible in the case of the GSI. In both cases, there is an expectation that the students who participate will go on to put the skills and knowledge they acquire to work, either through promoting a free-market vision or through replenishing the stock of text critics in the academy. And in both cases there is an evangelical vision working in the background, easily identifiable in the sources of financing but somewhat more implicit in the hands-on education being financed.

The Christian orientation of the GSI is discernible in one of its subsidiary projects. Every summer since 2012, the GSI has sponsored a two-week trip to England for a select number of GSI-affiliated students, for what is called the "LOGOS in Oxford" program, in conjunction with an organization called Scholarship and Christianity in Oxford (the UK branch of the Council for Christian Colleges and Universities). The LOGOS program was created by Pattengale for the explicit purpose of exploring the intersection of scholarship and Christian faith. "Many people in this field have a real interest in it because of their faith interest, so it seemed like a very natural thing to do," he told us. A student participant described it this way: "LOGOS' aim is about facilitating an environment where the young, Christian mind can flourish academically, socially, and spiritually. We (as the GSI) seem unapologetic about the Christian bent that LOGOS takes." Another participant was clear that this was a faith experience first, and an academic one second: "I found myself drawn to the professors whose lectures were not simply sound arguments, but visible representations of a vibrant faith. They were pastoral first, academic second; that is, they cared more about the body of Christ than their own academic prowess."

For many in the academy, the notion of a specifically Christian scholarship—like a specifically Jewish, or Muslim, or any other type of scholarship—is at odds with the basic notion of critical scholarship altogether. As "critical" generally signifies the distancing of oneself (or at least the attempt to do so) from that which is being studied, the explicit linking of faith and scholarship, especially in a program oriented at younger minds, is something of a challenge. The application form for the LOGOS program asks the question, "What impact has your Christian faith had on your academic studies, and vice versa?" In 2013, those students who attended heard lectures on such topics as "An evangelical approach to textual studies of the Bible," "Textual criticism and the inspiration of Scripture," and "The book of Daniel and Christian vocation for young academics," as well as a series of lectures under the heading "The vocation of Christian scholars in the modern university." Steve Green spoke one morning at chapel.

It seems almost comical now, but originally Pattengale envisioned running two parallel programs: one for Christian students and one for Jewish students. The Christian program has been very successful: they have sent more than a hundred students to Oxford, and have had twice that many applicants. The Jewish version, on the other hand, has yet to really find its feet. As Pattengale said, "We hope that we'll have students this year that actually will apply to that program." It's hard to see how: by his own admission, "Part of it is that in our programs there's predominantly audiences that came out of Christian backgrounds." That demographic reality, of course, is no accident.

LOGOS is like the study guide for the GSI program: while GSI students learn their ancient alphabets and manipulate their digital images, LOGOS in effect answers the question of "What are we really doing here?" The answer is, "Training a new generation of Christian scholars." And this raises the question: what, from the evangelical perspective of the Green family, constitutes "Christian" scholarship?

A key can be found in the comments of the student quote above: "Pastoral first, academic second." As Mark Noll put it, "Evangelical self-definition . . . hinges upon a specific conception of Scripture more than upon a specific approach to research. Evangelical scholars are not professors who happen also to be conservative Protestants, but conservative Protestants who find themselves engaged in scholarship."[58] A program like LOGOS—as well as the various Christian institutions of higher education with which the Greens have been financially involved—creates a sense of community not primarily of scholarship, but of Christian identity. In the previous chapter, we noted the general evangelical mistrust of expertise; here we may point to the other side of the same coin: the idea that, for evangelicals, the authority vested by other traditions in religious leaders or in scholarly experts is placed instead on the larger body of "the church"—that is, on the popular opinions of the evangelical masses. Noll writes, "While the evangelical community respects its scholars, it also expects them to communicate the results of research in a style that is both understandable and supports treasured beliefs."[59] Such an attitude is obviously prejudicial for the results of "Christian" or "evangelical" scholarship. By limiting LOGOS (and, for the most part, the GSI) to a self-identified Christian participant pool, its founders avoid the complications of differing intellectual perspectives that come with religious diversity; they reinforce a faith-driven scholarship, rather than a scholarship-informed faith.

Even while the Mustang public school district was debating whether to move forward with Steve Green's Bible curriculum, the Museum of the Bible was in the process of testing a version of the program in a different school system: that of Ramat Gan, a small city just outside of Tel Aviv in Israel. The choice of Ramat Gan is less arbitrary than it might first appear: the city is the home of the Israeli company Compedia, which designed the augmented reality technology used in the MOTB curriculum. In its first trial year, fifteen-hundred Israeli ninth-graders used the curriculum; in its second year, that number quadrupled; and it is expected that thousands more will be using the program in the near future. The program has been publicly lauded by the Israeli Ministry of Education, Youth, and Society.[60]

The success of the curriculum in Israel, despite having failed in the United States public schools, is due to a confluence of factors both curricular and structural. The Museum of the Bible did not simply take the Mustang curriculum and translate it into Hebrew. Rather, they took the core format of the course and adopted it for a specifically Israeli audience. This meant removing all the references to Jesus and the New Testament, as well as increasing the material relevant to Judaism: not only supplementing the occasional mentions of tradition Jewish interpretations (midrash), but also expanding discussions of central Jewish traditions, such as Shabbat. What they created, in the end, was essentially a Jewish Bible curriculum, one that not only concentrates exclusively on the Jewish parts of the Bible but also conforms to a fairly standard set of Jewish traditions about the Bible.

The Israeli curriculum is, in short, precisely the type of course that would be impossible to use in American public schools, as it is written for and from the perspective of a single religious tradition. (It would be quite usable in Hebrew schools in the United States, however, though there is no evidence that MOTB has looked into such a possibility.) What makes such a program viable in Israel, of course, is the fact that Israel is a self-defined Jewish state; though

Judaism is not its sole official religion, there is no equivalent of the ACLU to challenge the teaching of Judaism as normative. Quite the contrary: the Hebrew Bible is not only welcome in Israel's public schools, it is compulsory: all Israeli high school students must pass a Hebrew Bible exam in order to attend university, and every public school is required to offer classes in it. (Given the fact that Bible is a required topic, however, it might be going too far to say, as did the CEO of Compedia, that "what we are seeing in Israel is a Bible revival as a result of this curriculum."[61]) The Israeli market was tailor-made for the MOTB curriculum—it was competing not against the very concept of teaching the Bible in public schools, but merely against other Bible curricula. With an Israeli technology firm helping, and with advisors ensuring that the material was suitably de-Christianized, all the pieces were in place for a successful program.

In the past year, the Museum of the Bible has taken a new approach to promoting its Bible curriculum in the United States. Rather than attempting to breach the public school system, and the Supreme Court rulings that govern such efforts, MOTB has instead begun marketing its curriculum to the home-schooling crowd.[62] Though relatively small (approximately 3 percent of all Americans), this is a natural audience: home-schooling is particularly popular among evangelical Christians suspicious of the secular public schools. A 2009 report from the U.S. Department of Education revealed that the most common reason parents gave as the most important for choosing to home-school was "a desire to provide religious or moral instruction."[63] The Green family itself chose to home-school its children.[64]

To this end, the Museum of the Bible released in 2016 the first volume of its new home-school curriculum: Genesis to Ruth. It is clear from comparison with the Israeli curriculum that this program is close to the base curriculum from which the Israeli version was created. It is equally clear that the home-school curriculum has gone to some efforts to address the problems highlighted by Mark Chancey in his evaluation of the original public-school draft. On legal grounds, this was probably not necessary—there are no centralized policies governing home-school curricula, no church-state issues to be wary of. In theory, the home-school curriculum could be explicitly evangelical. But, in fact, it looks very much like an attempt to conform to the kinds of restrictions MOTB would encounter in a public school system. It looks, in short, like precisely the curriculum they would like to place in a public school, should another one be willing to give them the opportunity. (At the very least, the home-school curriculum contains little that could be identified as specifically tailored to the home-school audience, in contrast with the explicitly Jewish Israeli version.) This is sensible: the Museum of the Bible is very clear that it considers itself to be a nonsectarian organization. Nevertheless, even the newly scrubbed curriculum suffers from a Protestant Christian bias, if not to the degree that the first draft did.

The home-school curriculum—at least the first quarter of it that has been released at the time of this writing—can be evaluated in light of the categories used by Chancey in his report on the public school draft: the promotion of the idea that the Bible is historically accurate and reliable; the use of Christian concepts as a framework and the presence of theological concerns; a favoring of the Protestant form of the Bible; the implication that the Bible is a source of cultural good and a tone of religious triumphalism; and errors and idiosyncrasies. The following overview, admittedly extensive, is meant to be illustrative: what the curriculum reveals is the fault line between the desire to present the Bible in a nonsectarian manner and the deeply ingrained Protestantism of the Green family and MOTB.

The reliable historicity of the Bible is a central idea for evangelical Christianity, and for Steve Green in particular, as he has repeatedly made clear: in conversation with us about biblical scholarship, he said, "What we keep finding is, boy, it validates what the book says." Although the home-school curriculum is less direct about this than its earlier incarnation, it still reveals a sharp slant in the direction of historical accuracy. The issue is raised most prominently in the chapter entitled "Bible History." Here the curriculum compares the historical evidence for three figures: King David, Jesus, and—oddly—Martin Luther King, Jr. Students read that "the process for examining the historical reliability of the accounts of Dr. King in the Birmingham jail" is "essentially the same" as that for looking into the historicity of David and Jesus. In the case of the biblical figures, the curriculum uses the references to David and Jesus in the Bible as a primary piece of evidence for their historical reality. The ninth-century BCE Tel Dan Stele, which mentions "the house of David," is the only extrabiblical source for David; for Jesus, we are told that "archaeological remains verify numerous locations and events." No serious scholar denies the existence of Jesus, and only a minority think that David is entirely fictional; yet putting them together with Martin Luther King, Jr. suggests an equivalence of historicity that is decidedly inappropriate. The summary at the end of the chapter suggests that "if we keep our eyes open—checking everything for reliability, authenticity, and accuracy—ancient kingdoms, mighty kings, and passionate prophets can come alive!"

Later chapters continue in this vein. A chapter devoted to the Sumerian King List, an ancient Mesopotamian text listing the kings of Sumer from the mythic past to approximately 1750 BCE, might seem an odd topic at first; its purpose in the curriculum becomes clearer, however, when the textbook uses the possibility of gleaning historical information from the Sumerian King List as a model for doing the same with the biblical flood story. The teacher's guide for this chapter suggests the following discussion prompt: "Historians and archaeologists are always looking to verify historical claims and details. The more times we see a name or place mentioned, the more likely that it is a historical reality. In your opinion, what does it mean that the flood story appears in more than one source?" This is an interesting rhetorical trick. The existence of multiple versions of the flood story has frequently been a source of concern to faith groups, because it highlights inconsistencies or contradictions with the biblical record. But in this instance it is used in order to meet the historical "criterion of multiple attestation."

In the chapter on Abraham, a handout is provided for the sole purpose of countering the common scholarly claim that the presence of camels in the stories of Genesis is anachronistic and evidence of a later authorship.[65] The chapter on the Exodus contains a number of problematic features in this regard, among them the suggestion that the Merneptah Stele—a record from the late thirteenth century BCE enumerating the various conquests of the Egyptian Pharaoh Merneptah, which is famous for containing the first extrabiblical mention of "Israel," in a list of subdued lands and peoples—is somehow a piece of evidence for the historicity of the Exodus. In a chapter on "Egyptian Texts"—another that might seem off-topic—it is again suggested that the Merneptah Stele might be a clue for dating the Exodus. More directly—so much so that it looks like a holdover from the first draft—the teacher's guide to this chapter says, "Archaeological discoveries help us to confirm the Bible's account of events."

The method of introducing a chapter that is not directly related to the Bible and then using it as a back door into the issue of historicity seems to be an intentional one throughout the curriculum. A chapter on "Lost Civilizations," which presents the stories of the Minoans, the Egyptian city of Amarna, the Mycenaeans, the Trojans, and the Hittites, is used to counter the stark lack of archaeological evidence for biblical stories. "Does the fact that unambiguous proof has not been found of their existence mean they didn't exist? Is there a chance that in the near or perhaps distant future proof will be found?" We are told that the biblical stories in question took place in the Late Bronze Age, and that at that time other civilizations were flourishing that subsequently "vanished from the surface of the earth, only to be recovered as archaeologists dug a little deeper." The chapter summary makes the essential argument clear: "Absence of evidence is not the evidence of absence." Yet the logic here is less than convincing: even if we concede that Troy existed and that there was a war there, we would still be a long way from confirming that Achilles died after sustaining a wound to his ankle. The quiz at the end of the chapter claims that learning about lost civilizations both "provides tools for investigation of biblical events" and "provides evidence for the reliability of some biblical events"—though the chapter does not offer an example of the latter.

Within the academy, the biblical story of Joshua and the conquest of Canaan is one of the most famous loci for challenging the historicity of the biblical account with archaeological evidence. In the teacher's guide, we read that "according to Bible scholars, there was no central government in Canaan in the time period in which the Joshua story is set. Instead, groups lived in separate city-states. If there was no coordinated defense, this would have made it easier to conquer the land." This seems to take the historicity of the Bible at face value. Almost more troubling is when the curriculum deals directly with the question of archaeology and the conquest. "Scholars have questioned whether the archaeological record supports the biblical account of the Israelite conquest of Canaan," we are correctly informed, with specific mention of the conquest of Jericho. But this is followed by a caveat: "As is often the case, scholars have many opinions on the issue." This is true only if "scholars" is taken in the broadest sense. There is virtual unanimity among archaeologists and biblical scholars that Jericho was not and could never have been conquered by the Israelites.

What we see in this last example is a rhetorical technique that the home-school curriculum adopts repeatedly: the introduction of a scholarly opinion that potentially challenges the historicity or authenticity of the Bible, followed—always followed—by the minority perspective of other scholars who support the biblical account, or sometimes by the weight of traditional interpretation. "Some scholars argue that the Bible's description of the Hittites does not match the people the scholars began to call 'Hittites' in the 19th and 20th centuries," we are told. But the very next sentence undermines that scholarly position: "Other scholars believe the description does match."

Virtually all of these problems come to a head in the chapter entitled "The Origins of Writing: How Were the Earliest Books of the Bible Written?" The stated goal of this chapter, according to the teacher's guide, is "To learn when and how the Bible may have been written." This is obviously an enormously complex topic, one that stands at the center of numerous scholarly debates. The textbook's approach is signaled already by the title: somehow the origins of human writing are going to be brought into the discussion of the composition of the Bible, a connection that no serious scholar would endorse. It only gets more difficult from there. On the first page of the chapter, we read that some biblical stories "refer to very ancient times before reading and writing even existed. These stories would have been passed down the stream of generations through oral storytelling." This logic requires, erroneously, that stories that refer to preliterate eras must have been originally composed in preliterate eras.

On the next page, we learn that "the Bible claims that Moses wrote at least some key parts of the Torah." The passages referred to are those in which the Bible narrates Moses writing down words that were spoken to him by the deity, such as Exodus 17:14: "The Lord said to Moses, 'Inscribe this in a document.'" Though this verse and those like it are classic passages for apologists seeking to affirm Mosaic authorship of the Pentateuch, they are of course no such thing: they are third-person narrative descriptions of Moses, a character in the story, writing down something that was said to him by another character in the story. Yet the teacher's guide instructs the students to "search verses attributed to Moses, according to the Bible." There are no such verses. Remarkably, the teacher's guide, and an accompanying handout, also suggests that the verses "attributed to Moses" can be distinguished from the rest of the biblical text on the basis of "differences in style and linguistics." This is a point on which no reputable scholar would agree—nor does the curriculum offer any examples of such stylistic markers.

"It's certainly possible that Moses could have written parts of Genesis, and parts of all the first five books of the Bible. Whether or not it's likely is a matter of ongoing debate. Most modern scholars would agree that even if Moses was an author, he must have had a significant amount of help." So says the curriculum. In fact, the debate about Mosaic authorship effectively ended in the seventeenth and eighteenth centuries. Mosaic authorship is a total nonstarter in biblical scholarship. Yet the possibility of it is the entire focus of this chapter. While there is a page that reflects the common scholarly opinion that the Pentateuch is a combination of multiple sources, this idea is used to suggest only that "portions of the Torah must have been written, or edited, after the time of Moses." It is "portions" and "edited" that are the red flags here. What the curriculum is strongly suggesting is that Moses—who, as an author, is necessarily being treated as a historical figure—could well have written some of the Torah.

The textbook asks: "How Advanced Was Writing at the Time of Moses?" And, a few pages later, "Was Language Advanced Enough in Moses' Era to Account for the Narrative Found in the Torah?" These questions are red herrings: no scholar denies that writing was advanced enough in the wider ancient Near East in the period the Bible ascribes to Moses (though many question whether the relatively small and underdeveloped region of Israel had developed writing to the same degree, a problem that is unaddressed in the curriculum). They also, in the phrases "the Time of Moses" and "Moses' Era," take the biblical narrative and equate it with history: the era in which Moses lived according to the Bible gets pegged to a real-world chronology. Most standard scholarly introductions to the Bible discuss not whether or when Moses wrote the Torah, but how that traditional belief arose—and why it was abandoned in scholarship. By simply assuming the accuracy of the biblical dating for Moses, and the authenticity of Moses as a historical figure, the textbook ends up making arguments for Mosaic authorship that are thoroughly reactionary.

Though it admits that there is no direct evidence for Mosaic authorship, the curriculum engages in yet another typical false equivalency with the present day: although "we may never know who wrote what," it says, "this is not a problem unique to Moses and the Torah. We do not have video recordings to show who wrote any ancient text." The textbook falls back on classic apologetic tropes: the Torah contains "streams of tradition, some of them very ancient," and "we can say that the societies in which Moses and Abraham are said to have lived were literate societies." The chapter's final quiz gives away the game: Q: "What can the existence of ancient writing systems prove?" A: "That writing has already developed by the time of Moses." The entire chapter is prejudicial in the extreme, and completely unrepresentative of modern, or even eighteenth-century, scholarship. It flies very close to the border of apologetics.

The home-school curriculum, as a product of the Museum of the Bible, claims to be nonsectarian, and stresses that it is not a textbook of theology. (The teacher's guide even includes a section on "The Constitutional Approach" to teaching the Bible—perhaps another indication that this edition has a public school audience in mind.) Yet while it may trend more in that direction than it did in its initial draft, the current product retains distinct theological elements. All too often the curriculum seems designed to elicit reflection not on the Bible per se, but on present-day issues of morality. The idea that the Bible is indeed a guide to be followed is stressed repeatedly. "Rules express shared values, bring order, and encourage behavior that serves the common good." "According to the Bible even free people are subject to certain rules and moral constraints, and there's no contradiction between freedom and obeying the divine law because the divine law bids us"—note especially that "us"—"to do what is best." In a striking moment, the teacher's guide sets up a distinction between behavior that is "inappropriate" and behavior that is "immoral": "inappropriate" is defined as "a weaker version of immoral, or perhaps it is something more subjective, which depends on social norms." In other words, morality is a fixed concept, something objective.

Certain key conservative Christian topics find their way into the curriculum. According to the textbook, Genesis explains "where marriage comes from," with reference, in absolutely typical evangelical style, to Adam and Eve (a quiz tells us that Eve was created in order "to have a male and a female in the world," which is not quite what the Bible says). In a chapter on the relationship of the Bible to modern science (on which more below), the classic metaphor of God as "divine watchmaker," made famous by William Paley in the early nineteenth century, is mentioned repeatedly. Abraham's story is construed more than once as being all about faith—building explicitly on Genesis 15:6, a verse that was central to Paul's understanding of why Gentile converts to the Jesus movement did not need to follow the Jewish law. Abraham, we are told, was on a "journey of faith." Faith became a central category for thinking about obedience to God only with the composition of the Pauline epistles. This is Christianity's reading of Abraham, not the one presented in the Hebrew Bible.

The curriculum's aversion to the biblical laws is striking, especially as it contains a chapter titled "The Law of Moses" and another about "Ancient Near Eastern Law Codes." Yet it is abundantly clear that from the perspective of the curriculum, "the law of Moses" means not the dozens of chapters of legal code found in Exodus, Leviticus, Numbers, and Deuteronomy, but rather, almost exclusively, the Ten Commandments—that is, the only biblical laws by which Christians consider themselves still bound. The stated goal of the "Law of Moses" chapter, according to the teacher's guide, is "to introduce students to the Ten Commandments and their impact on history." The avoidance of the vast bulk of the laws is evident in the quiz: "Why are the Ten Commandments considered to be so important?" "Following them would allow the Israelites to receive God's blessings." This may be true in part, but it is far from complete: the Bible makes no distinction between obedience to the Ten Commandments and obedience to the rest of the commandments. (Indeed, traditional Judaism holds that it is mistaken to elevate the Ten Commandments above the rest of the laws—in part because this is precisely what Christians do.[66]) The curriculum suggests that the Ten Commandments are fundamental, and that the rest of the laws are a mere outgrowth of them: "From these Ten Rules, the Israelites developed a detailed system of regulations that bound the community together." This is false both on the level of the biblical narrative and in terms of the historical development of Israelite law.

The understanding of biblical law promoted in the curriculum is markedly Protestant in tone: "The Jewish law code"—and one may certainly quibble with the use of "Jewish" here—stressed the importance of loving God, loving your neighbor, and loving yourself." This sounds far more like a traditional Christian reading, filtered through the lens of Jesus's teachings, than it does a description of what is actually in the Bible. "Love your neighbor as yourself" occupies a single verse in the middle of Leviticus—it can hardly be considered a point of emphasis, at least in comparison to the chapter upon chapter dealing with far less feel-good concerns. No mention is made anywhere in the textbook of the cultic regulations found in Leviticus, for example. Even granting the difficulty of making them engaging for high-school students, the omission of these laws, which are so conceptually central to the Hebrew Bible, and to Judaism, results in a sharply skewed version of the Bible.

A prominent perspective in the curriculum is the idea that a direct encounter with the biblical text is somehow more authentic than one mediated through interpretation. The Bible is described as a "firsthand account," and students are to be told that although other people's interpretations can be valuable, going directly to the primary source might allow us to "see something no one saw before." This is certainly true of scholarship; but for ninth-grade students this seems less an encouragement to train as a biblical scholar and more a promotion of the idea that scholarship is not necessary to understand and engage with the biblical text. This approach to the Bible has deep evangelical roots, expressed by Dwight L. Moody in the late nineteenth century as the practice of reading the Bible "as if it were written for yourself."[67] Even before Moody, in the early nineteenth century, evangelicalism emphasized that the Bible can be understood just like any other book: that a common-sense rationalism, partaking of rather than standing in opposition to Enlightenment ways of thinking, will lead the reader—any reader—to the clear truth of scripture. "The clear, unperverted deductions of reason are as binding in their authority and not less truly to be relied on, than the Word of God; and . . . the former can never contradict the latter," wrote Nathaniel Taylor, an influential Yale seminarian.[68] This attitude was bound to an increasing sense of democratization across American society, and with it to a brand of populism that manifested in a biblical hermeneutic: personal judgment outweighs the accumulated generations of expertise, be it clerical or scholarly.[69] In line with this, the curriculum seems to maintain the position that there is such a thing as "interpretation-free" biblical reading.

In this one can also see a reflection of another standard evangelical perspective: not only that the Bible is the sole source of insight and influence when isolated from the historical and cultural conditioning that inevitably accompanies the interpretations of the past; but that, somewhat paradoxically, the Bible can be interpreted by today's readers free from any sense of historical and cultural conditioning that may obtain in the present. Perhaps the clearest expression of this ostensibly self-contradictory perspective can be found in a statement by the International Council on Biblical Inerrancy: "We further deny that the corruption of human culture and language through sin has thwarted God's work of inspiration."[70] In other words, culture is corrupt, and therefore culturally grounded readings are problematic; at the same time, however, the inspiration of the Bible is still discernible. This perspective goes hand in hand with the idea that, although transmitted by human agents, the Bible is fundamentally the word of God, and therefore unchangeable in its meaning and intent. Removing the notion of cultural context and interpretation from both the writing of the Bible in the past and the reading of it in the present, even in the more nuanced form evident in the home-school curriculum, is essentially a position on inerrancy.

Moreover, this attitude fits into a trend in evangelical, and specifically fundamentalist, thinking described by the scholar Mark Noll as an "uncritical adoption of intellectual habits from the nineteenth century."[71] This manifests in a continuing, though unsustainable, concept of objectivity in interpretation and scholarship; a "neglect of forces in history that shape perceptions and help define the issues that loom as most important to any particular age";[72] and a discounting of the accumulated wisdom of the past. These are the types of intellectual habits that are usually broken as individuals make their way through the halls of higher education—a path, however, that is mistrusted by many evangelicals (and that, as noted earlier, was not taken by the Greens).

In the very first chapter, the curriculum asks, "What is the Bible?" It then goes on to explain that the Jewish, Catholic, Protestant, and Eastern Orthodox canons are somewhat different, in number of books included and in their order. What those differences are (aside from the inclusion or exclusion of the New Testament), and where they come from, is not laid out for the student. Nor is it noted that the canon used in this curriculum is the Protestant one, even for the Hebrew Bible. "For our general purposes, 'the Bible' will refer to the Hebrew Bible's 39 books as well as the 27 books of the New Testament." Yet the curriculum sets the discussion of the book of Ruth after the chapter on Judges—which is the order not of the Hebrew Bible, but of the Christian canon. Less obviously, the textbook declines to mention that the numbering and verse division of the Ten Commandments differs from tradition to tradition—it simply presents, in a pictorial representation, the Protestant version, beginning with "You shall have no other gods before me," rather than, as in the Jewish tradition, with "I am the Lord your God who brought you out of Egypt." In both of these cases, it is clear that some choice must be made; whatever order of the biblical books and the Ten Commandments is chosen, however, transparency (or even awareness) regarding the decision seems necessary.

Steve Green is convinced that the Bible is a source of unmitigated good—and that any bad that has been done with it is a result of bad people with bad interpretations. The book itself is blameless, and is responsible for many of the cultural values we hold dear. This view is still represented in the latest version of the curriculum. Its chapter on "Modern Science" states that "some belief systems create a friendlier intellectual environment for scientific investigation than others. . . . This is not to say that societies that believed in multiple gods could not achieve remarkable scientific advances"—the ancient Greeks come immediately to mind—but that some religious beliefs "better lend themselves than others to a view of physical reality that behaves in rational and orderly ways." The argument of this chapter is that the Bible "encourages 'scientific curiosity.'" Modern science, we are told, "developed in Western Europe"—seemingly ignoring, say, the deep foundations of modern mathematics in Arab culture—not because of the superiority of Western Europeans per se, but "because of a complex history that begins largely in cultures shaped by the Bible." The chapter goes on to describe the religious beliefs of early scientists—with special reference to the "divine watchmaker" metaphor—and then lists "Major Figures in the Rise of Western Science Who Were Also Members of the Clergy" (the Christian clergy, to be specific). The chapter ends with a quote from the physicist Richard Feynman in which the rules governing the universe are described as "a miracle." Never mind the fact that Feynman was an avowed atheist.

The relationship of the Bible to slavery has its own devoted chapter. To its credit, the curriculum recognizes that many people used the Bible to support slavery—but it goes on to say that "large numbers of people eventually agreed that an appropriate interpretation of the Bible demands the end of slavery." This suggests that it was biblical interpretation that drove opinions on slavery, rather than, more accurately, the other way around. In the teacher's guide, Moses is compared with Lincoln, a comparison that highlights the curriculum's selective reading of the Bible itself. Although the biblical Exodus narrative does indeed emphasize the freeing of the Israelites from slavery, the laws that follow make clear that slavery was an accepted institution for the Israelites themselves. The textbook correctly identifies the biblical distinction between Hebrew and Canaanite slaves, and holds up the humane laws governing the treatment of Hebrew slaves by fellow Israelites. But it says nothing about the biblical treatment of the Canaanites—the much better parallel to modern-day slavery, especially in the American South—which is constrained by no such humanitarian rules.

Biblical law—what little of it is discussed—is presented as a great advance over contemporary ancient law codes and as the foundation of all Western law. "The Ten Commandments are often credited as the moral and legal foundation of Western civilization." This is a theological position taken by certain conservative legal commentators, not a historical fact—the most influential legal thinkers of the Enlightenment, like Mill and Rousseau, were far more focused on Greek and Roman law. (One might also note that the curriculum has the teacher ask "Why do some people object to quotations from the Bible being displayed in public places?" just as the students have been shown an image of a biblical verse from Micah displayed at the Library of Congress.) The great cultural advance of biblical law is evident from an exercise in which students are to role play the part of a sales rep for the biblical law: "The mission is to pitch this law system to customers and convince them that it is better than the other law codes known from the ancient Near East." (It is noteworthy that no student is asked to take the opposite position.) Sometimes this preference results in what appear to be simple errors of fact: "In the Bible," in contrast to the laws of its neighbors, "the laws require impartial treatment of all, regardless of social status." This again ignores entirely the category of the Canaanite slave, and no mention is made here (or anywhere else) of the question of how and whether women fit into any of the legal categories in the Bible. Following one of Steve Green's regular talking points, the curriculum suggests that "the rights and freedom of the individual" are biblical in origin; the two pages of legal history that accompany this suggestion, however, demonstrate no such thing, as is only to be expected, considering that the claim is virtually impossible to maintain.

In a chapter on "Crime and Justice," we find a section that feels oddly out of place, even in the context of this curriculum. An entire page is dedicated to the "Impact of Bible Study on American Prisoners." It cites studies that show a lower rate of recidivism for prisoners who participate in Bible study programs; it then uses its standard rhetorical technique of saying that while "some scholars criticize these kinds of studies," "many scholars conclude, however," that such programs are helpful. There follows a description of one such program: InnerChange Freedom Initiative. The choice of one specific program to highlight feels almost like an advertisement; the choice of this particular program, however, is significant. InnerChange Freedom Initiative, founded by Nixon's "hatchet man" and prominent evangelical Charles Colson, is not a group that promotes the Bible and its study, at least not primarily: it is an organization "based on values reflected in the life and teaching of Jesus," according to their website, which includes a story about a Muslim prisoner who converted to Christianity after participating.[73] This is not a Bible study program; it is quite openly a Christian ministry program. (The first item listed on the website under "What We Do" for in-prison programming is "Evangelism Events"; the page also says that the program "shar[es] the good news of Jesus Christ with those behind bars."[74]) That this section of the curriculum is meant to promote a classic evangelical "biblical worldview" is clear from the teacher's guide: "Research seems to indicate that Bible study can reduce recidivism. Why? Changed values? Changed beliefs?"

The last chapter (so far) of the curriculum is again not really about the Bible, but about the good that is understood to come from the Bible: "Charitable Giving and the Bible." The aim of this chapter is to teach students that charity is a concept derived from the Bible. The teacher is to explain to the students that "the idea of charity was foreign to the Roman culture"—a historical claim that is difficult to maintain. To be sure, the term charity is derived from the Christian usage of the Latin word *caritas,* but the "idea of charity" has antecedents in the Greek and Roman concepts of *philanthropia* (philanthropy) and *humanitas* (humanness). Not only was love of humanity idealized by Greek philosophers, Roman emperors saw themselves as practicing philanthropy when they donated baths, gymnasia, fountains, and gladiatorial games to the people. Roman law even made provisions for philanthropic acts by granting legal status to charitable endowments and mutual-aid societies.[75] It is true that philanthropy as a concept referred to more than giving to the poor and the needy, but it would be a grave mistake to say that the idea of charity was foreign to the Romans or, for that matter, to ancient Jews. Our modern language of charity is Christian, but the idea is classical.

Indeed, this section seems particularly riddled with historical errors, perhaps because it strives so hard to make an argument that does not hold up particularly well. We are told that in the great Roman plague of 165 CE, "a minority of people in that society, Jews and Christians, was familiar with biblical standards of social and ethic behavior" and took it upon themselves to care for the sick, unlike their pagan Roman contemporaries. There is no evidence that this is true. (There is evidence to suggest that during the Plague of Cyprian, in the middle of the third century, healthy Christians provided basic care for those who were sick, but we have no similar documentation for the middle of the second century.[76]) Later in the chapter, on a page about the Roman emperor Julian, the reader is told that "although the polytheists outnumbered Christians, the Christians were unified by their common creeds and by their special allegiance to one book, the Bible." This too is misleading at best: the Christian canon had not even been established by the time of Julian, and there is no indication that early Christians considered allegiance to the Bible as a central plank of their common cause; indeed, Christianity was already so diverse at that time that the very idea of being unified under common creeds is ahistorical.[77] Oddly, it is left to the teacher to explain why Julian is being mentioned in this chapter at all: because "Julian pioneered the use of governmental institutions to help the poor." This would seem relevant information to include in the textbook; it might, however, have contradicted the central thrust of the chapter: that the Bible is fundamentally responsible for the concept of charitable giving.

In the end, the chapter has a goal beyond simply informing the student about the Bible and its impact on charity in the modern world. It wants also to change student behavior. A question on the test that accompanies the chapter asks, "How does the Bible's attitude toward the poor differ from Greco-Roman polytheism? How do you think this attitude could be applied to the problem of poor people today? Give a few practical suggestions in the spirit of the Bible." More directly, the final assignment of the chapter has the students engaging in charitable activities and reporting back to the class about what they have done. Again, the curriculum seems to have a purpose in mind that goes well past mere education. It is hard not to see here a direct reflection of the Green family's long-standing philanthropic efforts.

Beyond the many elements of the curriculum noted above that illustrate the continuing difficulty it seems to have with the concept of "nonsectarian," the textbook contains a bewildering variety of what Chancey aptly termed "errors and idiosyncrasies." First, and least important, it is riddled with typographical errors. The voice-over used for the augmented reality segments seems to be a non-native English speaker (if it isn't just computer-generated), which makes it distractingly difficult to listen to. But these are technical issues. The curriculum also contains some strange mistakes (beyond those mentioned above): At one point the teacher's guide, in suggesting how the Israelites might have reconciled the promise made to Abraham, that he would have many descendants and that they would possess the land of Canaan, with the hundreds of years of slavery in Egypt, offers as a "possible answer" that "God never gives Abraham a timeline for his promise," although in fact God does just that in Genesis 15: "Your offspring shall be strangers in a land not theirs, and they shall be enslaved and oppressed four hundred years." Later, in describing the apostasy of the Israelites at Sinai, the curriculum says, "They have reverted to the culture of their former Egyptian oppressors and have chosen to worship a golden calf," even though calf worship was a Canaanite practice, not an Egyptian one. The fourth commandment is translated as "thou shalt not kill," in line with the KJV, rather than the more accurate "thou shalt not murder"; biblical references to skin disease are translated, in the traditional manner, as "leprosy," and are even equated directly with modern Hansen's disease, despite scholarly unanimity that the condition(s) described in the Bible cannot be identified with the modern medical diagnosis of Hansen's disease. These are all the kinds of errors that a competent biblical scholar would catch immediately.

Other aspects of the curriculum perhaps fall better under the category of "idiosyncrasies," sometimes with identifiable perspectives standing behind them, sometimes not. At one point, the literature of the ancient Near East is classified as belonging to one of two possible categories: "creative prose" or "poetry"; this is an awkward and artificial division, especially in the case of "creative prose"—one wonders, for instance, whether the Bible, as ancient Near Eastern literature, should also be described as "creative prose." In saying that "God requires only one act of obedience from Abraham and his descendants" (which is not a particularly good reading of the Bible to begin with), we are told that that one act is "circumcision (ouch!)"—the parenthetical commentary feels unnecessary at best and insulting at worst.

The curriculum digresses from its main topic—the Bible—a number of times, to treat issues that are perhaps related, but for which one would not normally turn to a Bible textbook. In the discussion of creation, students are encouraged to think about whether there is extraterrestrial life. At the story of Jacob and Esau, there is a significant amount of material on the psychology of sibling rivalry. Similarly, the Joseph story contains a segment on the psychology of dreams. Students are taught about the psychologist Victor Frankl, and are then given a handout with suggested biblical verses to use "to find meaning in their lives." These all point to a curricular design that looks far beyond the Bible and attempts to shape the lives of its users.

An aspect of the curriculum that is consistent throughout the textbook is the white European faces that appear on its pages. It is certainly possible that the choice of primarily Renaissance images is intended to illustrate the impact of the Bible on Western art, but it does leave the impression that the biblical figures were white Europeans, rather than of Middle Eastern descent. It is difficult to find even a single brown face in the curriculum—with the one exception of the photograph accompanying a brief description of ancient Jewish marriage traditions, which features, bizarrely, a modern-day Bedouin woman. The textbook is dependent on a modern, Western, and, it seems fair to say, Christian concept of what the biblical figures looked like. (In one image, the divine beings that go up and down the ladder in Jacob's famous dream are depicted as pure white human forms with wings—a familiar image to us today, but one thoroughly foreign to the Bible, and, for that matter, to Judaism.)

The detailed attention given to the curriculum in the preceding pages is not merely for the sake of pointing out problems—though it should be remembered that the available curriculum is only a quarter of the intended final product, and covers only part of the Old Testament. It is the types of problems that the curriculum continues to suffer from that are revealing. The Museum of the Bible has made an explicit attempt here to overcome the overt sectarian evangelicalism of its original public school curriculum. Yet even after multiple rewrites, the sectarian perspective proves to remain deeply ingrained. Where errors appear and oversights glare they always benefit the general perspective that Christianity, and Protestant Christianity in particular, is superior to the worldviews that preceded and grew up alongside it. This is unlikely to be evidence of a nefarious scheme to convert users to the worldview of the Greens. On the contrary, a good-faith effort seems to have been made here: the continuing problem, here and throughout the various Green/MOTB enterprises, is an ongoing lack of self-awareness, a basic inability to recognize which aspects of their ideas about the Bible are defensible from a secular, scholarly perspective, and which emerge from their faith tradition.

In 2016, the Republican Party's platform for the presidential election, at over 35,000 words, covered an enormous amount of material. Tucked away about halfway through, however, was a single striking sentence: "A good understanding of the Bible being indispensable for the development of an educated citizenry, we encourage state legislatures to offer the Bible in a literature curriculum as an elective in America's high schools." In its almost constitutionally old-fashioned wording, strongly reminiscent of the Second Amendment, the line reads a bit like a holdover from previous party platforms. But it is not; in fact, this is the first time in United States history that any party platform has included a call for the Bible to be taught in America's public schools. Indeed, the Bible has gone almost entirely unmentioned in these party documents, with two exceptions: on the Republican side, a promise not to ban Bibles from military facilities, which first appeared in 2012 and then again in 2016; and on the Democratic side, only in a statement from 2000 on climate change, which, in attributing it to human factors, says, "These are not Biblical plagues."

Given the reasonably lengthy history of efforts to push the Bible into the public schools—the NCBCPS has been active since 1993—it is noteworthy that the movement should have achieved a place in the Republican party platform only in 2016.[78] Whether or not the inclusion of the sentence in the platform is a direct result of the Green family's involvement (in the 2016 primary season almost every GOP presidential candidate made the pilgrimage to Oklahoma City to seek the Greens' blessing), it is clear that the MOTB Bible curriculum is being produced and promoted at a meaningful moment in American culture. Though it is being marketed only to home-schoolers for now, MOTB has not given up its dream of seeing the Bible taught across the country—not just as literature, or for its historical value, but as the core of where America came from and what its values ought to be.

4

THE MUSEUM OF THE BIBLE

ON A SWELTERING AFTERNOON IN JUNE 2015, WE TRAVELED TO Washington, D.C., to tour the Museum of the Bible construction site and meet with Cary Summers, the president of Museum of the Bible, Inc. The museum itself was in development, so we met Summers at 409 3rd Street, the building that abuts the construction site, where the museum's offices were located. In many ways, 409 3rd street is a typical office building: there's a large entryway space outside that serves as a shady refuge for smokers. Inside there's the customary mish-mash of offices, perched atop the service providers that cater to employee needs: there's a deli, a daycare center, a FedEx, even a Gold's gym. The large entranceway is somewhat misleading, as visitors are siphoned through the security checks and X-ray machines that act as the omnipresent gatekeepers for buildings that house federal offices.

We were greeted by Shannon Bennett, Director of Community Relations for Museum of the Bible, and, we later a learned, a Bible student herself. She ushered us into an inconspicuous conference room in the basement for our meeting with Summers. Over the course of the next five hours, Summers generously provided us with a tour of the site and a lengthy interview about the Museum's mission and purpose. He was friendly and charismatic; his charm and personality are convincing and congenial. He is clear and believable; he's the kind of man you want to represent your organization.

Wearing Museum of the Bible–branded hardhats, we made our way through the construction site. It would become an eight-story 430,000-square-foot museum, but at the time it was like any other building zone: in the heat, nondescript liquid was pooling on the floors of the lower levels. Summers chatted enthusiastically, detailing the plans for the forty-foot bronze doors at the entryway, the replica of the ceiling of the Sistine Chapel inside the doors, and the exhibits, theater, and lecture hall on the floors above. As we climbed the ladder to the roof of the building, he told us about the rooftop garden and biblically themed restaurant on the top floor. The highest floor had yet to be constructed, but off in the distance we could see the dome of the Capitol. The Museum of the Bible was facing down the highest levels of government. The arrangement was deliberate, as Steve Green would later tell us: one purpose of the museum is to educate legislators about the biblical foundations of American government. The museum has come a long way from its roots in America's religious heartland.

The idea for the museum, as mentioned in the first chapter, was initially Johnny Shipman's, intended for his hometown of Dallas. It was a natural location for a museum of this kind: evangelical-rich states like Kentucky and Florida already house Bible museums and theme parks, and Protestants have been trying to bring the physical world of Jesus to people for over a hundred years. In the 1870s, the Chautauqua Institution, an educational institute based in Chautauqua, New York, and founded by a Methodist bishop, built a large-scale model of the Holy Land known as Palestine Park.[1] The park is open to this day, but when visitors came there in the nineteenth century they would arrive by boat in order to mimic the journey of pilgrims arriving in the Holy Land. In this way, Palestine Park was both an educational resource for Sunday school teachers and a way to place pilgrimages to the Holy Land within the financial reach of average Americans.

In 2001, the Holy Land Experience opened in Orlando under the direction of Christian television mogul Jan Crouch. Billed as a theme park, the Holy Land Experience attempts to recreate the setting of first-century Jerusalem. Like the Museum of the Bible, it is home to a substantial collection of biblical manuscripts—the Van Kampen collection, Scott Carroll's former project—which are on display for the public attending the theme park. Like the Museum of the Bible, the Holy Land Experience is geographically positioned alongside its secular neighbors. It jostles for position and competes for visitors with Disney World and Universal Studios.

The rolling hills of Kentucky are home to no fewer than two museums that explicitly invite visitors to believe in the truth of biblical events. The first, the Creation Museum, presents a vision of the earth's beginnings that accounts for the conflicting evidence offered by theories of evolution and paleontology.[2] Alongside its apologetic exhibits demonstrating the veracity of the biblical six-day creation is an exhibit called "Culture in Crisis," which demonstrates "what happens when the Bible is taken out of a culture" and gives "real-life" examples of how "compromising God's Word has harmed the Church and the Family." Abortion, pornography, violence, and social decay are, the exhibit argues, the effects of secularization. More recently, in 2016, Ken Ham's Answers in Genesis, the same group that is responsible for the Creation Museum, built a museum dedicated to the biblical flood story, called Ark Encounter.[3] The conceit and centerpiece of the museum is a life-sized replica of Noah's ark, constructed using the book of Genesis as its blueprints. The museum is far from nonsectarian; its goal is connecting the flood story, which Ham believes took place in 2348 BCE, to Christ.[4]

The Museum of the Bible could easily have ended up as one of these rural museums, in an evangelical-friendly community and with a strongly Christian supersessionist bent. But as the collection grew and as Steve Green, in his words, "started taking ownership of the project," he began to think bigger. The Greens and Cary Summers hired a consulting firm to survey the viability of a museum in Washington, D.C., New York, or Los Angeles. The consultants determined that Washington, as the museum capital of the country, would yield the highest rates of attendance. It was a decision that made sense to Green, he told us, because his Hobby Lobby stores did best when they were located close to other big box retailers.

The only unknown was the specific location for the museum. For Green, the opportunity had to be financially right. In July 2012, MOTB purchased the Washington Design Center from the Vornado Realty Group for slightly less than $50 million. The large red brick structure was originally built in 1919 as a refrigerated warehouse. It was only later that it became the home of furniture, lighting, and textile makers. The history of the building suited the Green's needs: located a mere two blocks from the Mall, the former warehouse had been built without windows, making it the ideal location to house ancient photosensitive artifacts.

As plans for the museum began to take shape, the Greens decided to begin sharing their collection with the world. In March 2011 the traveling *Passages* exhibition was announced to a gathering of academic, religious, business, and government leaders in Washington, D.C., at the home of the Apostolic Nuncio to the Holy See, otherwise known as the Vatican Embassy. Designed by Scott Carroll, the exhibit debuted in Oklahoma City in May 2011 before travelling to Atlanta, Charlotte, Colorado Springs, Springfield, Missouri, and Santa Clarita, California. *Passages* was in many ways a dry run for Museum of the Bible: not only was it filled with many of the artifacts that would come to make up the museum, its gift shop sold Museum of the Bible apparel.

If *Passages* was a foreshadowing of the eventual museum, other exhibits signaled an interest in ecumenical dialogue and collaboration. Two exhibitions, *Verbum Domini* and *Verbum Domini II*, were organized at the Vatican; the first in February 2012 and the second in April 2014. (It was during the latter that papyrologist Roberta Mazza first saw the Coptic fragment of Galatians that had previously been up for sale on eBay.) The Vatican exhibits were a coup for the Museum of the Bible: never before had the Vatican allowed a double page of Codex Vaticanus, one of the oldest and most important copies of the New Testament, to be included in an independent exhibition. Codex Vaticanus did not have far to travel, as the exhibition was hosted inside the Vatican itself, in the Braccio di Carlo Magno, an event venue that opens directly onto St. Peter's Square.

The connection with the Vatican was negotiated by Mario J. Paredes, American Bible Society Presidential Liaison for Roman Catholic Affairs. While the Greens did not have the opportunity to meet with then-pope Benedict XVI in 2012, when they returned in 2014 for the opening of the second exhibition, representatives of the Museum of the Bible spoke with Pope Francis, and not only about ancient artifacts. The visit was auspiciously timed: only a week earlier President Obama had visited the Vatican to meet with the Holy Pontiff. In news briefings, President Obama suggested that "social schisms" had not been a prominent topic of discussion with Francis. But media interviews with Steve Green told a different story. Green, whose family was at the time in the midst of suing the government over the HHS mandate, told MSNBC news that he had spoken with the Pope about their shared concerns about contraception. He added that he had thanked the Pope for raising the issue with President Obama. Almost inevitably, the political and personal interests of the Green family were associated with Museum of the Bible.

In October 2013, the *Book of Books* exhibit in Jerusalem opened. In January 2014, a Spanish-language exhibition called *La Biblia* debuted in Havana, Cuba. A revival of *Verbum Domini* was organized in Philadelphia in 2015 to coincide with the World Meeting of the Families (a triannual gathering of Catholic leaders and laity to discuss, protect, and promote the family) and Pope Francis's visit to the United States. This special exhibit, Cary Summers told us, was organized at the request of the Vatican. But other exhibits were not officially sanctioned by the events with which they were ostensibly affiliated. In the summer of 2015, members of the Society of Biblical Literature, the professional organization for biblical scholars, were invited to attend a reception and to visit a special *Highlights of the Green Collection* exhibition in Buenos Aires. The exhibit was arranged to coincide with the SBL's annual international meeting there, and the marketing that surrounded it implied that it was an SBL-endorsed event (the MOTB press release proclaimed, "Forty-eight Items on Display at Society of Biblical Literature's Annual Meeting"[5]). But John Kutsko, the president of the society, was insistent that the organization had not approved or sanctioned the Museum of the Bible's event—indeed, he emphasized that the use of SBL's name in the exhibit's materials was against SBL's expressly stated wishes.[6]

The *Passages*, *Verbum Domini*, *Book of Books*, and *La Biblia* exhibits were all well-publicized events approved by host institutions. But if the path to the Museum of the Bible was paved with traveling exhibits, many of these steps were unmarked. Green Collection artifacts have appeared at fund-raising dinners in support of the Becket Fund, the legal-aid charity that promotes religious freedom and defended the Greens in their Supreme Court fight. In 2012, the *Verbum Domini* exhibition moved to Ken Ham's Creation Museum, which markets itself as a defense of biblical inerrancy. The media release for the arrival of the collection there leveraged the prestige of the exhibit's previous location: "Moving From the Vatican to the Bible-Upholding Museum." At the opening of the exhibit in Kentucky, Steve Green commented about the two museums: "We are like-minded. Our purpose in opening the Museum of the Bible and in loaning a part of our collection to the Creation Museum is to show visitors the value of the Bible in society."[7]

Artifacts from the Green Collection have also found their way into Answers in Genesis's second Christian theme-park, Ark Encounter. Three of the bays on the second deck of the life-sized replica of the ark display Green Collection artifacts that are used to support the historicity and impact of the biblical Noah's ark story. Whatever Green and MOTB may say about the intentions of their museum, the mission and conclusions of these other, decidedly sectarian museums is abundantly clear.

The connections between the Museum of the Bible and the explicitly evangelizing projects of Ken Ham go beyond the mere lending of artifacts. Cary Summers, the president of MOTB, has served as a consultant for both the Holy Land Experience and Ark Encounter. In describing the purpose of the latter, he is considerably less circumspect than he is when describing the purpose of the Museum of the Bible. Of Ark Encounter he says, "The key will be massaging out the Christ aspect of it. . . . I think you can create a great storyline of the impact of the Bible that came out of Noah's lineage, and you could support it with hundreds of artifacts."[8]

The fact that the Greens are evangelicals who financially support and believe in the mission of Ark Encounter and the Creation Museum does not, of course, mean that they are insincere when they claim that their Museum of the Bible will be nonsectarian. As Steve Green himself told us, his family supports evangelical outreach programs, but MOTB is not supposed to be a part of that. Yet it is notable that the display of Green-owned artifacts at these more conservative and less intellectually credible theme parks goes unmentioned on MOTB's webpage. While the publicity for the museum proudly remarks upon its traveling exhibits in Atlanta, Charlotte, the Vatican, Jerusalem, and so on, there are no references to Kentucky. The presence of the artifacts there is a tangible link to an avowedly fundamentalist Christian world—a connection, and indeed a world, that MOTB chooses not to advertise to the broader public.

Unlike museums like the Creation Museum and Ark Encounter, MOTB does not appeal to its evangelical bona fides in order to leverage itself. Arguably, it doesn't have to: the involvement of the Green family and the celebrity pastor Rick Warren already telegraph that the museum has Protestant roots. Instead, the museum emphasizes its academic credentials. The first floor will feature exhibits from the libraries of some of the world's most prestigious and well-respected universities. According to Cary Summers, exhibits from seven libraries, including the Bodleian, the Sackler, the Parker, and Jewish Theological Seminary are slated to appear at MOTB. Upon first glance, the impression gleaned by a visitor will be that the exhibits and message of the Museum of the Bible are backed by intellectual superpowers.

But, as we saw in chapter 1, when MOTB was first envisioned, it was clearly evangelical in purpose: "to bring to life the living word of God, to tell its compelling story of preservation, and to inspire confidence in the absolute authority and reliability of the Bible." By 2012, this read, "We exist to invite people to engage with the Bible through our four primary activities: travelling exhibits, scholarship, building of a permanent museum, and developing elective high school curriculum." The organization's mission was condensed further the following year. In 2013, it read that MOTB sought only to invite people to engage with the Bible through "museum exhibits and scholarly pursuits." Education reappeared in their 2014 filing, but with no reference to the curriculum in particular.

The nonprofit filings tell the history of the organization's shifting view of the museum as it was shaped by forces both internal and external. When the high school curriculum slipped off the docket in June 2014, the organization was in the early days of the fight to place their Bible curriculum in American high schools. The more prominent shift, however, is from 2011 to 2012, the period that coincided with Scott Carroll's exit from the organization. The broad invitation to engagement with the Bible that emerged in 2012 does not even imply that the Bible is being treated as a holy artifact, much less as the "living word of God." The explicit faith commitment of the founding mission is replaced by a blander, broader invitation. It is one that can be understood as a subtle evangelical call, but to outsiders it could read as an intellectual invitation. The Bible could be understood as a historical curio, if one were so inclined.

When we asked Steve Green about the change in the mission of the museum, he denied that a shift had ever taken place. What had changed, he indicated, was mostly his personal perception of what it means to be nonsectarian. "I don't know that there was a big change. I think from day one now there's been a bit of a clarification for me in understanding what [nonsectarian] means, but from day one the idea was a nonsectarian museum," he told us. "I don't know if there was this big change but it was a process of understanding, clarifying where my fence posts are."

For Green a turning point in that educational process was a visit to the Billy Graham Library in Charlotte, North Carolina. When visitors leave the library, they receive a credit-card-sized description of God's plan of salvation. It is a pledge card; at the bottom, the visitor is invited to sign his or her name. It is a classic Graham formulation: people hear the Gospel during their visit, and as they leave they are invited to accept Christ as their savior. The notion appealed to Green: "I came out and said, 'Boy, I like that,'" he told us. But an ensuing discussion in an MOTB public relations meeting brought him to the realization that he could not issue an evangelical altar call and still claim to be nonsectarian. The idea was tabled, and in conversation with Green it was clear that he considers his willingness to put aside this idea to be an indication of the nonsectarian impartiality of the museum. "My family has no problem supporting those that are out there evangelizing—we do that," he told us, "but this one [the Museum of the Bible] is a different role, it has a different purpose. A public school is not the place to evangelize, that's what the church's role is; a public school is for education to teach the facts."

Representatives of the museum have been using the language of nonsectarianism since at least 2010.[9] But "nonsectarian," as already discussed, is not a synonym for either "nonreligious" or "open to all approaches." On the contrary, the nuances of the term imply both Christian and Protestant. As Cary Summers told us in our visit to the museum, "We're nonsectarian. We're not trying to buy items to tell the Catholic story. We're not trying to tell the Jewish story."

For both Green and Summers, being nonsectarian means "just telling the facts" or "just telling the story." In a discussion with us about the hugely successful History Channel television series *The Bible,* Green told us that he felt that the show was a bit too Catholic. This was something he wants to avoid, and it is something that is intrinsic to his understanding of what it means to be nonsectarian. "I just want to let the facts speak for themselves. So I don't know that there was necessarily a big change; there was a clarification in my mind of what that meant but from day one it was always a nonsectarian museum. . . . I think I've become one of the stronger proponents of making sure we don't cross that line."

The rhetoric of "merely telling the story" has been part of the program from the beginning, as we have seen: they understand themselves as storytellers, not collectors. Green and Summers occasionally describe the nonsectarian story as just the facts, just the narrative of the Bible, or just the elements upon which Jews, Catholics, and Protestants can agree.

It's a commendable goal, but the fissures in this strategy start to emerge when Green gets into the specifics of what it means to "just tell the facts." He cites the evangelical author and minister Josh McDowell—he of the mummy mask destruction displays—as someone who is "just putting the facts down." McDowell's books are available for sale in the *Passages* gift shop. The assessment of McDowell as a plainspoken facts-oriented author is an interesting one. McDowell is barely known outside of evangelical circles, and would not be considered a scholar by the vast majority of

American academics. He runs Josh McDowell Ministry, which, in its own words, "serves and equips the Body of Christ in raising generations of purpose-driven Christians who know what they believe, why it is true, and how to live it out."[10] A self-described Christian apologist, his best-known work, published originally by Campus Crusade for Christ, is called *Evidence That Demands a Verdict*—a book that Green specifically mentioned to us as informing his own understanding.[11] McDowell is a curious choice for a nonsectarian model.

Moreover, while the prospect of presenting the biblical story from Genesis through Revelation may seem straightforward enough, it is an idea that seems naive to biblical scholars, who would contest the idea that the Bible tells a single consistent story —to say nothing of the many places in which Jews, Catholics, and Protestants disagree on the meaning of that story. The Bible is not like a Shakespeare play. It is a library, a collection, and like any collection—except, perhaps, the Green Collection—it contains multiple perspectives and opinions, even about essential plot points. When trying to present the story of Noah's ark, for instance, do you say that Noah took two of every animal on earth, as it says in Genesis 6? Or do say that he took fourteen of every clean animal and two of every unclean animal, as it says in Genesis 7? When telling the story of Jesus, which Gospel account do you follow? The one from John, in which Jesus dies on the day before Passover, or the other three, in which Jesus dies on the first day of the holiday?

It is, of course, central to the literalist evangelical understanding that there are no contradictions within the Bible—that these and the myriad other ostensible problems can be explained or interpreted out of existence. In truth, there is something essentially evangelical about the entire project of telling "the" story—as if there is one single truth that can simply be presented, and in so doing overwhelm the messy complications of reality. Steve Green told us, "We can't really cross the line of faith—we don't want to. We just want to present the facts." This is a fine and noble sentiment, and given the number of times he repeated the theme, one that is clearly important to him. But it is one that glosses over the way that the presentation of "facts," the selection of and emphasis on certain "facts" to the necessary exclusion of others, is never without its own bias.

The idea that it is even possible to tell a story—any story, much less one as literarily and historically complicated as the Bible—on its own independent terms, without grounding it in any interpretive approach, is, for biblical scholars and literary critics alike, problematic and outdated. It resonates, as Mark Noll has shown in his work, with evangelical understandings of biblical criticism, but it is willfully ignorant of the fact that the Bible does not speak unless someone speaks with it. The Museum of the Bible's rhetoric of allowing the Bible to speak for itself and inviting people to engage with the Bible, as if there were not hundreds of years of cultural interpretation and clutter affecting both the museum's and each individual visitor's interpretation of the Bible, emerges out of a particular Protestant intellectual milieu, going back to the principle of *sola scriptura*. Noll describes this attitude, quoting the nineteenth-century Protestant theologian John W. Nevin, as understanding the Bible to be "a book dropped from the skies for all sorts of men to use in their own way." In the early nineteenth century, Alexander Campbell, one of the key figures in the founding of the Disciples of Christ movement put it this way: "I have endeavored to read the Scriptures as though no one had read them before me."[12] Noll further cites the *Systematic Theology* of Charles Hodge, from 1872: "The Bible is to the theologian what nature is to the man of science. It is his store-house of facts."[13] In her book *Apostles of Reason*, Molly Worthen describes the rise in evangelical Christian circles of "inductive" reasoning as the primary means of working through the Bible: "It restored the Bible to its rightful authority while assimilating—yet restraining—human rationalism." Worthen writes, "Inductive Bible study had long formed the core of evangelical and fundamentalist pedagogy. Students studied the 'facts' of the Bible for themselves."[14] Whether consciously or not, the Museum of the Bible participates in this "inductive" approach: as Green says, "We just want to present the facts."

When Steve Green talks about the Museum of the Bible, he describes it as a "broad tent" that is focused solely on the Bible. "We don't want to go outside the Bible," he says; "I can't bring in my Protestant tradition." He describes visiting the Vatican and seeing artwork in which biblical scenes are melded with portraits of medieval Popes. Everything there is interwoven, he told us, and the Bible is muddled with Catholic tradition. Moreover, Green is a realist about the difficulties in identifying one's own biases. He realizes that it is easier for him to detect Catholic influences than it is for him to see Protestant ones. He is charmingly humble about the frailties of human prejudice.

What he appears not to appreciate, however, is that the focus on the Bible as the exclusive touchstone for Christianity, divorced from some perceived denominational tradition, is itself a Protestant notion. *Sola scriptura*, the idea that Christianity should be grounded only in the Holy Scriptures, began as one of Martin Luther's axioms. The notion that tradition (which is often a form of biblical interpretation) and scripture (which has no meaning without an interpreter to read and understand it) are separate from one another is a religious commitment. The distinction between the text and readings of the text is also found in non-Protestant religious groups. Catholics too speak of scripture and tradition, and Jews refer to the written and the oral law. The notion that the Bible speaks in a coherent voice that stands apart from human history—this is a faith claim, not a scholarly or secular one. But the idea that the Bible can be understood apart from tradition, that a museum could be "just the Bible," or *sola scriptura*—this idea has a distinctly Protestant ring to it.

In the United States, the notion of presenting merely the words of the Bible has a storied history. The American Bible Society was founded with the intention of bringing the King James Version of the Bible to people without "note or comment."[15] The idea seems innocuous enough, but it was formed in distinction to the commentary that appeared in Catholic versions of the Bible.[16] For the founders of the American Bible Society, distributing Bibles without "note or comment" or, as the Greens might put it, "without interpretation," meant avoiding denominational bias. They saw commentary and marginalia as the cause of fractures and "jealousies" in the Church. Historically, the publication of the Bible without comment has been understood not only as a tool of conversion but also as a means of defeating Catholicism. In the nineteenth century, more than a few stories about the ability of the unadulterated King James Version to convert Catholics were published. The idea of publishing only the things about which Protestants, Catholics, and Jews agree is well-intentioned, but the history of the idea of telling the Bible's story without artifice has an intrinsic anti-Catholic bias.

This is not to say that MOTB organizers and curators intend to be anti-Catholic; on the contrary, the idea of showing the points on which Jews, Catholics, and Protestants agree is often tied to a sense of wonder that they can agree at all. Using the Protestant language of witness, Steve Green told us that "I think it will be powerful testimony to the world to say: 'Here's these people, what we hear about in the news is their fights, but here they come together because they agree upon something that can be powerful.'" For Green, presenting Jews, Protestants, and Catholics in agreement with one another is itself proof of the importance of the Bible. That conclusion, too, supports the essential Protestant idea of the primacy of the Bible: ultimately the presence and participation of Jews and Catholics in MOTB is used to reinforce both Protestant theology and Protestant claims to superiority.

It also has a subtly antielitist and anti-intellectual tone. In his history of the American Bible Society, John Fea quotes Jeremiah Day, a president of Yale College, who remarked in 1824, "So far as commentators enable us to understand what we read, we may be grateful for their aid. But we are not to look for improvements on a revelation from heaven. The volume of immutable truth is not to be wrought into a more perfect form by metaphysical refinement. It will not be in a higher degree, the wisdom of God, and power of God to salvation, when translated into the technical language of modern theological systems."[17] The idea that the Bible does not need interpretation, commentary, or scholarly explanation is in its origins Protestant and asserts that the authority, meaning, and message of the Bible is self-evident. The King James Version was novel among early printed Bibles for, by order of the Bishop of London, it contained no marginal theological notes to help guide the reader through the text, such as were found in the most significant previous English-language versions: the Great Bible, the Bishop's Bible, and the Geneva Bible. Sheltering the Bible from commentary is not about protecting it from critical analysis; it is a theological statement about the value of the Bible itself.

For Green and Summers, what should be left out of a nonsectarian Bible museum is not only specific denominational emphasis, but indeed any and all human interpretation. Summers told us, "Man has misused the book, but the book is rock solid. That's what nonsectarian is. It's not a denomination, it's not a faith, it's the book." This is a revealing stance. Summers seems to be unaware that the statement "The book is rock solid" is itself a faith claim. Even referring to the Christian Bible, as he does here, as a single book, rather than a collection of books, is a faith statement; one that presumes that the speaker is not, for example, Jewish. It is hard to imagine a Jew agreeing that the New Testament, with its denunciation of the Jews as offspring of Satan (John 8:40–48), is "rock solid," or that a museum that argues as much is nonsectarian.

In our conversations with both Summers and Green, they exhibited an interesting double-read of the way that the Bible both can and cannot be held responsible for events and trends in human history. On one hand, there is a distinction between the Bible itself and humanity's "misuse" of it. Green agrees when he refers to the Jonestown mass suicide and the cult leader Jim Jones: "Don't blame the Bible because he's misused it." Implicit in such statements is the notion that the Bible and humanity are somehow distinct —as if the Bible itself is not a human product.

On the other hand, there is the way that Green and Summers describe the Bible's impact in the world. Our history, culture, literature, health system, ethics, values, familial structure, and government, they correctly note, have all been fostered and shaped by the Bible. An entire floor of the museum is dedicating to showing the impact that the Bible has had in the formation of modern society. Individual displays will include the Bible's influence on the formation of the family, healthcare, charity, and government. Steve Green told us that there will be a section called "The Bible in America"—which also happens to be the title of a book that Green authored—that will demonstrate that the government is built on biblical principles. In particular, he identified the principle that all men are created equal, the principle of religious freedom, and "economic private property rights" as key biblical concepts that contributed to the success of the nation.

These certainly are principles that Christians have claimed originate in the Bible, but they have a particular history to them. Even if the notion existed, there is little evidence that, prior to the Reformation, anyone would have ascribed to "private property rights" the import later endowed by John Locke.[18] Moreover, the centrality of these rights would be contested by other groups of Christians—for example, Latin American Roman Catholics, especially those associated with liberation theology movement—who would point to passages in the New Testament about care for the poor and holding goods in common.[19] It is not necessary to adjudicate between these sets of claims or evaluate which is a "better" reading of the Bible, especially since each group grounds its perspective in different scriptural texts. Indeed, the salient point is that both interpretive traditions can claim biblical foundations—but only one set of claims is represented at the Museum of the Bible. There's no disputing the difficulty inherent in curating a museum, but this museum's interpretive decisions lean in the direction of Protestantism.

The museum will not shy away from some of the hard truths about how the Bible has been interpreted: there will be exhibits dedicated to the Holocaust and slavery in America. But there is nevertheless a rhetorical distinction between the way that Summers and Green describe man's "misuse" of the Bible, which is divorced from the inanimate pages of scripture, and the Bible's "impact" on our society, which is something for which the Bible should be credited. After describing the widespread ignorance in America about the content of the Bible and its impact on society, Green concluded, "Our goal is to cause people to realize this book's impacted your life now; you can believe that it's been the scourge of the earth, that's your right, but believe that knowing fully its impact. And I think the answer to that is that yes, there have been men that have used this book for their own selfish ill intent; my argument is that we don't blame the book for man's misuse of it."

Built on eight levels, the museum is structured to present the Bible in three different ways: the narrative presented in the Bible itself, the history of the Bible—both the history behind the text and the history of the text's transmission and translations—and the impact of the Bible on society.

The narrative floor, Green astutely recognized, is an important part of the museum. Modern museum-goers are woefully undereducated about even the contents of the Bible, and thus it is necessary and appropriate to begin with the story. In his description of this section, Green likened it to a Cliff's Notes version of *Romeo and Juliet*. This floor will include "the narratives of the Hebrew text from Genesis to Chronicles and then through first-century Nazareth, ending with the story of the New Testament." Visitors will walk through a life-sized reproduction of Nazareth, an aspect of the museum whose origins lie, it seems, in the tourist attraction known as *Nazareth Village*, of which Cary Summers was previously CEO. Located within the modern city of Nazareth, the purpose of the village "from the beginning" was "to help pilgrims see the Nazareth Jesus knew and hear Jesus' words."[20]

In describing the purpose of the history floor, Green told us that it would present the archaeological and manuscript evidence for the events and world described in the Bible. "All we can do is present the facts—we really can't cross the line of faith. We don't want to, we just want to present the facts." Among the exhibits found here will be artifacts that "document the Bible's preservation, translation, and transmission across centuries and cultures." Included among them will be "writings dating to the time of Abraham" (cuneiform tablets), fragments of the Dead Sea Scrolls, and early New Testament manuscripts.[21]

Finally, the impact floor would discuss the many ways in which society, American society in particular, is underwritten by biblical concepts and values. The notion that America was self-consciously founded as a Christian country is not unique to the Greens. It has colonial and nineteenth-century roots but blossomed, as Kevin

Kruse has shown, in vitriolic clerical responses to the New Deal and in the tightening of the relationship between the Republican party and religious right during the 1980s.[22] In highlighting those aspects of society that he feels have been particularly shaped by the Bible, Green singled out our "freedoms" and "private property rights" as two elements that stem from the Bible. Green is not wrong: American interest in individual property rights has historically been tied to Protestant readings of the Bible. Demonstrations of the Bible's impact will include exhibits on the fine arts, science, and government.

The impact floor is, in some ways, a more upbeat reflection of an exhibit at the Creation Museum that aims to show how society would crumble without the Bible. At the Creation Museum, visitors are led through corridors depicting the effects of legalizing abortion, same-sex marriage, and euthanasia. The accompanying placard explains: "Scripture abandoned in the culture leads to . . . relative morality, hopelessness and meaninglessness."[23] Certainly this is a position with which Green would tacitly agree. He told us, "Our nation was built on a biblical worldview. If we walk away from it, let's walk away from it with our eyes wide open. Understand what you're walking away from, what is it you want to embrace. A secular worldview? Well let's look at other secular worldviews and see what that has created: it's created the greatest tragedies in the world."

The language used by Summers and Green in describing the museum is deliberately neutral. The conclusions that they want visitors to reach, however, are not. In a podcast about the museum's purpose, Cary Summers said, "Mounting manuscript and archaeological discoveries continue to affirm [the Bible's] accuracy." The presentation of the evidence will be strongly skewed in favor of a literal reading of biblical events. When it comes to the narrative floor, at least, this seems fair enough: Green explained to us that if he were organizing an exhibit on Harry Potter he would include Quidditch contests and flying broomsticks because they are an integral part of the narrative. Similarly, he feels that people who do not believe in the historicity of the Bible should understand the inclusion of miracles and the supernatural in the museum's presentation of the biblical narrative, because they are part of the story.

It's a crisp argument—though one may note the irony of Green using a work of fiction (one that has been condemned by many conservative Christians as advocating witchcraft) to justify the Bible. Where arguments about historical accuracy become more complicated is, perhaps unsurprisingly, on the history floor: after visitors have been introduced to the biblical narrative, presented as literally as possible, the next section of the museum does not seem to take the opportunity to present the abundant manuscript or archaeological evidence that calls the historicity of that narrative into question.

An obvious and significant test of the Museum of the Bible's impartiality is less in what evidence is included and more in what evidence the museum's curators and organizers choose to exclude. "There are holes in the collection that we would like to fill," Summers said. There are, to be fair, holes in the collections of many museums. But the Museum of the Bible, we were repeatedly told, wishes to acquire only those artifacts that support the story that it is trying to tell. It is noteworthy, for example, that the Museum of the Bible devotes so little space or attention to noncanonical and apocryphal texts, books, like the *Gospel of Judas*, that were considered religiously significant by some ancient Christians and Jews but which failed to make it into the canonical Bible used by most modern faith communities. Nor will there be any mention of the use of the Christian Bible in the scriptural traditions of Muslims or the Latter-Day Saints. The story of the Bible, we were told, will essentially end with the Reformation and the translation projects of modern missionaries. There is an ingrained assumption that from the ancient world to the present the text of the Bible has been fixed in stone. The Greens have happily purchased ancient cuneiform that tells us nothing about the Bible but that gestures to literacy in the ancient world, hinting at the possibility that the stories of Abraham are eyewitness accounts—preferring this over acquiring examples of noncanonical texts that were considered scriptural by generations of early Christians.

Similarly, the Green Collection contains an unusually large number of Torah scrolls from the sixteenth through nineteenth centuries—unusual because while a museum of the Bible might be expected to own and display a handful of Torah scrolls, as examples of the use of the Bible in Judaism, it is generally not common practice to have thousands of such scrolls in a museum's holdings. Summers describes the purpose of these acquisitions in altruistic terms: "We buy for three reasons; one is to tell the story, the second is to rescue items, and the third is research." The Torah scrolls, he told us, fall into this second category. They purchase the scrolls because they are going to deteriorate. "We are the hospital of the world for Torah scrolls," he said. Altruism aside, it is more difficult to imagine what place thousands of Torah scrolls would have in a museum display, or what role they might play in telling the story of the Bible.[24]

Steve Green, however, has no such difficulty. Green told us that he would like to use the collection's substantial assemblage of Torah scrolls to illustrate the permanency of the biblical text. "I think that there's a phenomenal story that they tell; there's a curiosity and intrigue for a Christian world with the Torah scroll." Seeing thousands of Torah scrolls laid out, he said, would help to demonstrate the inerrancy of the transmission of the biblical text itself. Summers clarified that he expects that this particular exhibit will display 640 scrolls.

The same message of inerrant transmission, Green added, can be inferred from other ancient Jewish manuscripts: "This is the story of the Dead Sea Scrolls. Let's take a look at the Great Isaiah Scroll," he said, referring to the remarkable, nearly complete text of Isaiah discovered at Qumran; "Let's put a percent on it. It's ninety percent what we have to this day. There's a thousand-year gap, and ninety percent of the [remaining] ten percent is, you know, they switched a word or something—instead of 'there' it's 'their,' and you know what it was. . . . So that's an exciting story to tell, and the Torah scrolls help tell that story."

In other words, the Torah scrolls—like those from the Dead Sea—will, from Green's perspective, help demonstrate the consistency of the biblical text, the accuracy of its transmission over the millennia. For Green, the Torah scrolls are a response to critics like Bart Ehrman. The ability of Jewish scribes over the last five hundred years to faithfully reproduce the standard text of the Hebrew

Bible is seen as evidence of the divine hand at work in the preservation of scripture. (It is probably worth pointing out that Green's understanding of the transmission of Torah scrolls is faulty, or at least incomplete. Until the Middle Ages, there was widespread disparity among Torah scrolls. When the great medieval Jewish scholar Maimonides attempted to clarify which text should be considered authoritative, he had to choose among various possible versions—and the one he chose, now known as the Aleppo Codex, did not in fact end up being the base text for modern Torah scrolls. Almost all modern Torahs are based on an edition produced in Venice in 1525—members of the Yemenite Jewish community continue to rely on the text chosen by Maimonides.) Leaning forward to us later in the interview, as he discussed archaeological ventures, Green said that it gives him chills thinking about the Dead Sea Scrolls: "God, I think, protected the Dead Sea Scrolls for when he was ready for them to be revealed. And I just wonder what he's still got buried under the ground and waiting for the right time for it to be revealed."

The avoiding of noncanonical texts, even those that were widely discussed and dispersed among ancient Christians, along with the explicit use of Jewish religious items to support an evangelical Christian position on the inerrancy of the Bible's transmission, gives us pause about the fate of two of the most high-profile "gets" in the museum.[25] On the fifth floor, the Museum of the Bible will lend space to exhibits drawn from and curated by the Israel Antiquities Authority and the Vatican Museum. The collaboration between these organizations and the Museum of the Bible is unprecedented: the Israel Antiquities Authority is famously strict about controlling the display of its more than two million artifacts; the Vatican, for its part, has never permitted its treasures to be loaned to a foreign institution. In both cases, the Museum of the Bible will cede control of the space to these world-renowned institutions. But even under such terms, questions of direction and intention still linger.

The partnership between the Museum of the Bible and the Israel Antiquities Authority is noteworthy primarily because the IAA has never before had a semipermanent outpost in a foreign country.

The director of the IAA acknowledged the uniqueness of this new venture: "The Israel Antiquities Authority is thrilled and proud to partner with the Museum of the Bible on this landmark project. Making the archaeological heritage of the Land of Israel and the vital archaeological work conducted by the IAA available and accessible to people around the world is our mission. The rare opportunity to have a long-term exhibition in the U.S. Capital of a large selection of archaeological treasures that were excavated in Israel and illuminate the story of the Bible is remarkable."[26]

The collaboration goes beyond the IAA-controlled display at the museum: MOTB has pledged $4 million to fund a new archaeological dig in Israel, at the previously unexcavated site of Tel Shimron in the Galilee. As part of the agreement, the artifacts unearthed in the excavation, though still technically under IAA control, will be displayed at the Museum of the Bible. The archaeologist heading the excavation, Daniel Master of Wheaton, is widely respected, and no one we have spoken to questions his integrity and commitment to running an independent and rigorously professional dig. For some scholars and academic organizations, however, the close collaboration between an archaeological dig and antiquities collectors—especially those who have been investigated for illicit importation—is a source of discomfort. Nevertheless, the IAA, Tel Aviv University, and Wheaton College have all provided institutional support for the project.

While the IAA sees the collaboration as a chance to finance and promote its mission of making Israel's archaeological heritage widely accessible, MOTB is participating in a long-standing evangelical program of support for Israel. As the scholar Timothy Weber wrote, in an article entitled "How Evangelicals Became Israel's Best Friend," for evangelicals Israel "is the Holy Land, the site of God's mighty deeds. In a way, they think the Promised Land belongs to them as much as it does to Israelis."[27] This attitude is manifested in the very public backing that evangelicals provide for the modern state of Israel. Originating in part in a fundamentalist notion of premillenialism—the belief that the end of time is fast approaching—the return of the Jewish people to Israel has been seen as a fulfillment of biblical prophecy. George Marsden, in his book *Fundamentalism and American Culture*, notes that "the practical result of these teachings was that American fundamentalists and most evangelicals were among the most ardent promoters of United States policies of support for Israel."[28] Although MOTB has an obvious programmatic need to engage with the artifacts excavated from Israel, this may not account fully for the organization's commitments, including the Covenant Journey and Bible curriculum projects described in the previous chapter.

In a similar manner, evangelicals have found common cause with Catholics going back to Vatican II in the 1960s. In particular, evangelicals were drawn to the Catholic intellectual framework of "natural law," an attraction that grew increasingly stronger as it became clear that this principle formed a mutual basis for opposition to abortion and gay marriage. As Molly Worthen puts it: "It enabled them to reject the secular insistence upon a neutral public sphere in which religion had no place."[29] D. Michael Lindsay points to the collaboration between evangelicals and Catholics as the production of a united front against liberal Protestantism.[30]

Lindsay also notes how this collaboration has benefited both sides, in a manner that closely tracks with the joint venture between the Vatican and the Museum of the Bible: "Catholics benefit from evangelicals' entrepreneurial creativity and ability to connect with popular audiences, while evangelicals have gained new bases of support. Evangelicals now draw on a vast array of source material that is rooted in the Catholic tradition."[31] In the Vatican-controlled exhibit, Cary Summers told us, artifacts would be on display illustrating how the Bible has been interpreted. But, given their insistence on telling "just the story," one has to wonder how much freedom will be granted to the curators of the Vatican space. Summers told us that the Vatican would have absolute freedom within their own exhibit, but added wryly that MOTB would have to approve it because "we can't have something goofy."

This kind of oversight should trouble those with a vested interest in Roman Catholic piety. The Vatican exhibit will become a pilgrimage site for American Roman Catholics: the fact that the exhibit will be curated by the Vatican lends it instant credibility and religious authority. It may, for those whose finances do not stretch to transatlantic airfares, become the premiere Roman Catholic pilgrimage site in the country. Summers told us that he hopes it will. To be sure, there are others: the Shrine of the Divine Mercy in Massachusetts; the Shrine of St. Elizabeth Ann Seton; the Shrine of Our Lady of Martyrs; the Shrine of St. John Neumann; and the Basilica of the National Shrine of the Immaculate Conception. But with the exception of the latter, none of these is located in the nation's capital, and not even the Sistine Chapel itself enables visitors to reach out and touch the hand of God so exquisitely rendered by Michelangelo some five hundred years ago. If for no other reason than that it promises to house one of the most significant Catholic pilgrimage centers in the United States, the question of whether the Museum of the Bible is subtly Protestant is a pressing one.

It is unfair, not to mention presumptuous and difficult, to criticize the shape and contents of a museum that no one has yet seen. We have only the statements of the Museum of the Bible's administrators—Cary Summers, David Trobisch, and Steve Green—and press releases as our firm guides. We can analyze their words, but there is always the possibility that their plans will change. It is possible, however, to evaluate *Passages*, the traveling forerunner of Museum of the Bible, and consider how this exhibition presents the story of the Bible.

When we visited *Passages* in 2015, it was situated in a former hardware store in a strip mall in Santa Clarita, California. Just across the parking lot from a Jack-in-the-Box, it seemed like an improbable venue for a Bible exhibit. Our guides for the day were Lauren Green McAfee and Michael McAfee, daughter and son-in-law of Steve Green, and directors of community engagement and Bible engagement for MOTB, respectively. Smiley, happy-go-lucky brunch lovers, they are charming and likeable. It would be unsurprising to see Michael run for public office one day.

The exhibit itself was organized chronologically, though it had the potential to be visited thematically. It began with ancient history and the world of Abraham, proceeded through rooms of ancient manuscripts, and moved to the Reformation and the translation of the Bible into English before briefly surveying the use and impact of the Bible. The climactic portion, which followed briefly on a "Controversies" section that discussed the Holocaust and slavery, was a discussion of the Bible in American history.

In its structure, and in many other ways, *Passages* was the heir to a number of other for-profit Bible exhibits. Throughout the 2000s, Bill Noah's *Ink and Blood* and Lee Biondi's *The Dead Sea Scrolls to the Bible in America* exhibits traveled throughout the United States, displaying artifacts that attested to the history of the Bible as a book. Though neither Noah nor Biondi recalls anyone from the Green family or organization ever visiting their exhibits, the two ventures were strikingly similar to what would eventually become *Passages*. All three began with cuneiform tablets demonstrating the origins of writing; all displayed Dead Sea Scroll fragments, as well as biblical manuscripts from the era of early Christianity. All came to a climax with the translation of the Bible into English, with emphasis on the works of John Wycliffe, William Tyndale, and the other vernacular translations that led to the King James Bible. Like *Passages*, Noah's *Ink and Blood* contained a full-scale working version of Gutenberg's printing press—even manufactured by the same person, Rusty Maisel—along with an actor portraying Gutenberg himself.[32] Noah also displayed multiple editions of the King James, including the "He" and "She" Bibles and the so-called Wicked Bible (a 1631 edition of the KJV that included a misprint in the Ten Commandments that seemingly encouraged readers to commit adultery), along with pages from a 1663 translation into Algonquin and the Bay Psalm Book, all of which are also part of *Passages*. Like *Passages*, Biondi's exhibit displayed the Aitken Bible, the edition approved by the United States Congress in 1872, as well as the Lunar Bible, a microfilm copy that was brought to the moon with the astronaut Edgar Mitchell in 1971. Most striking, perhaps, is the similarity in language used to describe the purpose of the exhibits, especially from Biondi: "This exhibition has been put together to tell the dramatic and inspirational story—the story of how we got the Bible—especially how we got the Bible in English and the influence of the Bible on the foundation of the American nation."[33]

Most striking to us, as historians, were the interpretive gaps in the museum. The importance and significance of the Bible's role in the important controversies alluded to in the exhibit went unexplained. Rather than discussing how anti-Jewish sentiment in the Gospels of Matthew and John fostered a negative and dangerous caricature of Jews throughout history, the artifacts bearing on this theme were presented without comment. The result was both that the controversy seems dislocated from the Bible and that apologetic narratives slip into the gaps in the museum's story. There is no link posited between the New Testament and anti-Semitic pogroms and the Holocaust. The biblical verses that would supply the link are nowhere mentioned, allowing the presumably Christian viewer to remain confident in the moral righteousness of their text. This exhibit is displaying evidence of the twentieth century's greatest atrocity; and yet here, of all places, the museum placates, but it nowhere unsettles.

Moreover, the Holocaust exhibit focuses not on the deaths of people (in contrast to the animatronic martyrdom of Tyndale), but on the destruction of Torah scrolls. This elicited an interesting parallel between Protestants and Jews: the Holocaust is, in *Passages*, refocused as a question of biblical fidelity and an example of the importance of defending one's scripture, rather than as an atrocity nurtured by a particular kind of biblically grounded religious and racial prejudice.

When *Passages* comes to treat the issue of the Bible and slavery, a similar sort of disconnect can be felt. The exhibit begins by admitting that the Bible condones slavery, and that it was a common, indeed almost universal, practice in the ancient world. The visitor is also told that "the Bible has been used both to justify and to condemn slavery," and can see a book from 1843 using the Bible to defend slavery. But this is about as even-handed as it gets. Case after case contains letters, books, and tracts written in opposition to the slave trade (many of which have no obvious biblical connection whatsoever). The series culminates with a first edition of *Uncle Tom's Cabin* and a first-series printing of the Emancipation Proclamation. Victory for the abolitionist movement is construed as victory for the Bible: "Ultimately," reads the signage, "it can be argued that the Bible and its followers were among the most important and instrumental influences in the abolishment of slavery in both Europe and the Americas."

Of course, the reverse would be equally true had the proslavery side prevailed—but this potential trajectory, and the Bible's role in it, is never considered. It seems to be the perspective of *Passages* that history and morality are inseparable, and that the Bible is responsible for both. "We don't make America the hero," Steve Green told us; "it's the Bible that's the hero." The Bible, it is suggested, leads only to good. The privileging of the Bible as an inherent force for good is, as we have seen, the perspective of Steve Green: "Yes, there have been men who have used this book for their own selfish ill intent. My argument is that we don't blame the book for man's misuse of it." And this is fair enough: the Bible doesn't enslave people, people enslave people. But it seems difficult to then claim that we should credit the Bible for man's positive use of it—especially when, in this case, the abolition of slavery goes directly against the biblical laws.

Throughout *Passages*, the only narrative and interpretation provided by holograms and animatronics are those that are focused on the importance of translation into the vernacular. This process was at the heart of the Reformation—Luther's translation was as influential for German as King James's was for English. The rendering of the Bible into common language was understood then, as it is still today, as a strike against the authority of the Catholic church, authority which derived from the church's unique position as the interpreter for the masses of the otherwise incomprehensible Latin of scripture and liturgy. It is ironic, then, but telling, that one of the animatronic characters encountered in the *Passages* exhibit is Jerome, the great fourth-century translator of the Bible into Latin. The monk who provided the world with the very Latin text so abhorred by Protestants is made to proclaim—in a clunky and slightly creepy way—how wonderful it is for everyone to be able to encounter the Bible in their native tongues.

After the translation and defense of the vaunted King James Version, we hear no more about any controversies or translational difficulties surrounding scripture. A brief exhibit of the translation of the Bible into the languages of the colonized—with special attention given to the 1836 translation into Mohawk—passes over the violence of the evangelizing efforts that stands behind these texts. Nor is there any mention of the thousands of other English versions of the Bible that followed the beautiful but flawed efforts of King James's servants. It is an exercise in Protestant triumphalism. It is the story of the Protestant Bible.

As with the Museum of the Bible, for *Passages* what is interesting is not what is included—which is presented with insights from both Protestants and Catholics—but what is excluded. Islam and the Book of Mormon are nowhere to be found, even though they are important parts of the history of biblical interpretation. The only gesture in the direction of Orthodox Christianity is found in the liturgy section. Perhaps even more remarkable for an exhibition about the history of the Bible, there is no reference to how, when, or by whom the books of the Bible were written. The exhibit jumps from cuneiform texts that predate the Bible to the Dead Sea Scrolls, which are used, as Green suggested, to illustrate just how similar our modern text is to the earliest versions we possess. In that two-millennium gap is the composition of the entirety of the Hebrew Bible. Perhaps even more striking is the leap from the Dead Sea Scrolls to early Christian scribes—again jumping over the actual writing of the New Testament. As far as the exhibit seems to be concerned, the Bible, both Old and New Testaments, simply appeared on the scene fully-formed, to be copied by scribes and worshipped by adherents. Given the vast reams of scholarship devoted to the questions of the Bible's origins, this omission is surprising; it is less so, however, given the traditional evangelical belief that the entire Bible is the word of God. The only mention of authorship is an oblique reference to God that appears on the lips of the creaky animatronic St. Jerome.

For all the textual material contained in the exhibit, there are no translations provided of the papyri, no references to variations in any of the texts. In the chronology of the museum, we follow the passage of a presumably singular text through history to its supposed *telos*, the King James Version. But in the Bible's history—or at least the history of our knowledge about it—the discoveries of these ancient papyri were important not for their proof of the text's consistency, but because they destabilized the idea that the received text accurately preserved the earliest version of the Bible.

The Protestant focus of *Passages* can be understood in light of its history: it began life as an exhibit about the King James Version of the Bible, and that commitment continues to shine through. But this is not how *Passages* is advertised to visitors: it is described on the MOTB website as an exhibit "chronicling the history of the Bible."

There is an interesting and revealing tension in the way that those involved in the Museum of the Bible talk about its potential influence in the world. When we traveled to Los Angeles to speak with him, Steve Green told us that he hoped to educate the nation's politicians about the Bible. When asked about the immediate context of the museum in Washington, D.C., he said, "I think our legislators ought to know the foundation of our government, they ought to know that that's what their role is and they need to know that this book speaks to life and it has advice; it advises how a good government should be: a government's role is to reward good and to punish evil at a high level. . . . Our founding fathers unabashedly looked to the Bible in founding this nation, so why wouldn't it be right for our legislators to know our history of our government?" It seems fair to assume that the advice that the Bible recommends for good government and the administration of justice is advice that Green would like to see implemented by legislators and government workers.

In slight contrast to this, Cary Summers denied that the museum was intended to influence people. "The idea that I can influence you is nuts . . . it's up to you." The idea of educating without influencing is conceptually similar to the idea of telling the story of the Bible without interpreting it. In each case, the former is understood as neutral, the latter as partisan. But beyond the *prima facie* absurd notion that it is possible to educate without also influencing, there is another reason that those involved in the museum are reframing their mission in the seemingly neutral language of merely inviting people to learn about the Bible: their commitment to the idea that the physical tangibility of the Bible itself has the power to spiritually inspire and even convert.

In an entry on his blog from July 2016, Cary Summers tells the story of an encounter he had with an Orthodox Jewish woman in

Israel.[34] She was visiting the collection and asked to be able to smell the 700–800-year-old scrolls that were on display. He offered to open one of the decommissioned scrolls for her and allowed her to touch it. The experience was a powerful moment for the woman: in her denomination of Judaism, women are never permitted to touch the Torah. Both the woman and Summers were profoundly moved by her experience touching "the Word of God." Summers concluded his entry saying, "Bringing people into closer contact with the Bible is one of the goals of the Museum of the Bible."

The aforementioned Torah scrolls, understood by Steve Green to be evidence of the Bible's perfect transmission, play a part also in this aspect of the museum's mission. We were told that the museum is considering housing their decommissioned scrolls in a single room where visitors will be able to touch the parchment of the scrolls themselves. The purpose of actual physical contact with the scrolls, both Green and Summers told us, was the impact it would have on people, like the impact Summers witnessed in Israel.

Using the scrolls in this way is controversial for both antiquarian and religious reasons. In the first place, the oils in human fingertips will over time inevitably degrade the scrolls themselves, leading to their eventual disintegration. The organization has spent time and money restoring these scrolls. As noted above, Summers described the Museum of the Bible as a hospital for the world's Torah scrolls—but it seems that it is a field hospital that plans to dispatch its artifacts back into the fray. With regard to the religious issues, generally a Torah scroll that can no longer be used in the synagogue, that is no longer kosher, is supposed to be buried in a special chamber known as a *genizah*—either a storage area in a synagogue (as in the case of the most famous of these, the Cairo Genizah) or, often, a reserved plot in a Jewish cemetery. Some exceptions to this may apply: scrolls that survived the Holocaust, for example, are often permitted to be displayed to the public, though this is to be done only for the express purpose of serving as a witness to the Holocaust. Some Jewish traditions also allow for displaying decommissioned Torah scrolls in museums. In such circumstances, however, it is understood that the scrolls will be treated with the utmost respect: "displayed in a museum case that would be appropriate to the sacred nature of the scroll."[35]

The Museum of the Bible's directors are not unaware of the controversy surrounding the use of the Torah scrolls. When we asked Steve Green if visitors would be able to able to touch the scrolls themselves, he said, "We have to think through that and make sure that we don't do something that would be offensive to the Jewish tradition. . . . If we feel that we can do that, where people can get a sense of touching [and] feeling, there's something to that. So there's ways of being able to use the Torah scrolls to have an impact on people's lives." Against the potential for accusations of religious insensitivity Green weighed the benefits of bringing people physically closer to the immutable biblical text.

For David Trobisch, the issue was more straightforward. "We've checked with different rabbis and [the scroll is not] a kosher item. . . . It's the prejudice of Christians that say you couldn't do that, you can't touch." The items available in the educational collection, he told us, would be things of which they have multiple copies. They would place these items in the collection where they don't have to "do all the security and theater stuff"; and "if [the Torah scroll] wears out, it wears out." Trobisch's nonchalance about the potential destruction of Torah scrolls is especially striking given his background. He was educated in Germany; he would know, therefore, of the scandal that plagues the memory of German theologian Otto Michel, founder of the *Institutum Judaicum* in Tübingen. Michel had styled himself as "a friend of the Jews" and a "Hebrew." After his death, it emerged that Michel had been a Nazi in his youth and had kept a wooden Torah disk, looted from a synagogue in Zgierz, in his office for over fifty years. No one knew how Michel (who had never mentioned being a Nazi in his autobiography) had come into possession of the religious relic. The revelations caused a scandal and made national headlines.[36] The optics of a Christian museum allowing the potential destruction of Torah scrolls for the purposes of educating a predominantly Christian audience are problematic for most people. But Trobisch should be particularly sensitive to this issue.

For Steve Green and Cary Summers, though, there is something bigger at stake. The tangible presence of scriptural texts contains its own kind of religious power—what Carroll described as "inspiring by touching and tasting and handling things." This may seem like magical thinking or a pseudo-Catholic fixation on relics, but the power of the word of God to transform the hearer has a particular history in American Protestantism.

John Fea includes in his book a number of stories in which, even when caught in glimpses, the Bible converted sinners and atheists. Fea tells the story of a Christian father preparing to send his son off to college. Worried that his son would lose his faith, he purchased a copy of the Bible and secretly placed it at the bottom of his son's trunk. As feared, when his son arrived at college "the restraints of a pious education were soon broken off," and the young man "proceeded from speculation to doubts and from doubts to denial of the reality of religion." One day the young man discovered the Bible in the trunk and petulantly decided to use it to clean his razor blade. Each day he would tear pages from the book and use them to wipe the blade clean, but one morning as he was completing the task several verses caught his eye and struck him "like a barbed arrow to his heart." The young man was converted. As Fea puts it, "There was no need to provide rational answers to the young man's skepticism—the 'Sacred Volume' had 'done its work.'" The power of the Bible was so great that in another instance the mere presence of scripture had a kind of miraculous power. In one narrative, an ABS (American Bible Society) agent left a copy of the Bible in a barn belonging to an antagonistic and irate farmer. After several days the farmer's spiritual distress overcame him and he went in search of the rejected book, found it in the manger, read, repented, and consecrated himself to God.[37] It is unlikely that most people hearing these stories thought that the Bible served a talismanic purpose. "Most ABS agents," Fea writes, "believed that the Bible's apparent magical powers could easily be explained by an appeal to the third person of the Trinity—the Holy Spirit."[38] The central message of these stories, and the conviction of the ABS, was that if the Bible was permitted to do its work, without interference from notes or commentary, and was placed "in the hands of every person in America, a slow and steady spiritual and moral transformation would capture the nation."[39]

The intrinsic power of the unencumbered biblical story and the unmediated biblical manuscript helps explain why the Greens are willing in principle to construct a nonsectarian museum. An interesting twist on the museum's mission statement can be heard on their one-minute blog series, "The Book." In an episode straightforwardly entitled "The Museum of the Bible," the narrator states, "It's not the goal [of the museum] to teach a specific interpretation of the Bible; rather, it's a mission very much like that of the parable of the sower: to sow a seed, to invite all people to engage with the Bible."[40] The museum's mission—its invitation to the Bible—is here construed in Christian terms. Even in their own self-professedly nonsectarian public face, the ultimate goal of the museum seems to be to proselytize.

The shift in the language describing the Museum's purpose is unproblematic for Green, because the physical presence of the Bible itself will do that work. Moreover, when Green told us that his vision for the museum hadn't changed, he was not being insincere. His description of using the Dead Sea Scrolls to prove that God protected the Bible is synonymous with the idea that part of the mission of the museum is tell the story of the remarkable preservation of the Bible. When Summers and Green say that they only want to tell the story, they do so in full confidence that the Bible itself will do the work of evangelization for them.

When we left the Museum of the Bible site in 2015 we were thoroughly impressed. Cary Summers, like so many involved in this project, is a sincere and charismatic man, intelligent and articulate. But there was much about the museum that was obscured from the public. What was not immediately apparent as we left 409 3rd Street that day was that the entire building, not just the basement offices that we visited, is owned by the Hobby Lobby corporation. Owning the adjacent building makes a great deal of practical sense for the Museum of the Bible: it enabled them to proceed with construction without having to worry too much about interference from the tenants next door, and it provided them with staging and planning space while construction was underway.

But it's also surprising: among other federal tenants, 409 3rd Street houses the offices of the Department of Health and Human Services—the very organization that Hobby Lobby, Inc. was suing in 2012, when their shell company, Washington Office Center, purchased the building. The Museum of the Bible site, 300 D Street, was purchased by the charitable organization on the same day, mere moments before: the numbers of the public documents recording the purchases are consecutive. Water and Sewer covenants between the city and Washington Office Center made in 2015 use plans that include the logo of the Museum of the Bible. They are the same plans utilized by the Museum of the Bible in their own covenant with the city.

The details of the purchase of the two buildings that sit on the corner of Avenue D and 3rd Street are architectural reminders of the relationship between the Green family and the Museum of the Bible organization. It is a relationship that goes beyond paperwork sharing. The museum is buttressed, quite literally, by Hobby Lobby, Inc. It is a foundational relationship that brings with it the constant reminder of Hobby Lobby's political ambitions. It is also a relationship that is not always apparent and that is often deliberately concealed.

The same concern with obfuscation surrounds the museum and the claims that it makes about itself. That the Museum of the Bible has an implicit faith bias is not the problem. Bias is inescapable; even in cases where we self-consciously try to educate ourselves about our own prejudices, we fail to see them in all their subtlety and complexity. Where the biases of the Greens' project start to become problematic is in the repeated self-description as nonsectarian; the selective use of scholarship and material evidence to support a particular interpretation of the text coupled with the refrain that they are not, in fact, interpreting the Bible at all.

The presentation of the history of the Bible from ancient writing systems to the Dead Sea Scrolls to Wycliffe, the King James Version, and Protestant missionaries has been told before. It is a narrative synonymous with that of smaller, less successful exhibits like Bill Noah's *Ink and Blood*. The story of the Bible's impact shadows the language of Lee Biondi's *Dead Sea Scrolls to the Bible in America*. The Museum of the Bible will be larger and flashier, but for all the academically accomplished consultants and employees, the conceptual map of the Museum of the Bible follows a course chartered by other self-educated Protestant businessmen. It is the Protestant story of the Bible—or the story of the Bible that appeals to and is held dear by Protestants. It is the only story of the Bible that Steve Green has ever known.

There seems to us to be no doubt that when Steve Green and Cary Summers say that the Museum of the Bible will be nonsectarian they mean it sincerely. Steve Green spoke to us at length about the difficulties of seeing one's own bias and was candid about the educational process he has undergone. Moreover, the Museum of the Bible has taken some steps to try and ensure that the museum truly is nonsectarian. Hiring and consulting with representatives of various religious denominations, as they have done, is an excellent start. We were told repeatedly that Jewish and Catholic scholars had been brought in to ensure that nothing in the museum was obviously wrong or offensive. It is hard to avoid the sense, however, that these other religious perspectives are not being given their own voice, nor are they being used to help temper the inherent Protestantism of the museum; rather, they are being folded into a presentation of the Bible that is still deeply Protestant in concept, but is now buttressed by being able to claim support from other communities as well.

Part of the problem with the Museum of the Bible's aspirations of impartiality is that they are grounded in a religiously derived understanding of the Bible's ability to speak apart from tradition. They have set themselves an impossible task, and they have done so for religious reasons. Religious commitments determine what is and is not included in the museum. We have to wonder about the religious traditions that have been excluded from this process. The lack of references to the expanded biblical canon of the Ethiopic Christian Churches; the glaring omission of the relationship between the Bible and the Qur'an, even in the impact section; the near silence about the various branches of Orthodox Christianity; and the refusal to engage with the use and expansion of the Bible in Latter-Day Saints tradition all demonstrate the limits of the claims that the museum makes about itself.

"Nonsectarian," for the Greens and the museum, means Jewish, Roman Catholic, and Protestant. It is these traditions that are represented and respected. The afterlife of the Bible among other groups and denominations is not something in which the museum is especially interested. Perhaps this is because adding other branches of Christianity and other lines of tradition would disrupt the subtly supersessionist chronological narrative that takes the visitor from Judaism through Catholicism to Protestantism. Perhaps it is because in the past thirty years conservative Catholics, Protestants, and Jews have become politically united in opposing liberal social reforms on hot-button issues like abortion, contraception, and same-sex marriage—issues, of course, about which the Green family has fought or indirectly funded lawsuits.[41]

More likely, the focus on these three groups reflects an idea, originating in the 1950s, that the United States is a "triple melting pot" in which Jews, Catholics, and Protestants preserved their identities and achieved equal status and acceptance in post-war America. This theory is most closely associated with Will Herberg's *Protestant-Catholic-Jew*, a book that, to this day, remains a classic in the field of American religious history, but the phrase "triple melting pot" was borrowed from an article by sociologist Ruby Jo Kennedy, which examined intermarriage in New Haven and concluded that "religious barriers are holding fast."[42] Herberg was not alone in dividing Americans into this tripartite schema; the sociologists August Hollingshead and George Stewart had done the same, the latter arguing that even if American culture expected people to adopt a new language, it did not expect people to give up their individual faiths.[43] Herberg's book was written the same year that "under God" was added to the Pledge of Allegiance, and he harnesses the pluralistic Zeitgeist when he concludes, "To be an American today means to be either a Protestant, a Catholic, or a Jew."[44] His theories have been criticized by subsequent generations of sociologists, but the basic distinction has had a lengthy and influential afterlife, including, one might argue, at the Museum of the Bible.

If the museum's nonsectarian claims are difficult to parse, its legal and practical distinction from the Green family is even more difficult to ascertain. When the Museum of the Bible nonprofit was established, it became legally distinct from the Green family. It was this legal distinction that allowed both the museum to apply for tax-exempt status and the Green family to claim millions of dollars in charitable tax deductions for its donations to the museum. But the legal distinction does not bear out in the administration of the museum or the way its representatives talk about it. One difficulty we encountered in talking to representatives from the Green family is that they often refer to the collection and museum as theirs. Even though the museum was not established until 2010, the landing page of the Museum of the Bible lists the acquisition of the first artifact in 2009 as the first "major milestone" in its history, with no reference to the Greens. The collection itself, which is usually numbered at around 40,000 artifacts, has always been the property of the Green family. But from its inception the Museum of the Bible has claimed that it owns the same 40,000 artifacts. The confusion may arise from complicated loan agreements between the two, but it raises the question: where does the Museum of the Bible begin and the Green Collection end? Or, more precisely, how much influence does Hobby Lobby have over the Museum of the Bible?

In an interview with the *Washington Post* in September 2015, David Trobisch said that he only has occasional contact with the Greens and that the family has no direct influence over the curation of the museum. "The decisions about the collection are made by me and my team."[45] These statements are in tension with others made by Trobisch, who acknowledges that the Green family decided upon expensive purchases that would later be donated, and vetted those scholars who serve as academic advisers to the museum. It was not unusual, we learned, for scholarly advisers to have lengthy conversations with Steve Green in which they found themselves trying to persuade him of the accuracy of their historical arguments. At least one such scholar, who cannot be named because of the terms of the nondisclosure agreement they signed, came to the realization that they were fighting a losing battle, and that the museum's exhibits would represent a Christian view of history.

Practically speaking, electronic footprints inextricably link the two companies and trace out the tendrils of their more conservative connections. The Museum of the Bible domain name, in effect their website, continues to be owned and administered by Hobby Lobby, Inc. And both the Museum of the Bible and Hobby Lobby list the same correspondence address—7707 S.W. 44th Street, Oklahoma City, OK 73179, the general address of Hobby Lobby, Inc.—for concerns about their respective websites.

In 2015, once the news of the federal investigation into the imported cuneiform tablets hit the media, both the Greens and MOTB tried to sever any connection that might be assumed to exist with regard to these cuneiform tablets: Hobby Lobby's official statement to the press emphasized that MOTB was "a separate not-for-profit entity made possible, in part, by the generous contributions of the Green family." Virtually identical statements were given from the MOTB side, with further attempts to keep the two entities as separate as possible: "We understand that Hobby Lobby is cooperating with the investigation related to certain biblical artifacts." Yet when we were first alerted to the federal investigation, we called Cary Summers to ask him if he knew about the investigation. He quickly clarified, "These were before I was involved with Museum of the Bible." But he went on: "Hopefully we'll get this resolved one way or the other." And further: "There's been nothing else since then at all. We've never had anything even close to a blip like that, ever." And: "We'll have to see if we can get it worked out." The federal investigation, as everyone was keen to emphasize after the news came out, is into Hobby Lobby, not the Museum of the Bible. But Summers, as the head of MOTB, was both knowledgeable about the situation and able to speak about the investigation—repeatedly using the first-person plural.

Some of these connections are explicable when set against the history of the organization. The Museum of the Bible is the brainchild of the Green family, and the enduring electronic and bureaucratic connections are evidence that the organization has yet to strike out on its own from its parent organization. At the same time, it is worth asking why Hobby Lobby continues to own the intellectual property rights to MOTB's website, or why both the Green family and representatives for MOTB refer to the same set of artifacts as their own 40,000-item collection. Throughout this book we have cited both Steve Green and Cary Summers as resources for information about both the Green Collection and the Museum of the Bible, despite that fact that the two are legally distinct. This was a conscious choice on our part, because both individuals speak as if the two entities are identical: the legal distinction is continually blurred by casual references to the collection and museum.

After our exposé of the investigation hit the news, the Museum of the Bible attempted to distance itself from the Greens. The Museum of the Bible website was scrubbed clean of explicit references to the Greens. The GSI and Green Collection, as noted in previous chapters, are now referred to as the"Scholars Initiative" and the "Museum Collection," respectively. This is despite the fact that the Green Family continues to own, as far as we can tell, almost all of the artifacts that make up the collection. The cyber-purge is not exhaustive: in a humorous copyediting slip in an article on the museum's website, the *Passages* exhibition is now described as drawn from "the Museum Collection. Named after the Green family . . . ," despite the fact that the collection no longer has the name "Green" in its title.[46] The Museum of the Bible's partners have also not changed the language used on their websites. The Creation Museum, for example, still refers to the Green Collection. What the new Green-free public image conceals is that Green and his immediate family continue to direct the museum. Steve Green is still chairman of the board of MOTB; museum offices are still based at the Hobby Lobby compound in Oklahoma City and in Hobby Lobby–owned property in D.C.; Green's daughter serves both as a brand ambassador for Hobby Lobby and as community outreach spokesperson for MOTB; and in fund-raising efforts in evangelical circles the Greens continue to be the face of the museum. On its Twitter and Facebook feeds, MOTB regularly pushes Steve Green's book, *The Bible in America*.

That the museum and the Green family continue to be close—one might say, inextricably intertwined—is understandable. It's even defensible: why wouldn't the Green family want to have a say in directing the mission of an organization that they funded and founded? The difficulty is that the museum portrays itself to the public as something else: it presents itself as a nonsectarian independent organization, intimates that it contains the best academic research available, and claims to issue an open invitation to everyone. These may be sincere and well-intentioned claims, but they are impossible to support.

CONCLUSION

IN THE BEGINNING WAS THE WORD, AS THE GOSPEL OF JOHN SAYS. The Green family of Oklahoma, as much as anyone, has lived in accordance with their understanding of the Word. But for the Greens, as for billions of other Christians worldwide, the biblical structures within which they live are not really founded on the turns of phrase or narrative plot twists that pepper the Christian canon. The interpretive moves and historical circumstances that molded and compressed the variegated biblical perspectives into a monolithic biblical worldview have receded into the past. For them the Bible is not, as it is to many scholars, a cacophony of voices that require adjudication or explanation; it is not a cultural artifact or historical curio; it is not even text: it is a symbol that signifies an already fixed message and story.

For the Greens to be who they are, it had to be this way: they built a crafting empire on biblical foundations, they dedicated their profits to evangelical outreach, and they took their religious principles to the Supreme Court. They did not become evangelical champions because of an ambivalent relationship with the New Testament. In the beginning—and, for the Greens, from the beginning—there was the message.

At no point have they concealed their belief that the Bible has a story to tell and a message to deliver, nor have they hidden their ambition to serve as conduits for that story. The oft-repeated statement by the Greens and their MOTB representatives, "We aren't collectors, we are storytellers," is central to their own self-understanding. It is also the key window through which all of their Bible-related ventures should be viewed. "We're just going to tell the story." "Just the facts." We all tell stories—narrative is the form by which we as human beings communicate. But the stories we choose to tell, where we choose to begin and end, what we emphasize, what we downplay, and our very modes of communication are reflections of our own social positioning. David Green's early instruction that his collection not be used to undermine the King James Version of the Bible is illuminating here. The story that the Greens purport to tell is merely the story of the Bible; the story they will actually tell is the complex product of their religious heritage. What they know and think about the Bible has been determined by their specific socio-religious context and particular historical moment. Their beliefs about the Bible, its message, and its impact are not unique to them as a family; many of them are standard assertions among a number of Protestant denominations. This is not necessarily a bad thing; this context is, however, an essential part of their story, and therefore of the story that they wish to tell.

Upon opening in 2017, Museum of the Bible will become the Christian Smithsonian. It will be the educational resource for the Bible for the museum-going American public. In 2014, former president George W. Bush spoke at an MOTB event in Dallas, where he said, "The museum is a great idea. It's very important that the Museum of the Bible invites and makes people of all faiths feel comfortable. It will be an important part of our capital."[1] But it is only in the past five years that MOTB the organization and Museum of the Bible the facility have begun to articulate their mission in terms of academic interest and general education. As recently as 2012 it was an explicitly religious evangelical organization. The shift in orientation is not an indication of a shift in aspiration. For the Greens, who remain at the helm of this project, the intent is still to return America to its Christian roots through evangelization and education. That the curriculum and museum are nonsectarian doesn't matter. They don't need to convert when they believe that the Bible will speak to people directly. It is precisely for this reason that they hope to open Torah scrolls for people to handle, because, MOTB executives told us, it makes a "difference" to people—a religious difference, that is.

That the Greens hope to elicit conversion through a nonsectarian museum is not in and of itself problematic. Though some might balk at their "hidden agenda," their ambition functions only within their own selective religious framework. To complain about the MOTB organizers' hope that supernatural powers will act to proselytize museum attendees is rather churlish, especially if one does not believe in those powers. What rankles is not their "agenda," be it overt or hidden; the issue is their self-description and self-presentation.

Many facets of their programs claim to be nonsectarian, but they are not the big tent they imagined or promised. Where they have faltered is in their belief that they could present the Bible without emendation or interpretation. In the eighteenth and nineteenth centuries, when officers of the American Bible Society distributed the King James Version of the Bible to the public, they believed they were presenting the Bible without annotation. It was a self-conception made possible by their faith-based belief that this particular English translation of the Protestant Bible had divine origins. MOTB is working within the explicitly interpretive settings of childhood education and museum curation to tell "just the story" of the Bible. Even in comparison to the American Bible Society, it is on a fool's errand.

Like all of the Green family's forays into public discourse about religion, the museum has ambitions that go beyond merely supplying information. Summers hopes that MOTB will become the premiere religious pilgrimage site for Roman Catholics in the United States. In structure and emphasis, however, this is a fully Protestant museum, and that should be a cause of concern to the Roman Catholic pilgrims Cary Summers hopes to attract. The cherry-picking of scholarship; the use of manuscripts to demonstrate the divine preservation of the Bible's message, rather than its diversity; and the rhetoric that surrounds the museum's emphasis on the centrality of the Bible to three major religious groups, and thus the primacy of an exclusively biblical religion, all speak to MOTB's denominational partisanship. The Vatican may well curate its own exhibit, just as Green Scholars will work on their individual manuscripts, but the presentation of those artifacts and the positioning of the exhibits will be circumscribed by a museum the arc of which curves towards Protestant triumphalism.

To this MOTB and Green family representatives would certainly protest; both Steve Green and Cary Summers claim that they are not there to convert or "persuade." One would have to be very naive indeed to think that museums, and curricula, do not influence and educate in ways that are formative. But this is the central problem: they are naive, and in many ways their naiveté has specific religious roots. Even with their shift to a nonsectarian model, the Green family and MOTB do not appear to appreciate that the Bible does not tell a single story and that religious instruction (and indeed instruction of all kinds) is always ideologically loaded. The notion of merely telling the story and allowing the Bible to speak has a storied history in the United States: one that is both implicitly anti-Catholic and is—from any reasonable academic perspective—completely impossible. That they believe it is possible to tell the story of the Bible without interpretation betrays not only their Protestant roots and bias but also their fundamentally anti-intellectual orientation.

The shape of both the MOTB's exhibits and its curriculum have been a source of concern to both academics and public advocacy groups. In their defense, MOTB has always protested that these projects are works in progress and that the more problematic aspects of their curriculum are mere drafts. But one wonders if the same mistakes would have been made if these ventures had, from the beginning, been truly interdenominational rather than ostensibly nonsectarian. The makeup of the MOTB board is telling: for an organization that prides itself on its interdenominational involvement, every member of the board is Protestant—and within that broader category, the majority are evangelical, with openly conservative social and political views. The principal members of their staff are also uniformly Protestant. One has to wonder why a nonsectarian museum has no Jews or Catholics in any of its leadership positions.

What became clear over the course of our conversations with Steve Green and others in the organization is that on a foundational level they identify the Bible with their own Protestant Christianity. This is nowhere more clear than in the regular references

Steve Green makes to a "biblical worldview"—an understanding of the millennia-old Bible as being the source of a very present-day way of life, and, from the other side, the belief that the way they choose to live is an expression of the Bible's message. But this equation, common though it may be, loses sight of its own history: of the myriad cultural forces, from the offenses of medieval Catholicism to the secularism of the present day, that have shaped the many forms of Protestantism and Protestant interpretive strategies, and that allow the Greens to conceive of their lifestyle and ideological positions as "biblical."

The clarity with which the Greens understand their biblical worldview produces an overly determined picture of both the Bible's story and its contents. Green in particular, but others in MOTB as well, exhibit this tendency not only when they talk about "just telling the story." It is apparent in their easy description of the story and morality of the Bible as singular, as if the Bible does not offer up complicated and difficult-to-digest stories about rape, incest, and child sacrifice. Such narratives can be rendered palatable by the larger interpretive tradition in which the Greens participate. But these stories, and the reading strategies that processed them, should not be obscured, as they undoubtedly are, by the conceptual homogenizing juggernaut that is "the singular story." It also emerges in their curriculum, when they import Christian understandings of the Ten Commandments into the Hebrew Bible without gesturing to the rich biblical and Jewish legal tradition of which the commandments are just one part, and without recognizing the historical conditions that led to this Christian hyper-interest in the tablets received on Mount Sinai.

It is evident in their appeal to the biblical origins of American society—as if it were the Bible alone that inspired the founders, rather than a notion of Bible refracted through the uniformly Protestant but otherwise diverse culture of America's early history. It can be seen in the way that all of their educational ventures avoid any discussion of Islam or Mormonism; a strategy that coaxes the history of the Bible's reception into an easy journey from ancient Judaism to Colonial-era Protestantism, from Old Jerusalem to New England, from one promised land to another.

And it is abundantly clear that when they appeal to the Bible as something held in common by Jews, Catholics, and Protestants, they effectively eliminate the importance of the concepts of tradition and interpretive authority central to both Judaism and Catholicism. With the elevation of biblical authority and the promotion of the idea that the Bible "speaks" without interpretation comes the implicit understanding that additional sources of authority are extraneous to the core revelation. This is a standard idea for Protestants but is a subtle denigration of Catholicism, in particular. Removing the millennia of tradition that have formed Catholicism, and Judaism as well, in order to get back to a shared biblical foundation is not ideologically neutral.

There are ostensibly ecumenical religious ventures that have at their core a desire to see the other destroyed. Much evangelical investment in Israel, for example, has as its goal the inevitable destruction of the Jewish people at the Apocalypse. MOTB is not one of those ventures. But the spiritual self-confidence and generosity of heart that led them to a "big tent" philosophy is in tension with a calcified understanding of the biblical message. When Catholics and Jews are brought in, when the irenic language of "what we all agree on" is used, it is not to undermine the Protestant viewpoint, but to reinforce it. Ultimately, if there are tensions between the Greens' reading of the Bible and those of their non-Protestant partners, it is safe to say that the Greens' position will not be the one that is jettisoned—in part precisely because they believe their position to be unqualifiedly "biblical."

When the "biblical worldview" coalesces around modern beliefs, it is no surprise that the historically and culturally conditioned distinctiveness of the Bible should fade away. Because the Greens, like so many others, believe that the Bible still speaks directly to us today, they often fail to see the many places where it is, in fact, very distant indeed—and the innumerable ways that modern readings of it, Protestant or otherwise, have been influenced by the very cultural factors that they are seeking to eliminate.

The Greens and MOTB credit the Bible with the more laudable ideals of modern society, but when the Bible is used to oppress others they claim that it is human beings who "misuse" it.

When the Bible was used to oppose slavery, the Bible was speaking; when it was used to support slavery, the Bible was being misused. A parallel double standard emerges when one tracks the discourse that surrounds Hobby Lobby's charitable projects. They claim that they intend merely to educate, but they also aspire to influence politicians and return the United States to its Christian roots. They present themselves as a small family defending their religious rights and with no interest in tampering with the rights of others, but they also fund lawsuits to protect traditional marriage. They seem to view themselves, as they do the Bible, as curiously innocent of efforts to influence or control other people.

The origins of this self-perception seem to lie in the essential difference between the church/state divide and the rights of private religious individuals to try and influence politics in general. Historically, the separation of church and state in the early years of the U.S. allowed for the initial flourishing of evangelicalism in America. Moreover, as Mark Noll has pointed out, the need for churches, disentangled from the apparatus of the state, to compete for members also meant that religious leaders could turn their attention to more widely promoting their own perspectives: "Now they tended to ask, What would most readily promote expansion of the church? What would most forcefully advance the cause of the church in society?"[2] In this light we can understand how, for the Greens, there is no contradiction between exercising their constitutional rights to religious freedom and attempting to evangelize a country through various educational programs. They might protest, quite correctly, that their projects are purely optional. Even though their Bible curriculum was designed to monopolize the space of biblical instruction in public schools, it was still intended to be an elective course. The curriculum and museum are alarming because they are misadvertised: what is billed as education is, in fact, subtle religious indoctrination. Whether the Greens would acknowledge their own bias, or even object to this kind of thing on the basis that they believe that America was founded as a Christian country, this is what should trouble interested observers.

The double standard becomes double-speak when they describe the purpose of their educational projects. They are not here to influence or persuade, they protest, and yet their projects are about education. The slippery rhetorical distinction between education and persuasion, information and indoctrination, does real work for them here. Most people would agree that whatever one's pedagogical philosophy, the purpose of education is intellectual formation, but it inevitably involves moral formation and the creation of communal identity. Steve Green himself acknowledges this when he wrote, "The American educational system has become instrumental in defining who we are."[3]

In his book *The Bible in America*, Green lays out the history of biblical education in the United States. Most of his chapter on education involves block quotations from prominent eighteenth- and nineteenth-century thinkers, educators and politicians about the centrality of the Bible to American education. Toward the end, after describing the legality of a secular Bible curriculum, he objects to the growing trend to prevent the Bible "from having any direct influence on student's moral choices."[4] The chapter closes with the hope that "the Bible be restored to the place it once had in American public education, when it was not only respected for its academic value but also revered and cherished for its message."[5] That Green wants to see the Bible be (re)instated as the moral touchstone in public education is hardly surprising. What is revealing is his awareness that education in general serves this purpose. It does more than instruct; it defines who we are. It is precisely this awareness that bankrupts the claims of MOTB executives that their nonsectarian projects do not exist to persuade anyone. One cannot both claim that the Bible must be taught in schools, because education is instrumental in defining who we are, and simultaneously claim that one's educational initiatives are devoid of efforts to shape or define people. On this point they are not merely naive, they appear disingenuous.

Their own intersectionality—as patriots, as evangelicals, as Oklahomans, as Pentecostals, as business owners—makes the task of separating their patriotism from their Christianity impossible. For the Greens themselves, though, it offers a far greater challenge. The Greens hope to restore America to its biblical roots. But how can anyone hope to reverse-engineer a system when they do not acknowledge the ways in which they are both products and consumers of a fictionalized historical marriage of faith and founding fathers? To put this less abstractly: as people of faith the Greens are within their rights to try to influence politics and education in accordance with their beliefs, but when they do not see that their beliefs are already the product of a deeply politicized religious formation process, they inevitably run into difficulties.

It is because this is so difficult to see that they unwittingly make hypocrites of themselves. Green told us that he does not want his child "going to a public school and being proselytized by someone" and that he recognizes that he cannot do the same. But he does not see the ways that MOTB's museum and curriculum continue to rehearse Protestant tropes in ways that are, for example, mildly anti-Catholic. The Greens cannot be said to be unaware of the centrality of education to the formation of individual and civic identity; they are ignorant, rather, of the ways that their own identity as both Christians and Americans is the product of a contested narrative about the nation's founding. As a consequence, they are unaware that the claim that America is a Christian country is as much a faith statement as a historical claim, and that in using this as the premise for performing an intervention in our country's system of education they are engaged in a form of evangelization.

Steve Green has been open about his own educational journey during the process of putting the Museum of the Bible together. He speaks frankly about learning to understand what "nonsectarian" means, and how to apply those lessons to this venture. Though his journey is laudable, it appears to be incomplete. Neither Green nor Cary Summers seems to have made the intellectual leap that accompanies the essential task of critical thinking: the recognition of one's own cultural situatedness, and with that recognition the active attempt to overcome the biases and predispositions inherent in each person. Even when, as in the case of the curriculum, those biases are explicitly pointed out, they are not assimilated; Green has made the transition from openly evangelizing to merely "presenting the facts," but has not come to terms with the ingrained confessional stance of his message.

Indeed, we have been struck by the fact that, despite his language of learning as he goes, what Green has actually learned is fairly narrow. It is telling that he refers to learning what it means to be nonsectarian, but never refers to a shift in his understanding of the Bible's nature, story, or message. He has come to realize that he cannot try to directly convert anyone to his worldview, but the worldview itself has remained entirely unchanged. Given that Green is involved not only in collecting biblical artifacts but also in the academic study of them, and in the presentation of those artifacts to the wider public—and though he has been advised by dozens of scholars, formally and informally—it seems that Green's understanding of the Bible itself, the focus of all of his efforts, is exactly the same as it was when he started. This may not be all that surprising: from the very beginning, Green used the language of "storytellers, not collectors." They have always known what story they wanted to tell; that story was a faith commitment. And while the way they tell the story has become more polished, and while more details have been added to the narrative along the way, the underlying message has been utterly consistent.

It is possible to read the story of the Greens and MOTB as a case of well-intentioned self-deception and large-scale naiveté. It is likely that they are truly unaware of the way that their religious commitments undergird virtually every aspect of their activities: they believe that they are engaging in nonsectarian efforts.

Perhaps as a result of this central misapprehension, however, they have also ended up misleading their constituents and stakeholders at virtually every level. They have promoted a Protestant Bible curriculum in the guise of secular education. They have created a museum that speaks the language of religious pluralism but that in fact rehearses the standard Protestant story of the Bible. They have taken advantage of undergraduate and graduate students, offering the promise of important scholarly work; but often the only benefit for students has been a bolstering of their own faith commitments, without any professional advancement or formation. They have misled the evangelical community by suggesting the potential for amazing new discoveries, remarkably early biblical texts, only to retract those claims or burying those artifacts out of sight. They have misled the scholarly community by offering access but then denying intellectual control, and by promising full disclosure but then maintaining near-complete secrecy about their holdings. And they have misled the public at large by promoting a curriculum and a museum that tell only the story that the Greens want to tell, without acknowledging that scholars and experts have spent decades, indeed centuries, laboring to provide very different accounts of the Bible and its history. We can agree with the Greens, and those others who have championed widespread biblical literacy, that the Bible is central to Western culture, and we can agree that it should be more broadly understood by contemporary society—indeed, we do agree with them on these points. But it is not elitist to think that the most prominent source of information about the Bible in the United States should not be filtered through the perspective of one particular religious tradition.

In all of this—or at least most of it—there are few grounds for claiming that the Greens and MOTB are engaging in any truly nefarious behavior. They are not, as some have portrayed them, maliciously inclined. If the Greens are anything, they are true believers: their understanding of the world, of right and wrong, is self-consciously colored by their faith. And this speaks positively to the fact that they are sincere and coherent individuals. The scope of faith is expansive and extends into every recess of human life: the church/state divide cannot be replicated on the level of the human person. We might add, as a matter of fact, that the cultural determinedness of their expression of Christianity does not bankrupt either the content of their faith or their sincerity. They believe that they are doing God's work in the world: they act not for themselves, but for a higher cause.

They are, in that sense, just like everyone else. There is not a person alive who has not at some point operated with unexamined assumptions. And not every one of those people can be said to be as altruistic as the Greens. Where the Greens differ from the average person is in reach. They have the resources to influence law-making, education at high school and university levels, and the broader public perception of the Bible. It is not despite their good faith efforts, but actually because of them, that the Greens are able to exert real influence and have made, and continue to make, a significant impact.

One might object that their impact will not really be that far-reaching—that this is just another museum, or just another educational curriculum, among many. There are numerous resources for religious education, to say nothing of the superabundance of material on the internet—so why so much hubbub about a single organization? Have we been seduced by their public relations team's hype?

Time will tell, but they have certainly laid the groundwork for something that goes well beyond any similar ventures in recent memory, and perhaps longer. Definite article or not, Museum of the Bible will be *the* Museum of the Bible. To be sure, there is the flotsam of information one can find on the choppy waves of the internet, but sheer size and location will guarantee it a place of significance among America's historical museums, to say nothing of the authority it has leveraged from its association with the Vatican and the Israel Antiquities Authority. These alliances, along with the ability to cheaply acquire legitimacy through partnerships with scholars at Yale, Oxford, and Cambridge, means that it cannot be easily dismissed as a fringe religious venture. MOTB's association with the Green family has given it authority among those evangelicals who normally eye the ivory towers with suspicion. They have invested all of this cultural capital in the museum-going capital of the United States. The Green family has purchased leverage in diverse markets, and their technical savvy, which is unmatched by comparable educational products, coupled with their resources will allow them to flood the internet with their seemingly authoritative content. There were small traveling Bible exhibits before the Greens, but their collections have largely been absorbed by the Museum of the Bible. They will share with trusted partners—be they universities, the Vatican, or Ken Ham's museums—but it would not be an exaggeration to say their market share of the American religio-industrial complex approaches a monopoly.

Because of their wealth and generosity, the Greens have had an outsized effect on the world of antiquities, both within the smaller world of biblical scholarship and in the global market. But the nature of their primary occupation and their undoubted success in employing particular business strategies has had a detrimental impact on the worlds that they have annexed.

One consequence of bringing corporate structure and business principles to the collection of biblical artifacts is the way that concerns about scholarly ethics and individual responsibility have been diffused within the organization itself. When we inquired about the acquisition of the Galatians fragment, every person we spoke to protested that they were not involved in the purchase, and not one suggested that they were responsible for trying to answer the questions that surrounded it. No individual scholar or editor is responsible for researching the provenance of the artifacts they publish. The final decision seems to rest in the hands of Michael Holmes, a brilliant and generous individual who, in 2015, was still in the process of formulating his own ethical position on these questions.

The hiring of Michael Holmes and David Trobisch in 2012 signaled a desire to move in a more careful and scholarly direction, but even as he laments the lack of scholarly perspective among his new employers Trobisch does not appear to understand what provenance actually is. The promises to be transparent have failed to materialize. Even after being subject to a federal investigation, Steve Green dismissed the general problems with the collection as a simple mistake, comparable to copyright infringement. He was unaware that while he could simply compensate those who own a Christmas-themed pattern, no one is able to reverse the loss of knowledge, and potential loss of life, that accompanies the illicit antiquities trade. Paying relatively small fines to the U.S. government and forfeiting ownership of certain artifacts does not come close to repairing the damage that is done when one participates in the market. Even if the pieces in the Green Collection were legal acquisitions that simply lacked proper documentation, the willingness of its owners to purchase without provenance signals implicit support for the illicit antiquities trade. This is not about the practices of the past; it is about repercussions in the future: whenever an illicit or unprovenanced artifact is purchased, it supports and enhances the market for more such items. No one has boosted the market for biblical antiquities more than the Greens, but they are troublingly blasé about their holdings. Summers's only defense is to appeal to those university collections amassed in the nineteenth and early twentieth centuries by colonialist archaeologists. Such explanations only highlight their lack of understanding of the issues involved: ancient artifacts are not Christmas tins, and the cultural values of collectors working before women could legally vote should not set the standard.

By their own employee's admission the Collection includes crates of unprovenanced papyri. Thus, the questionable artifacts dealt with in this book are only the tip of the iceberg; but the displacement of scholarly autonomy seems to have eroded individual scholarly accountability. The collections process hides behind walls patrolled by flimsy references to the desires of private sellers and robust nondisclosure agreements. Those overseeing the process are reluctant and perhaps incapable of doing the necessary work on provenance, and in the vacuum created by the absence of qualified scholarly objections inappropriate analogues from the world of business have been allowed to rule the day.

As academics, we are particularly attentive to the way that the Greens and MOTB have affected the revelation and distribution of information. As the Green family has journeyed from occasional Bible collectors to national storytellers, they and those who work with them have contributed to the privatization of a body of knowledge that is of pressing importance to everyone. It is not only Christians who are stakeholders in the artifacts that they control and carefully curate—the history of the Bible, as the Greens have gone to such pains to argue, is a history that is shared by anyone invested in history and culture. And yet the knowledge inherent in the artifacts that the Greens possess is tightly controlled by the Scholars Initiative. Other academics are prohibited from accessing the collection's holdings unless they join the GSI and bind themselves to the terms of Hobby Lobby's nondisclosure agreement. Tersely worded agreements are common enough, but scholars are ordinarily at liberty to decide where, when, and how to publish their findings. Moreover, once an academic argument enters the world, others are free to test and revise its findings. There has been no guarantee that future generations of scholars will be able to reexamine the manuscripts published by the Scholars Initiative.

Even as MOTB privatizes academic work, it capitalizes on the culture of shared knowledge that underwrites the academy. Undergraduate and graduate students are put to work as apprentices in the sealed workshop that is the Scholars Initiative, but it is questionable whether they reap professional rewards from the project. When research is sequestered behind a nondisclosure agreement and the choreographed timing of publication lies beyond their control, there is questionable advantage to participation. In the case of some students, even the skills that they acquired are disputable. When a student claims, as one did, to have learned nine ancient languages in the course of a summer and cites transcribing letters as evidence of her accomplishments, it is certain that she has not learned enough even to know why such a thing is impossible.

Even in the case of graduate students and scholars who receive compensation from the organization, that compensation appears enticing because of the manner in which scholars are, broadly speaking, undercompensated. Academia, and the humanities in particular, is one of the last monastic disciplines: it offers long hours, a hermetic lifestyle, and low pay in exchange for a life of the mind. Against this backdrop, the possibilities of free trips to conferences in Europe, research expenses, and expensive meals are beguiling. The founding purpose of the GSI was to inform the Greens about the nature of their collection, a process that significantly raised the value of their holdings. But, with the exception of a few key individuals, participants are not being compensated in a manner commensurate with the economically valuable work they perform for Hobby Lobby. And, in the process, they have forfeited ownership and control of their ideas and work. Intellectual independence has been exchanged for magic beans.

This new model has worked for the Greens only because academia ordinarily functions with a free flow of ideas. It is easy enough to exploit the largesse of academics, who generally share ideas and operate with notions of collective knowledge and community. One scholar told us that he agreed to help MOTB with the placards for their exhibits free of charge, because he could not, for ethical reasons, accept their money but is nevertheless committed to providing the public with accurate information. It's an impulse on which MOTB is able to capitalize, even as the organization asserts ownership of information that is of significance beyond the borders of the academy.

At the same time, for many academics, the mere promise of gainful employment by an organization with deep pockets has encouraged their participation in the Green family projects. In many cases those most prominently employed by the Greens have been constrained by their own financial dependence. David Trobisch joined the program after a period of academic unemployment. For junior scholars like Josephine Dru, Lance Allred, and Christian Askeland, these were their first permanent full-time positions. Of the central group only Michael Holmes, a remarkable text critic who is arguably underemployed and overworked at Bethel University, has a full-time academic post. Silent complicity in questionable ventures is a common phenomenon in the business world, but it is antithetical to academia, a sphere in which tenure acts as the guardian of academic freedom.

Certainly the importation of business practices into academia did not begin with the Greens; industry exerts disproportionate influence on the generation of scientific knowledge, and critics have protested the impact that pharmacological companies have on academic research and the way that drug patents restrict and control access to life-saving drugs. There is nothing sinister about the Green family and MOTB's desire to run the Scholars Initiative in this way. The Greens and Cary Summers come from the business world. It is understandable that the Greens and the museum's other religiously conservative donors should wish to have some control over the way that their collection is used, especially when the academic study of the Bible has a history of challenging, antagonizing, and degrading religious beliefs. It is arguably for this reason that the carefully selected members of the Scholars Initiative have been brought on merely to identify and translate manuscripts. Ironically, debates over the significance of these artifacts—issues of what to think about variants in biblical manuscripts and how to read the

Bible itself, the very questions that the participants were actually trained to answer—are not in view. They can publish, within the confines of a MOTB-controlled series, on the academic value of their artifacts, but they do not set the tone for the broader public conversation. Those larger questions—that is, the overarching narrative of the story the Greens want to tell—were settled beforehand. The scholars employed by the Greens have effectively been reduced to the status of copyeditors: they might correct an obvious error or augment the phrasing here and there, but they cannot alter the fundamental nature of the story itself.

It is difficult to blame the Greens for their desire to run their biblically oriented ventures in the same way they have their businesses. The idea that success in one area of life qualifies one for success in other areas of life is almost axiomatic in American society. When flailing universities have come to them for help in the past, it has been Green money, harvested in accordance with biblical principles, that has rescued those institutions. Divine guidance has helped them succeed in the past; surely it is even more appropriate in a context in which they are dealing with the word of God? In no other museum would the perspective of a high school–educated billionaire be allowed to trump the learning and evidence of scholars and experts. That this is the case is the consequence not only of the Green family's wealth—donors are courted at every museum, after all—but also of the more general principle that as successful businessmen their opinions and success enjoy divine backing. One wonders not only what the place of academia is when billionaire craft store owners dictate and determine public education, but also what is the place of expertise in general.

One question we asked ourselves in the course of writing this book was from where our discomfort with the Greens' various Bible-related projects arose. Were we as biblical scholars being snobbish? Were we trying to safeguard our ivory towers and scholarly production methods against a new, democratizing model for engagement with the past? Were our concerns just a rehearsal of secular discomfort with sacred interests; academic resistance to business models of education; elitist complaints about amateur engagement; or the objections of old-fashioned humanists to a new era of digitization?

Our answer was no. Not only because skill sets, if not the credentials earned while acquiring them, matter, but also because the Museum of the Bible positions itself as the academy facing outward to the world. But MOTB seriously misrepresents the diversity of thought in biblical scholarship; elides the complicated relationship between archaeology, history, and the text; and problematically describes interpretively founded positions in the language of scientific certainty. In a similar way, the publicizing of the "oldest copies" of Gospel texts at evangelical gatherings does a disservice to those attending. No one benefits when inaccurate information is disseminated. The stakes are too high to make sloppy mistakes. Exaggeration, when it comes to the biblical artifacts, actually threatens to discredit Christian claims about their past.

The Green projects highlight a culture clash, not between the sciences and the humanities, but between the educated and the uneducated, between the scholar and the lay observer, and between the free flow of ideas and the ownership of knowledge. In evangelical circles, academic approaches to the Bible have generated suspicion for over a century. Among some Roman Catholics too, caricatures of "the liberal academy" and laments over the decline of orthodoxy at Catholic universities have contributed to the notion that, when it comes to religion in particular, the intellectual elite are not to be trusted. Paradoxically, the Greens are funding academic enterprises, but these projects are meant to provide the evangelical answer to the advance of secularism. They are, in effect, raiding the storehouses of academic knowledge for those ideas and arguments that fit their story.

Setting a soft-focus lens, in their curriculum and museum exhibits, on classic evangelical tropes such as American exceptionalism, Lockean property rights, a Victorian vision of the family, and presenting the result as the timeless "biblical worldview," is acceptable in a particular kind of explicitly confessional context—at the Creation Museum, for instance. But it is not acceptable in contexts that claim to be nonsectarian. To be sure, in both the museum and the curriculum there will be gestures towards diverging opinions, but those disagreements are tamped down by the rhetorical weight of appeals to "Christian tradition" and the arguments of evangelically friendly academics.

The Green family means well: they are sincere Christians who want to make the world better. They have been poorly advised and have, at times, hired individuals who are unqualified and ill-equipped to do the work required of them. It is difficult to maintain intellectual standards when the unofficial hiring criteria are predominantly religious, rather than academic. We can even try, as we have, to understand from where their arguments originate and to empathize with their motivations. But ultimately, these caveats and explanations are inadequate. Those whose ambitions extend to shaping the values of a nation have higher standards to meet. In the context of public education, unchecked confidence looks a great deal like hubris. The Greens are free to use their considerable wealth to exert influence over politics and legislation; they are welcome to run their company according to their interpretation of biblical principles; and they are at liberty to try to evangelize. But when they, however unwittingly, disguise evangelization as education and fortify their beliefs as religio-academic consensus, they are doing more than merely misleading the public. When it comes to educating our children, informing our citizens, and serving as a resource to our politicians, accuracy and balance require more than notional guiding principles. At a certain juncture, after multiple false starts, vocal public and academic objections, and several public relations makeovers, the naiveté begins to look willful. It is of this that the Greens are most guilty.

NOTES

INTRODUCTION

1. Richard Cunningham McCormick, *The Young Men's Magazine* 1 (1957): 17–18. Many of the specifics were drawn from Colgate's obituary. Colgate became an iconic figure in contemporary and later discussions of Christian business principles. He is used as an example in G. Ernest Thomas, *Spiritual Life Through Tithing* (Nashville: Tidings, 1955).
2. See Timothy Gloege, *Guaranteed Pure: The Moody Bible Institute, Business, and the Making of Modern Evangelicalism* (Charlotte: University of North Carolina Press, 2015), esp. ch. 1.
3. William R. Leach, *Land of Desire: Merchants, Power, and the Rise of a New American Culture* (New York: Vintage, 1993), 211.
4. The popularization began ca. 1870 and following, but the identification of Christianity and business came earlier. See Stewart Davenport, *Friends of the Unrighteous Mammon: Northern Christians and Market Capitalism, 1815–1860* (Chicago: University of Chicago Press, 2008).
5. Bruce Fairchild Barton's *The Man Nobody Knows* (Indianapolis, IN: Bobbs-Merril Company, 1925) was an overnight bestseller and one of the best-selling nonfiction books of the twentieth century.
6. Gloege, *Guaranteed Pure*, 118.
7. Both David Green and his son Steve Green, current CEO of Hobby Lobby, have used the expression "black sheep" to describe David Green's position among his siblings. We interviewed Steve Green at The Redbury Hotel in Los Angeles; all further unattributed quotes from him are taken from that interview. David Green's use of the term comes from an interview with Voices of Oklahoma in 2009 (http://www.voicesofoklahoma.com/wp-content/uploads/2013/09/Green_Transcript.pdf; last accessed September 6, 2016).
8. For Green, the Air Force reserves were a stepping stone to management; for his employer they were a way to keep a valuable employee out of the draft for the Vietnam war. In an interview with Voices of Oklahoma David Green told the interviewer, "I wanted to be a store manager for McClellans and they said, you know, 'You cannot be a store manager if you haven't done your military service.' And back then they were drafting people. So they didn't want me to become a store manager and then I'd get drafted and then they'd have no store manager. So I said well I'm going to go into the Air Force Reserves. And then that way I could take and become a manager and serve during the weekends" (Voices of Oklahoma; see n. 7 above).

9. Brian Solomon, "Meet David Green: Hobby Lobby's Biblical Billionaire," *Forbes*, September 18, 2012 (http://www.forbes.com/sites/briansolomon/2012/09/18/david-green-the-biblical-billionaire-backing-the-evangelical-movement/#151223313462; last accessed October 24, 2016).
10. David Knowles, "Hobby Lobby accused of anti-Semitism over lack of menorahs, Chanukah decorations," *New York Daily News*, October 1, 2013 (http://www.nydailynews.com/news/national/hobby-lobby-accused-anti-semitism-article-1.1473330; last accessed October 24, 2016).
11. In 2012 Felicia Allen filed a complaint in the Circuit Court of Hinds County, Mississippi, claiming that she had been wrongfully discriminated against because she was pregnant. Her lawsuit was swiftly thrown out, her lawyer Nick Norris told Vice, when she realized that she had signed a document mandating her to pursue arbitration and was in breach of contract. See Mary Emily O'Hara, "Former Hobby Lobby Employee Claims She Was Fired for Having a Kid," Vice, July 30, 2014 (https://news.vice.com/article/former-hobby-lobby-employee-claims-she-was-fired-for-having-a-kid; last accessed January 15, 2017).

    Other documented lawsuits include a suit lodged by Roxanne Feeling in Kansas alleging discrimination under the Americans with Disabilities Act and a class action lawsuit filed by Scott Cole & Associates in California on behalf of workers accusing Hobby Lobby, Inc. of wage-and-hour violations (*Fardig et al. v. Hobby Lobby Stores Inc. et al.*, case number 8:14-cv-00561, in the U.S. District Court for the Central District of California).
12. In the case of *Fardig et al. v Hobby Lobby* a counter suit lodged by Hobby Lobby, Inc., noted that similar claims had already been forced into arbitration by the federal court. See Aaron Vehling, "Hobby Lobby Says Scott Cole Defied Court by Filing Wage Suit," *Law360*, October 28, 2014 (https://www.law360.com/articles/590976/hobby-lobby-says-scott-cole-defied-court-by-filing-wage-suit; last accessed January 15, 2017). Roxanne Feeling's lawsuit was suspended and she was compelled into arbitration in 2005.
13. A copy of the binding mutual arbitration agreement signed by Allen in 2010 was included as part of *Allen v. Hobby Lobby* and published online by *Rewire* on July 29, 2014 (http://rewire.news/wp-content/uploads/2014/07/Allen-v-Hobby-Lobby-Mutual-Arbitration.pdf; last accessed Feb. 14, 2017). The agreement reads:

    > any dispute, demand, claim, controversy, cause of action, or suit (collectively referred to as "Dispute") that the employee may have, at any time . . . with or against the Company [Hobby Lobby, Inc.] . . . be submitted to and decided by final and binding arbitration."

    The agreement further stipulates that this includes disputes arising from "sexual harassment, harassment and/or discrimination based on any class protected by federal law.
14. Links to all four of these organizations have at one time or another been found on the Hobby Lobby Incorporated "Donations and Ministry page," which now includes Museum of the Bible (http://www.hobbylobby.com/about-us/donations-ministry; last accessed Feb. 14, 2017).
15. Solomon, "Meet David Green" (see n. 9 above).

16. Darren Dochuk, *From Bible Belt to Sun Belt: Plain-Folk Religion, Grassroots Politics, and the Rise of Evangelical Conservatism* (New York: W. W. Norton, 2011), 185.
17. Solomon, "Meet David Green," *Forbes* (see n. 9 above).
18. Ibid.
19. Ibid.
20. Ibid.
21. Ibid.
22. In 2009, David Green said that the mission coordinator for Hobby Lobby, his grandson, received an average of 300 requests per month (Voices of Oklahoma; see n. 7 above).
23. *Hobby Lobby v. Sebelius,* No. CIV-12-1000-HE (W.D. Okla. Sept. 12, 2012).
24. Whether the devices concerned are all abortifacients has been contested by some. See Pam Belluck, "Abortion Qualms on Morning-After Pill May Be Unfounded," *New York Times,* June 5, 2012 (http://www.nytimes.com/2012/06/06/health/research/morning-after-pills-dont-block-implantation-science-suggests.html; last accessed February 14, 2017). For its part, the Hobby Lobby suit referred to the FDA-approved labeling, which specified that these products prevented the implantation of a fertilized egg.
25. For an excellent primer on religious freedom legislation in the United States and the issues at hand, see Emily Bazelon, "What Are the Limits of 'Religious Liberty'?" *New York Times Magazine*, July 7, 2015 (https://www.nytimes.com/2015/07/12/magazine/what-are-the-limits-of-religious-liberty.html?_r=2; last accessed February 3, 2017).
26. *Burwell v. Hobby Lobby*, 573 U.S. ___ 2014 (https://www.supremecourt.gov/opinions/13pdf/13-354_olp1.pdf; last accessed February 14, 2017).
27. For a discussion of the significance of this decision, see Micah Schwartzman, Richard Schragger, and Nelson Tebbe, "The New Law of Religion," *Slate,* July 3, 2014 (http://www.slate.com/articles/news_and_politics/jurisprudence/2014/07/after_hobby_lobby_there_is_only_rfra_and_that_s_all_you_need.html; last accessed February 3, 2017).
28. In an interview with Michael Barbaro for "The Daily," a New York Times podcast, on February 1, 2017, David Green explained his position on the lawsuit and his subsequent support of Donald Trump as grounded in the Constitution and the First Amendment (https://www.nytimes.com/2017/02/01/podcasts/the-daily-gorsuch-supreme-court.html; last accessed February 1, 2017).
29. David Green, Press Statement September 13, 2012 (http://www.becketfund.org/davidgreenpressstatement/; last accessed February 14, 2017).
30. "Hobby Lobby: A Family Business" (https://www.youtube.com/watch?v=empZxxB19nU; last accessed February 14, 2017).
31. David Green interview with Michael Barbaro (see n. 28 above).
32. On occasion, the Greens themselves have hinted that they have been treated unfairly by the media. In a 2017 interview about the lawsuit (see n. 28 above), David Green complained that "the liberal press" neglects to mention the excellent health insurance coverage Hobby Lobby offers its employees or the fact that the Greens provided a generous minimum wage long before the law required them to do so. It is worth noting that the Greens' generosity

has been mentioned in numerous "liberal" publications, including that of the journalist Green was criticizing at the time: see Alan Rappeport, "Hobby Lobby Made Fight a Matter of Christian Principle," *New York Times*, June 30, 2014 (https://www.nytimes.com/2014/07/01/us/hobby-lobby-made-fight-a-matter-of-christian-principle.html; last accessed February 14, 2017) and Mark Oppenheimer, "At Christian Companies, Religious Principles Complement Business Practices," *New York Times*, August 2, 2013 (http://www.nytimes.com/2013/08/03/us/at-christian-companies-religious-principles-complement-business-practices.html; last accessed February 14, 2017).

33. Among many other appearances, Steve Green spoke at Dallas Baptist University's Christian Business Owners Conference on April 9 2015 and at the Christian leadership conference America's Best Hope in 2015.

34. Lydia Bean, *The Politics of Evangelical Identity: Local Churches and Partisan Divides in the United States and Canada* (Princeton: Princeton University Press, 2014); Molly Worthen, *Apostles of Reason: The Crisis of Authority in American Evangelism* (New York: Oxford University Press, 2013).

35. David Green, "One judge away from losing religious liberty: Hobby Lobby," *USA Today*, September 1, 2016 (http://www.usatoday.com/story/opinion/2016/09/01/hobby-lobby-religious-freedom-liberty-obamacare-christian-david-green/89597214/; last accessed February 14, 2017). Green has repeatedly stated that the endorsement was grounded in his family's beliefs about religious freedom and should not be understood as an endorsement of every position Trump holds. "We voted for Trump, not that we agree with everything he does" (Barbaro interview, see n. 28 above).

36. Kate Bowler, *Blessed: A History of the American Prosperity Gospel* (New York: Oxford University Press, 2013).

37. Dochuk, *From Bible Belt to Sun Belt*, 169.

38. David Green with Bill Nigh, *Giving It All Away . . . And Getting It Back Again. The Way of Living Generously* (Grand Rapids, MI: Zondervan, 2017).

39. See James P. Byrd, *Sacred Scripture, Sacred War: The Bible and the American Revolution* (Oxford and New York: Oxford University Press, 2013), which opens with a compelling example from the Connecticut minister Samuel Sherwood, who wrote, "God Almighty, with all the powers of heaven, are on our side. Great numbers of angels, no doubt, are encamping round our coast, for our defense and protection. Michael stands ready; with all the artillery of heaven, to encounter the dragon, and to vanquish the black host." Samuel Sherwood, "The Church's Flight Into the Wilderness: An Address on the Times," in *Political Sermons of the American Founding Era, 1730–1805*, 2d ed.; ed. Ellis Sandoz (Indianapolis, IN: Liberty Fund, 1998), 523, cited in Byrd, *Sacred Scripture*, 1. On Hebrew Bible elements in Revolutionary-era thought see Mark Noll, *America's God from Jonathan Edwards to Abraham Lincoln* (New York: Oxford University Press, 2002), 83–85; and idem, "The Bible in Revolutionary America," in *The Bible in American Law, Politics, and Political Rhetoric,* ed. J. T. Johnson, 29–60. The Bible in American Culture Series (Philadelphia: Fortress, 1985), 39.

40. David Green interview with Michael Barbaro, n. 28 above.

41. Gloege, *Guaranteed Pure*, 4: "Corporate evangelicals, in contrast, largely abandoned their unquestioned allegiance to a particular denominational tradition."
42. "Statement of Faith," http://www.councilroad.org/statement-of-faith; last accessed February 14, 2017.
43. See Donald W. Dayton and Robert K. Johnston, eds., *The Variety of American Evangelicalism* (Knoxville: University of Tennessee Press, 1991).
44. On Schaeffer and his influence, see Barry Hankins, *Francis Schaeffer and the Shaping of Evangelical America* (Grand Rapids, MI: Eerdmans, 2008).
45. Worthen, *Apostles of Reason*, 253.
46. Del Tackett, "What's a Christian Worldview?" Focus on the Family (http://www.focusonthefamily.com/faith/christian-worldview/whats-a-christian-worldview/whats-a-worldview-anyway; last accessed February 14, 2017).
47. Joel Baden and Candida Moss, "Can Hobby Lobby Buy the Bible?" *The Atlantic*, January/February 2016, 70–77.
48. According to the Museum's website: https://www.museumofthebible.org (last accessed February 14, 2017).
49. Voices of Oklahoma (see n. 7 above).
50. According to the Form 990 filed by One Hope in 2013.
51. Arguably, this use of the term "nonsectarian" and its interest in prescribing the reading of the King James Version in public schools carried with it an anti-Catholic animus. See the discussion of the Eliott School Rebellion that opens John T. McGreevy, *Catholicism and American Liberty* (New York: W. W. Norton, 2004) and the ensuing discussion of the nexus of the King James Version, patriotism, and Protestantism.
52. For this understanding of "nonsectarian," we are grateful to Prof. Melanie Ross (personal communication).
53. Nathan O. Hatch, *The Democratization of American Christianity* (New Haven: Yale University Press, 1989).
54. In 2016, it emerged that the Sugar Research Foundation had sponsored research into the connection between dietary fat and cholesterol and coronary heart disease (CHD). This move followed the discovery of a potential relationship between CHD and sugar in the 1950s. The authors of this study revealed that two of Harvard's most prominent nutritionists had collaborated with the sugar industry to downplay sugar's role in CHD. See Cristin E. Kearns, Laura A. Schmidt, and Stanton A. Glantz, "Sugar Industry and Coronary Heart Disease Research: A Historical Analysis of Internal Industry Documents," *JAMA Intern Med* 176 (2016): 1680–85. In a similar vein, Jane Mayer's article "How Right Wing Billionaires Infiltrated Higher Education," *Chronicle of Higher Education*, February 12, 2016, examined the influence of the Koch brothers on university education and research in the United States (http://www.chronicle.com/article/How-Right-Wing-Billionaires-/235286; last accessed February 14, 2017).

CHAPTER 1. THE COLLECTION

1. Carroll received his doctorate from the University of Miami, where he studied with the prominent ancient historian Edwin Yamauchi.
2. We spoke with Scott Carroll twice, on July 24, 2015, and August 18, 2015. All quotes from him are taken from those interviews, unless otherwise noted.
3. Mart Green's response to the question "would you do this [hire the same cast] again" was, "To be honest I would not have hired Chad [the gay actor about whom the controversy emerged] had I known everything about him. But God had to work around me to get Chad on this project. So I learned that God loved Chad more than I did and that He wanted Chad on this project" (http://www.epm.org/resources/2006/Feb/21/end-spear-controversy-mart-green-and-steve-saint-o/; last accessed January 17, 2017).
4. We spoke with David Trobisch on November 23, 2014, and again on June 4, 2015. All quotes from him are taken from those interviews, unless otherwise noted.
5. Both Trobisch and Carroll told us that final decisions about acquisitions for the Green Collection are made by the Green family.
6. Green said this to Sandra Hindman (herself a Green Collection employee) in a piece entitled "We Are Storytellers First" that was published in *Fine Books and Collections* in Autumn 2013 (http://www.lesenluminures.com/enlu-assets/media/press/2013–10-finebooks/2013–10-finebooks.pdf; last accessed February 14, 2017).
7. P.PalauRib. inv. 183. The codex is part of the Palau-Ribes Collection, which is currently housed at the Historic Archives of the Society of Jesus in Catalunya. Details of this manuscript can be found in Hans Quecke, "Eine koptische Bibelhandschrift des 5. Jahrhunderts III (PPalau Rib. Inv.-Nr. 183)," *StudPap* 20 (1981): 7–13; Hans Quecke (ed. pr.), *Das Johannesevangelium saïdisch: Text der Handschrift Palau Rib. Inv. Nr. 183 mit den Varianten der Handschrift 813 und 814 der Chester Beatty Library und der Handschrift M 569* (Rome: Papyrologica Castroctaviana, 1984); and Pasquale Orsini, "La maiuscola biblica copta," *Segno e Testo* 6 (2008) 121–50.
8. The hammer price for the Wyman fragment was £301,250 (http://www.sothebys.com/en/auctions/ecatalogue/2012/the-history-of-script-sixty-important-manuscript-leaves-from-the-schyen-collection/lot.3.html; last accessed October 17, 2016). Technically Hobby Lobby purchases all artifacts.
9. See, for example, Phyllis Mauch Messenger, *The Ethics of Collecting Cultural Property: Whose Culture? Whose Property?* 2nd ed. Albuquerque: University of New Mexico Press, 1999); Kate Fitz Gibbon, *Who Owns the Past? Cultural Policy, Cultural Property, and the Law* (New Brunswick: Rutgers University Press, 2005).
10. See Rachel Shabi, "Looted in Syria—and sold in London: The British antiquities shops dealing in artefacts smuggled by Isis," *The Guardian*, July 3, 2015 (https://www.theguardian.com/world/2015/jul/03/antiquities-looted-by-isis-end-up-in-london-shops; last accessed February 14, 2017); Andrew Osborn, "Islamic State looting Syrian, Iraqi sites on industrial scale—UNESCO,"

Reuters, July 2, 2015 (http://uk.reuters.com/article/uk-mideast-crisis-unesco-idUKKCN0PC1OS20150702; last accessed February 14, 2017).

11. Robert J. Kraft, "Pursuing Papyri and Papyrology by Way of eBay: A Preliminary Report," report given to the 25th International Congress of Papyrology in Ann Arbor, August 3, 2007 (http://ccat.sas.upenn.edu/rak/papyri/ebay/report-2007/report-2007.html; last accessed October 8, 2016).
12. On the complicated history of the codex Tchacos, the book that contained the *Gospel of Judas*, see Herbert Krosney, *The Lost Gospel: The Quest for the Gospel of Judas Iscariot* (Washington, DC: National Geographic, 2006); James M. Robinson, *The Secrets of Judas. The Story of the Misunderstood Disciple and His Gospel* (San Francisco: HarperOne, 2007); and N. Brodie, "The Lost, Found, Lost Again and Found Again Gospel of Judas," *Culture Without Context: The Newsletter of the Illicit Antiquities Research Centre* 19 (2006): 17–27.
13. "The Coptic pieces . . . sold for more on average than the Greek, probably because it was rumored that Ferrini still possessed pieces of the Gospel of Judas, the Epistles of Paul, and some other Sahidic works of similar value." Kraft, "Pursuing Papyri" (http://ccat.sas.upenn.edu/rak/papyri/ebay/report-2007/report-frame.html; last accessed April 10, 2017).
14. See Hany N. Takla, "The Massacre in San Jose—The Sale of Dismembered Manuscripts of Christian Egypt on eBay," in *Synaxis katholike*, eds. Diliana Atanassova and Tinatin Chronz, 705–16 (Vienna: LIT, 2014), 705–16.
15. Christine M. Thomas, speaking at the "Provenance in an eBay World: Does the Provenance of Ancient Artifacts Matter?" Panel hosted by the Student Advisory Board, Society of Biblical Literature Annual Meeting, Atlanta, November 23, 2015.
16. See the recent policy statements of both the American Schools of Oriental Research, the leading academic society for the archaeology of the Middle East (http://www.asor.org/about/policies/conduct.html), and the Society of Biblical Literature (https://www.sbl-site.org/assets/pdfs/SBL-Artifacts-Policy_20160903.pdf). It should be noted that despite the positive moves toward greater accountability by these professional societies, their policies remain riddled with loopholes: exceptions are made for cuneiform texts, which, given the regions currently most disturbed by looting, seems unaccountable; and any artifact that has already been published, regardless of whether it is provenanced, is allowed to be presented at conferences. This policy effectively permits unprovenanced materials to enter the public domain, with institutional approval.
17. For Schøyen, see Torleif Elgvin, Michael Langlois, and Kipp Davis, eds., *Gleanings from the Caves: Dead Sea Scrolls and Artefacts from the Schøyen Collection* (London: Bloomsbury, 2016).
18. Owen Jarus, "Are These New Dead Sea Scrolls the Real Thing?" Live Science, October 10, 2016 (http://www.livescience.com/56429-are-new-dead-sea-scrolls-forgeries.html; last accessed February 14, 2017).
19. Nina Burleigh, "Newly Discovered Dead Sea Scrolls Are Skillfully Crafted Fakes, Experts Suspect," *Newsweek*, October 18, 2016 (http://www.newsweek

.com/2016/10/28/dead-sea-scroll-fragments-fake-experts-suspect-511224.html?rx=us; last accessed February 14, 2017).

20. On the practical means of determining forgeries in ancient manuscripts, see Joel Baden and Candida Moss, "The Curious Case of Jesus's Wife," *The Atlantic*, December 2014, 74–81.
21. In numerous media outlets, Carroll is described as a "real-life Indiana Jones." He swears that he did not give himself this nickname. While we were speaking with him, however, his cell phone rang—to the Indiana Jones theme music.
22. Geraldine Fabrikant, "Craft Shop Family Buys Up Ancient Bibles for Museum," *New York Times* June 11, 2010 (http://www.nytimes.com/2010/06/12/business/12bibles.html; last accessed February 14, 2017).
23. Roberta Mazza (www.facesandvoices.wordpress.com; Brice C. Jones (bricecjones.com); Paul Barford (paul-barford.blogspot.com); Dorothy Lobel King (phdiva.blogspot.com).
24. This information is freely available on Carroll's CV "highlights" section and his Facebook feed: https://www.facebook.com/heydoc.
25. We spoke with Cary Summers on June 11, 2015, August 24, 2015, and October 14, 2015. All quotes from him are taken from those interviews, unless otherwise noted.
26. Josh McDowell, "Living Treasures Hidden Within Ancient Artifacts," *Charisma Magazine,* April 1, 2015 (http://www.charismamag.com/spirit/evangelism-missions/560-evangelism/22947-josh-mcdowell-living-treasures-hidden-within-ancient-artifacts; last accessed February 14, 2017). Similar claims have been made by Carroll. In a presentation delivered at the University of the Nations on September 6, 2013, Carroll announced the discovery of "the earliest text in the world of Luke 16," "the earliest text of Timothy," a manuscript containing Second Corinthians chapter 6 through Galatians 3 (which would necessarily be several pages long), "the earliest text in the world of Genesis 17," and "the earliest text of Second Kings 9" (https://www.youtube.com/watch?v=CSUzWsuLpso–2013; last accessed February 14, 2017).
27. "Mummies in Morrison," Newsletter of the Baylor Department of Classics, vol. 8, Fall, 2011.
28. We interviewed many students who were involved in GSI projects in the course of researching this book. Because of their vulnerable status, we have chosen to keep all of their names private, even when they were willing to speak on the record with us.
29. https://www.museumofthebible.org/news/passages; last accessed February 14, 2017.
30. The question of whether antiquities held outside their country of origin should be repatriated is a fraught one. See Sharon Waxman, *Loot: The Battle over the Stolen Treasures of the World* (New York: Henry Holt, 2008). A controversial new book arguing against repatriation is Tiffany Jenkins, *Keeping Their Marbles: How the Treasures of the Past Ended Up in Museums . . . and Why They Should Stay There* (Oxford: Oxford University Press, 2016); see the devastating review by Johanna Hanink: http://bmcr.brynmawr.edu/2016/2016-12-06.html.
31. Carroll's Facebook feed, October 18, 2012.

32. Roger Bagnall, *Everyday Writing in the Graeco-Roman East* (Berkeley: University of California Press, 2011), 32–33.
33. For an indication of the type of conversations that were happening around this fragment among papyrologists and scholars, see the blog posts and subsequent discussions from the Evangelical Textual Criticism blog site: http://evangelicaltextualcriticism.blogspot.co.uk/2015/01/questions-about-first-century-mark.html; http://evangelicaltextualcriticism.blogspot.co.uk/2014/05/breaking-news-first-century-fragment-of.html; http://evangelicaltextualcriticism.blogspot.co.uk/2015/01/has-anyone-seen-first-century-mark.html (all accessed February 14, 2017).
34. Uploaded by Hezekiah Domowski on November 13, 2015 (https://www.youtube.com/watch?v=RD9CIH-l25Y; last accessed October 4, 2016). In the video, Carroll does not confirm that the fragment is currently owned by the Greens.
35. We spoke with Michael Holmes on June 3, 2015 and October 15, 2015. All quotes from him are taken from these interviews, unless noted otherwise. Holmes indicated that he didn't know if the papyrus was in the Green Collection or not, and added: "I don't know if what [Dan Wallace] saw is one of the fragments that GSI has."
36. Candida Moss and Joel Baden, "Exclusive: Feds Investigate Hobby Lobby Boss for Illicit Artifacts," *The Daily Beast*, October 27, 2015 (http://www.thedailybeast.com/articles/2015/10/26/exclusive-feds-investigate-hobby-lobby-boss-for-illicit-artifacts.html; last accessed February 14, 2017).
37. https://www.ice.gov/news/releases/ice-returns-stolen-picasso-painting-valued-15-million; last accessed February 14, 2017.
38. Ed Pilkington, "Hobby Lobby investigated for trying to import ancient artifacts from Iraq," *The Guardian*, October 28, 2015 (https://www.theguardian.com/us-news/2015/oct/28/hobby-lobby-investigated-ancient-artifacts-iraq; last accessed February 14, 2017).
39. Carroll's Facebook feed, August 19, 2012.
40. http://trobisch.com/david/wb/pages/curriculum-vitae.php; last accessed February 14, 2017.
41. David Trobisch said in November 2014, "I respect [Steve Green] very much and [his perspective is] certainly not a scholar's version of the Bible."
42. On the identity and background of "MixAntik," see Paul Barford, "Mixantik Papyri Online Again (Would You Buy Kiswa From this Man?)," December 14, 2012 (http://paul-barford.blogspot.com/2012/12/mixantik-papyri-online-again_14.html; last accessed February 14, 2017), and the various links provided there.
43. Brice C. Jones, "A Coptic New Testament Papyrus Fragment (Galatians 2) For Sale on eBay," originally posted on Quaternion on October 29, 2012; it was reposted on his new blog at http://www.bricecjones.com/blog/a-coptic-new-testament-papyrus-fragment-galatians-2-for-sale-on-ebay; last accessed October 4, 2016.
44. See Dorothy Lobel King, "The Tale of the Very Dodgy Papyri," December 14, 2012 (http://phdiva.blogspot.co.uk/2012/12/the-tale-of-very-dodgy-papyri.html; last accessed October 4, 2016).

45. "Galatian Papyrus on Sale," October 30, 2012 (http://evangelicaltextualcriticism.blogspot.co.uk/2012/10/brice-jones-has-identified-galatians-22.html; last accessed February 14, 2017).
46. William H. Willis, "Duke Papyri: A History of the Collection," *Duke University Library Notes* 51/52 (1985): 35–50:

    > As mentioned above, the source of the first literary papyri acquired by Duke was the small private collection formed by the renowned archeologist David M. Robinson, who bequeathed it to the writer in 1958. . . . Robinson's 75 papyri, however, had been left in their raw state unrestored in boxes and folders containing a miscellany of hundreds of small bits. As these are sorted by style of writing, cleaned, assembled, restored and identified, a process requiring many years of patient effort, they are being given to the Duke Collection. By [1985] 24 have been accessioned, including two Homer fragments and a Homer commentary, a doctor's prescription for a disease of the spleen, and other interesting texts (44).

    Willis's own description seems to rule out the possibility that the Galatians text would have gone unrecognized: it is substantially larger than the tiny fragments Willis mentions, and indeed larger than most of the other texts in Duke's Robinson Collection holdings.
47. Personal communication, J. Andrew Armacost, Curator of the Rubinstein Rare Book and Manuscript Library, Duke University, and Joshua D. Sosin, Associate Professor of Classical Studies, Duke University.
48. For an account of the scholarly arguments and a history of the debate that surrounded the publication of this text, including the important role that gender played in the assessment of the evidence, see Caroline T. Schroeder, in Tony Burke, ed., *Fakes, Forgeries, and Fictions: Writing Ancient and Modern Christian Apocrypha.Proceedings from the 2015 York University Christian Apocrypha Symposium* (Eugene, OR: Cascade, 2017), forthcoming.
49. Ariel Sabar, "The Unbelievable Tale of Jesus's Wife," *The Atlantic*, July/August 2016 (http://www.theatlantic.com/magazine/archive/2016/07/the-unbelievable-tale-of-jesus-wife/485573/; last accessed February 14, 2017).
50. What follows is taken from interviews conducted with William Noah on October 3 and October 20, 2016.
51. Subsequent to our first conversation with him Dr. Noah told us that he had contacted a mutual friend of the Greens to tell them about the mistake. He did not want to be associated with a controversial artifact.
52. Adam Klasfeld, "Looted 200 A.D. Sarcophagus Returned to Greece," Courthouse News, February 10, 2017 (http://courthousenews.com/looted-200-a-d-sarcophagus-returned-to-greece/; last accessed February 15, 2017).

CHAPTER 2. THE GREEN SCHOLARS INITIATIVE

1. The description above was taken from two emails to us by Jennifer Larson, on May 14 and 20, 2015.

2. Published by McGraw-Hill, Triangle, and Barge Canal Press, respectively.
3. On The Holy Land Experience, see their website, www.holylandexperience.com (last accessed February 14, 2017); see also some of the news stories about the park's ideological and financial status: Dana Canedy, "A Biblical Theme Park in Florida Begets Ill Will," *New York Times*, February 3, 2001 (http://www.nytimes.com/2001/02/03/us/a-biblical-theme-park-in-florida-begets-ill-will.html; last accessed February 14, 2017); Paul Brinkman, "Holy Land Experience to unload furniture, statues amid financial turmoil," *Orlando Sentinel*, July 20, 2016 (http://www.orlandosentinel.com/business/brinkmann-on-business/os-holy-land-auction-20160719-story.html; last accessed February 14, 2017).
4. We spoke with Jerry Pattengale on July 29, 2015. All quotes from him are taken from that interview unless otherwise noted.
5. We spoke to Askeland on July 16, 2015. All quotes from him are from that interview unless otherwise noted.
6. http://cccu.org/about (last accessed February 14, 2017).
7. http://www.baylor.edu/classics/index.php?id=89582 (last accessed February 14, 2017).
8. Mark Noll, *Between Faith and Criticism* (San Francisco: Harper & Row, 1986), 135.
9. https://shepherds.edu/about/doctrinal-statement/ and https://shepherds.edu/policies/statement-on-women/ (last accessed February 14, 2017).
10. Noll, *Between Faith and Criticism*, 138.
11. Sean Savage, "World's oldest siddur slated for future D.C. Bible museum," Jewish News Service, November 10, 2013 (http://www.jns.org/latest-articles/2013/11/11/worlds-oldest-siddur-slated-for-future-dc-bible-museum#.WQjjDje1vEs=; last accessed February 14, 2017).
12. https://www.cfnp.org/policy-counsel/pc---march-2013---green? (last accessed February 14, 2017).
13. We spoke with Lisa Wolfe on May 19, 2015.
14. We spoke with Emanuel Tov on June 29, 2015.
15. A copy of the Green Scholars Initiative NDA was provided to us by a participant who wishes, for obvious reasons, to remain anonymous.
16. In one notable instance in which NDAs were used, the preparation of the translation of the Gospel of Judas for *National Geographic*, it could be argued that the NDAs undermined the scholarly process. The initial translation contained a number of errors and was strongly criticized by scholars including April DeConick: "Gospel Truth," *New York Times*, December 1, 2007 (http://www.nytimes.com/2007/12/01/opinion/01deconink.html; last accessed February 14, 2017).
17. The Dead Sea Scrolls, for example, are freely available online in remarkable high-definition images (http://www.deadseascrolls.org.il/?locale=en_US), though the images are under copyright.
18. https://www.sbl-site.org/meetings/Congresses_Abstracts.aspx?MeetingId=21 (last accessed February 14, 2017).
19. We spoke with Karl Kutz on June 8, 2015.
20. Bethany Moreton, *To Serve God and Wal-Mart: The Making of Christian Free Enterprise* (Cambridge: Harvard University Press, 2010), 173–92. On

the adherence to free enterprise principles among evangelicals, see Dochuk, *From Bible Belt to Sun Belt*, 187–89.

21. Per an email from MBTS professor Stephen Andrews, who was the scholar assigned to work on the manuscript, May 29, 2015.
22. See chap. 1, n. 8.
23. Gareen Darakjian, "Pepperdine professors and students get a never-before-seen look at ancient religious artifacts using an innovative imaging technology," *Pepperdine Magazine*, Summer 2013 (http://magazine.pepperdine.edu/2013/08/illuminated-discoveries/; last accessed February 14, 2017); email from Natalie Lewis, May 19, 2015.
24. Speech to the Council for National Policy; see chap. 2 n. 12.
25. John J. Collins, *The Dead Sea Scrolls: A Biography* (Princeton: Princeton University Press, 2012), 20.
26. Collins, *Dead Sea Scrolls*, 213.
27. Noll, *Between Faith and Criticism*, 157.
28. Noll, *Between Faith and Criticism*, 152.
29. Randall J. Stephens and Karl W. Giberson, *The Anointed: Evangelical Truth in a Secular Age* (Cambridge: Harvard University Press, 2011), 3.
30. Ibid., 10.
31. George M. Marsden, *Fundamentalism and American Culture: The Shaping of Twentieth-Century Evangelicalism 1870–1925* (Oxford: Oxford University Press, 1980), 212.
32. On the Gnostic Gospels, see Bentley Layton, *The Gnostic Scriptures: A New Translation with Annotations and Introductions*. Anchor Yale Bible Reference Library (New Haven: Yale University Press, 1995); Elaine Pagels, *The Gnostic Gospels* (New York: Random House, 1989); Christoph Markschies, *Gnosis: An Introduction* (London: T&T Clark, 2003); David Brakke, *The Gnostics: Myth, Ritual, and Diversity in Early Christianity* (Cambridge: Harvard University Press, 2010).
33. This can be deduced by tracking Scott Carroll's movements and meetings as he describes them on his Facebook feed.
34. Hindman, "We Are Storytellers First" (see chap. 1, n. 6).
35. Among scholars this passage is widely regarded as an interpolation (a secondary addition) to the text of the Gospel of John. It began life as a note in the margins of a manuscript and, over time and with copying, worked its way into the manuscripts. For the fullest treatment of the manuscript history of this passage see Jennifer Wright-Knust, "Early Christian Re-Writing and the History of the *Pericope Adulterae*," *Journal of Early Christian Studies* 14 (2006): 485–536.
36. See, e.g., Roy E. Beacham and Kevin T. Bauder, eds., *One Bible Only? Examining Exclusive Claims for the King James Bible* (Grand Rapids, MI: Kregel, 2001).
37. Answer: 0.015 manuscripts.
38. Take for example the *Gospel of Judas*, the provenance of which is hotly contested. Yet, despite the controversy that surrounds the manuscript, scholars continue to publish and, thus, profit from its discovery. It is difficult to blame some of those involved: for junior scholars, failing to mention the Tchacos

Codex (the name of the physical book in which the *Gospel of Judas* was found) might prevent one's work from being published or accepted.

39. Michael W. Holmes, "How Soon Will It Be Published?" (https://michaelwholmes.com/posts-and-comments-2/; last accessed February 14, 2017).
40. Emanuel Tov, Kipp Davis, and Robert Duke, eds., *Dead Sea Scrolls Fragments in the Museum Collection* (Leiden: Brill, 2016).
41. Tov, Davis, and Duke, *Dead Sea Scrolls Fragments*, 5–6.
42. Owen Jarus, "25 New 'Dead Sea Scrolls' Revealed," Live Science, October 10, 2016 (http://www.livescience.com/56428-25-new-dead-sea-scrolls-revealed.html; last accessed February 14, 2017).

CHAPTER 3. EDUCATION

1. David Van Biema, "Hobby Lobby's Steve Green launches a new project: a public school Bible curriculum," Religion News Service, April 15, 2014 (http://religionnews.com/2014/04/15/hobby-lobbys-steve-green-another-project-public-school-bible-curriculum/; last accessed February 14, 2017).
2. http://bibleinschools.net/ (last accessed February 14, 2017).
3. Jon Watje, "School district considering adding Bible course," *Mustang Times*, November 13, 2013.
4. Van Biema, "Hobby Lobby's Steve Green" (see chap. 3 n. 1).
5. David Van Biema, "Hobby Lobby's Green family postpones launch of public school Bible curriculum," Religion News Service, July 16, 2015 (http://religionnews.com/2014/07/16/hobby-lobbys-green-family-postpones-launch-public-school-bible-curriculum/; last accessed February 14, 2017).
6. "Hobby Lobby's Bible course cancelled by Oklahoma school district," *Christianity Today*, November 29, 2014 (http://www.christiantoday.com/article/hobby.lobbys.bible.course.cancelled.by.oklahoma.school.district/43668.htm; last accessed February 14, 2017).
7. Bailey Elise McBride, "School Board Members Met Privately on Bible Class," Associated Press, May 21, 2014.
8. Ibid.
9. Ibid.
10. Ibid.
11. *Abington School District v. Schempp*, 374 U.S. 203 [1963] at 225.
12. *Wiley v. Franklin* 474 F. Supp. 525 [E.D. Tenn. 1979] at 531.
13. Available at https://www.youtube.com/watch?v=awrALVLc2zo (last accessed February 14, 2017).
14. Ibid.
15. Viewable at http://www.hobbylobby.com/about-us/holiday-messages (last accessed February 14, 2017).
16. Van Biema, "Hobby Lobby's Steve Green" (see chap. 3, n. 1).
17. Quoted in Stephens and Giberson, *The Anointed*, 258.
18. Quoted in Worthen, *Apostles of Reason*, 252.
19. Bailey Elise McBride, "Oklahoma District Bible Class: Sinners Will Suffer," Associated Press, April 25, 2014.

20. Mark Chancey, "Can This Class Be Saved? The 'Hobby Lobby' Public School Bible Curriculum," Report from the Texas Freedom Network Education Fund, May 2014.
21. Watje, "School district" (see chap. 3, n. 3).
22. McBride, "Oklahoma District Bible Class" (see chap. 3, n. 3).
23. Adelle M. Banks, "Hobby Lobby president's Bible curriculum shelved by Oklahoma school district," Religion News Service, November 26, 2014 (http://religionnews.com/2014/11/26/hobby-lobby-presidents-bible-curricu lum-shelved-oklahoma-school-district/; last accessed February 14, 2017).
24. Carla Hinton, "Mustang Schools still plan Bible class, but not with controversial Green scholars' curriculum," NewsOK, December 11, 2014 (http://newsok.com/article/5375150; last accessed February 14, 2017).
25. McBride, "Oklahoma District Bible Class" (see chap. 3, n. 3).
26. Hinton, "Mustang Schools" (see chap. 3, n. 24).
27. See Worthen, *Apostles of Reason*, 241–42; D. Michael Lindsay, *Faith in the Halls of Power: How Evangelicals Joined the American Elite* (Oxford: Oxford University Press, 2007), 80–85.
28. Colleen Flaherty, "Banking on the curriculum," *Inside Higher Ed*, October 16, 2015 (https://www.insidehighered.com/news/2015/10/16/new-paper-de tails-extent-bbt-banks-ayn-rand-inspired-grant-program; last accessed February 14, 2017).
29. David Levinthal, "Spreading the Free-Market Gospel," *The Atlantic*, October 30, 2015 (http://www.theatlantic.com/education/archive/2015/10/spreading -the-free-market-gospel/413239/; last accessed February 14, 2017).
30. http://www.baylorisr.org/programs-research/the-religious-freedom-project/; last accessed February 14, 2017).
31. Elmer Townes, *How God Answers Prayer (How to Pray)* (Shippensburg, PA: Destiny Image, 2009).
32. Elisha Fieldstadt, "Liberty University President Jerry Falwell Urges Students to Carry Guns," *NBC News*, December 5, 2015 (http://www.nbcnews.com /news/us-news/liberty-university-president-jerry-falwell-urges-students-carry -guns-n474886; last accessed February 14, 2017).
33. https://en.wikipedia.org/wiki/Liberty_University; last accessed February 14, 2017.
34. http://northpoint.edu/fast-facts/; last accessed February 14, 2017.
35. https://www.abhe.org/about-abhe/tenets-of-faith/; last accessed February 14, 2017.
36. "Massachusetts: Christian College Wins a Free 217-Acre Campus," Associated Press, September 21, 2012. http://www.nytimes.com/2012/09/22/us /christian-college-wins-free-massachusetts-campus.html.
37. https://www.gcu.edu/Documents/Doctrinal-Statement.pdf; https://www.gcu .edu/Documents/Ethical-Positions-Statement.pdf; last accessed February 14, 2017.
38. G. Jeffrey MacDonald, "After winning free campus, Grand Canyon University says 'no thanks,'" Religion News Service, October 29, 2012 (http://religionnews.com/2012/10/29/after-winning-free-campus-grand-canyon-uni versity-says-no-thanks/; last accessed February 14, 2017). An example of a

more successful donation by the Greens would be the $10 million they gave to Southeastern University in Florida, a Pentecostal school that, like Grand Canyon University, holds as doctrine that sex should be exclusively "between one genetic male and one genetic female within the covenant of marriage" (https://www.seu.edu/about/what-we-believe/; last accessed February 14, 2017).

39. http://www.northfieldopportunity.org/; last accessed February 14, 2017.
40. Lindsay, *Faith in the Halls of Power*, 86.
41. https://www.indwes.edu/academics/jwhc/christian-askeland; last accessed February 14, 2017.
42. Lindsay, *Faith in the Halls of Power*, 162–70.
43. https://www.ncfgiving.com/about; last accessed February 14, 2017.
44. Solomon, "Meet David Green" (see Intro., n. 9).
45. Voices of Oklahoma (see Intro., n. 7).
46. http://www.oru.edu/about-oru/mission.php; last accessed February 14, 2017.
47. Stephens and Giberson, *The Anointed*, 231.
48. http://covenantjourney.com/; last accessed February 14, 2017.
49. Sarah Pulliam Bailey, "Birthright for evangelicals? Hobby Lobby family funds new Israel trips," *Washington Post*, May 8, 2015 (https://www.washingtonpost.com/news/acts-of-faith/wp/2015/05/08/birthright-for-evangelicals-hobby-lobby-family-funds-new-israel-trips/?utm_term=.74a9ec722a25; last accessed February 14, 2017).
50. http://demoss.com/newsrooms/museumofthebible/news/New-Covenant-Journey-Program-Unveiled-at-Israeli-Embassys-Annual-Christian; last accessed May 21, 2015.
51. http://covenantjourney.com/itinerary; last accessed February 14, 2017.
52. Dan Bahat, "Does the Holy Sepulchre Church Mark the Burial of Jesus?" *BAR* 12 (1986): 26–45.
53. Gabriel Barkay, "The Garden Tomb: Was Jesus Buried Here?" *BAR* 12 (1986): 40–57.
54. https://www.splcenter.org/fighting-hate/extremist-files/group/liberty-counsel; last accessed February 14, 2017.
55. On the history of evangelicalism and Protestantism more generally in the context of the American university, see the important study of George Marsden, *Soul of the American University: From Protestant Establishment to Established Nonbelief* (Oxford: Oxford University Press, 1994).
56. See especially Noll, *Between Faith and Criticism*, 186–98.
57. Lindsay, *Faith in the Halls of Power*, 89–93.
58. Noll, *Between Faith and Criticism*, 142.
59. Ibid., 151.
60. https://www.museumofthebible.org/news/israel-museum-bible-and-city-ashkelon-announce-winner-its-bible-bee; last accessed February 14, 2017.
61. Ibid.
62. https://www.museumofthebible.org/homeschooling-curriculum; last accessed February 14, 2017.
63. http://nces.ed.gov/pubs2009/2009030.pdf; see also http://www2.ed.gov/about/offices/list/oii/nonpublic/statistics.html#homeschl; last accessed February 14, 2017.

64. In her blog post, "Six ways I engage with the Bible: Part One: Daily Reading" (http://laurenamcafee.com/?s=homeschool; last accessed October 18, 2016), Steve Green's daughter, Lauren McAfee Green, describes her education in the following way: "Growing up being homeschooled, my Dad taught my math lesson every morning before he left for work. And every morning as I walked into my Dad's study, half-asleep, to start my math lesson, he was already there reading his Bible. Seeing my Dad prioritize this book, even amidst his busy schedule—president of a large privately-owned company and a homeschooling father of four (at the time)—made a lasting impression on me." There is no doubt that the Greens are dedicated parents.
65. The handout brings three arguments against the charge of anachronism in the camels of Genesis. The first is that the camel was domesticated in the southern Arabian peninsula by 2000 BCE (or, as the curriculum calls it, BC). Though this is quite likely true, it has no bearing on when camels were introduced into the Levant, where the stories of Abraham both take place and were written. The second is the claim that "camels did not serve as pack animals in the stories of Genesis"—a claim that can be falsified with even the briefest of glances at the biblical text (see, e.g., Gen 24:32; 24:61; 31:17; 31:34; 37:25). The third argument is that "the Bible avoids mentioning animals that would be anachronistic"—which is simply a circular argument. The handout then concludes by asking the student to "summarize the approach that is taken"—note "is taken"—"to reconcile the seeming"—note "seeming"—"contradiction between archaeology and the Bible.
66. See *b. Ber.* 12a; *y. Ber.* I.8, 3c; *Song Rab.* 5:14. Maimonides also opposed the idea that "some parts of the Torah are of a higher degree of importance than others"; for this and further discussion, see Ephraim Urbach, "The Decalogue in Jewish Worship," in *The Ten Commandments in History and Tradition*, ed. Ben-Zion Segal (Jerusalem: Magnes, 1990), 161–89.
67. Gloege, *Guaranteed Pure*, 37.
68. Quoted in George M. Marsden, *The Evangelical Mind and the New School Presbyterian Experience: A Case Study of Thought and Theology in Nineteenth-Century America* (Eugene, OR: Wipf and Stock, 1970), 47.
69. On this populist movement in American Protestantism, see Hatch, *Democratization*, 162–89.
70. Cited in Noll, *Between Faith and Criticism*, 148.
71. Mark Noll, *The Scandal of the Evangelical Mind* (Grand Rapids, MI: Eerdmans, 1994), 126.
72. Ibid., 127.
73. https://www.prisonfellowship.org/2016/03/the-cost-of-saying-yes/; last accessed February 14, 2017.
74. https://www.prisonfellowship.org/about/in-prison/; last accessed February 14, 2017.
75. David Johnston, "Munificence and Municipia: Bequests to Towns in Classical Roman Law," *JRS* 75 (1985): 105–25.
76. This extrapolation follows the argument made in Rodney Stark, *Rise of Christianity: How the Obscure, Marginal Jesus Movement Became the Dominant Force in the Western World in a Few Centuries* (San Francisco: Harper San

Francisco, 1997), 73–94. Though not himself a Christian, Stark's stable of books about Christianity have been well received by conservative Christians.

77. Athanasius's Festal Letter, listing the twenty-seven books of the New Testament that correspond to our modern canon, was not published until 367 CE, four years after the death of Julian. Even then, Athanasius's letter is unlikely to represent a consensus on the matter. The Nicene Creed was first adopted in 325 CE, but Christian theologians continued to debate its significance and meaning for centuries. While it is common for modern Christians to identify the Nicene Creed as a point of theological agreement, it would be a mistake to say that Christians were united by this common creed. Many rejected it at the time, and everyone continued to debate it, in the same way as many other Christians added to or subtracted from the canonized New Testament.
78. On this process, and reactions to it, see Emma Brown, "GOP platform encourages teaching about the Bible in public schools," *Washington Post*, July 14, 2016 (https://www.washingtonpost.com/news/education/wp/2016/07/14/gop-platform-encourages-teaching-about-the-bible-in-public-schools/?utm_term=.56857f338495; last accessed February 14, 2017).

CHAPTER 4. THE MUSEUM OF THE BIBLE

1. Burke O. Long, *Imagining the Holy Land: Maps, Models, and Fantasy Travels* (Bloomington: Indiana University Press, 2002), 28.
2. On the Creation Museum, see the website, creationmuseum.org, and Jeffrey Goldberg, "Were There Dinosaurs on Noah's Ark?" *The Atlantic*, October 2014 (http://www.theatlantic.com/magazine/archive/2014/10/the-genesis-code/379341/); A. A. Gill, "Roll Over, Charles Darwin!" *Vanity Fair*, February 2010. (http://www.vanityfair.com/news/2010/02/creation-museum-201002), last accessed February 14, 2017; Susan L. Trollinger and William Vance Trollinger, Jr., *Righting America at the Creation Museum* (Baltimore: Johns Hopkins University Press, 2016).
3. See www.arkencounter.com; Laurie Goodstein, "A Noah's Ark in Kentucky, Dinosaurs Included," *New York Times*, June 26, 2016 (https://www.nytimes.com/2016/06/26/us/noahs-ark-creationism-ken-ham.html?_r=0); Carmine Grimaldi, "The Obsession with Biblical Literalism," *The Atlantic*, August 21, 2016 (http://www.theatlantic.com/politics/archive/2016/08/ark-encounter-kentucky/495707/), last accessed February 14, 2017.
4. For Ham's claim, see, e.g., his book *The New Answers Book 2* (Green Forest, AR: Master Books, 2008), 55, 249, 262.
5. https://www.museumofthebible.org/news/buenos-aires-gets-special-look-rare-biblical-artifacts; last accessed February 14, 2017.
6. We spoke with John Kutsko on October 28, 2015.
7. https://answersingenesis.org/ministry-news/creation-museum/rare-bible-manuscripts-on-display-at-creation-museum/; last accessed February 14, 2017.
8. Corinne Ramey, "Meet the Creationist Group Building a Life-Size Noah's Ark," Curbed, July 8, 2015 (http://www.curbed.com/2015/7/8/9943156/answers-in-genesis-ark-encounter; last accessed February 14, 2017).

9. On social media Carroll described the museum as nonsectarian in September 2010, a detail that supports Green's statements that he always conceived of the museum in this way. Summers tells a slightly different story, in which there was a gradual education.
10. www.josh.org; last accessed February 14, 2017.
11. Josh McDowell, *Evidence That Demands a Verdict* (San Bernardino, CA: Campus Crusade for Christ International, 1972).
12. Noll, *Scandal of the Evangelical Mind*, 98.
13. Ibid., 97–98.
14. Worthen, *Apostles of Reason*, 110.
15. In August 1914, the board of managers of the New Jersey Bible Society approved the founding of an organization for disseminating the Gospel of Jesus Christ throughout the world. Elias Boudinot, then president of the New Jersey Bible society, distributed a circular asking for delegates and announced that the society would "disseminate the Scriptures of the Old and New Testament, according to the present approved edition, without note or comment, in places beyond the limits of the United States, or in them." Elias Boudinot, "To the Board of Managers of the New Jersey Bible Society," August 30, 1814, cited in Eric M. North and Rebecca Bromley, "The Pressure Toward a National Bible Society, 1808–1816." ABS Historical Essay 9 (New York: American Bible Societies, 1963), 8–41 (at 41–42).
16. John Fea, *The Bible Cause: A History of the American Bible Society* (New York: Oxford University Press, 2016), 65.
17. Ibid, 63.
18. John Locke, "Of Property," *The Second Treatise of Government*. On the relationship between private property and the common good prior to Locke, see Diana Wood, *Medieval Economic Thought* (Cambridge: Cambridge University Press, 2002), 17–41; and Christopher A. Franks, *He Became Poor: The Poverty of Christ and Aquinas's Economic Teachings* (Grand Rapids, MI: Eerdmans, 2009), 53–66.
19. Catholic social teaching in general asserts that the right to private property is not absolute, but is subordinate to common goods. While often associated with Pope Francis's *Laudato Si*, this theme runs throughout papal documents; see Leo XIII's *Rerum novarum* (1891), the documents of Vatican II, John Paul II's *Centesimus annus* (1991), Benedict XVI's *Caritas in veritate* (2009).
20. http://www.nazarethvillage.com/about/vision-and-purpose/; last accessed October 7, 2016.
21. According to the updated MOTB website, https://www.museumofthebible.org/museum; last accessed October 7, 2016.
22. Kevin M. Kruse, *One Nation under God: How Corporate America Invented Christian America* (New York: Basic Books, 2015). On the nineteenth-century invention of the idea of a Christian America, see also Steve K. Green, *Inventing a Christian America: The Myth of Religious Founding* (New York: Oxford University Press, 2015). For an even-handed treatment of the subject, see John Fea, *Was America Founded as a Christian Nation?: A Historical Introduction* (Louisville, KY: Westminster John Knox, 2011).

23. Casey Ryan Kelly and Kristen E. Hoerl, "Genesis in Hyperreality: Legitimizing Disingenuous Controversy at the Creation Museum," *Argumentation and Advocacy* 48 (2012): 123–41.
24. Representatives of MOTB and the Green Collection provide varying figures for the number of Torah Scrolls in the Collection, ranging from 3500 to 8000 scrolls. The discrepancies can in part be attributed to the fact that, according to Summers, they continue to acquire scrolls at a rate of 500 a year, predominantly from Europe.
25. It is of course difficult to gauge the status and level of interest in ancient texts that did not make it into the canon. The preservation of multiple copies of an ancient text does not guarantee that it was important or influential. There are a number of noncanonical texts, for example the *Acts of Paul and Thecla*, *The Shepherd of Hermas*, and the *Apocalypse of Peter*, that are much discussed by ancient Christian writers.
26. https://www.museumofthebible.org/news/major-new-alliance-israel-antiquities-authority-will-fill-gallery-dcs-new-museum-bible-ancient; last accessed February 14, 2017.
27. *Christianity Today*, October 5, 1988 (http://www.christianitytoday.com/ct/1998/october5/8tb038.html; last accessed February 14, 2017). It is worth noting that the participation of some liberal Protestants in the BDS movement is tied to deeply problematic denials of the history of Judaism in Israel.
28. Marsden, *Fundamentalism and American Culture*, 249–50.
29. Worthen, *Apostles of Reason*, 246–47.
30. Lindsay, *Faith in the Halls of Power*, 96.
31. Ibid.
32. Maisel also constructed the Gutenberg Press used at the *Verbum Domini* event (https://www.ncregister.com/daily-news/interfaith-bible-exhibit-opens-in-st.-peters-square/blank.htm; last accessed February 14, 2017).
33. Lee Biondi, *The Dead Sea Scrolls to the Bible in America* (Biblical Arts of Arizona, 2004), 1. For the details from Noah's exhibit, see http://www.inkandblood.com/; last accessed February 14, 2017.
34. http://carysummers.com/226–2/; last accessed February 14, 2017.
35. From YD 282.1997, a ruling by the Committee on Jewish Law and Standards of the Rabbinical Assembly, the guiding organization of the Conservative Jewish movement (http://www.rabbinicalassembly.org/sites/default/files/assets/public/halakhah/teshuvot/19912000/abelson_pasul.pdf; last accessed February 14, 2017).
36. Gisela Dachs, "Otto Michel: Freund der Juden?" *Die Zeit*, 19 January 2012 (http://www.zeit.de/2012/04/Judaistik-Theologe-Michel; last accessed October 17, 2016).
37. Fea, *The Bible Cause*, 63–64.
38. Ibid., 65.
39. Ibid.
40. "Museum of the Bible" in *The Book Presented by Museum of the Bible*, accessed July 29, 2016.
41. The *Burwell v. Hobby Lobby* suit tackled the issue of funding abortifacients,

but this is not the limit of the Greens' legislative interest. A Salon investigation by Eli Clifton in 2014 revealed that the Green family had been using the National Christian Foundation to quietly fund anti–same sex marriage legislation since at least 2009. Eli Clifton, "Hobby Lobby's secret agenda: How it's quietly funding a vast right-wing movement," *Salon*, March 27, 2014 (http://www.salon.com/2014/03/27/hobby_lobbys_secret_agenda_how_its_secretly_funding_a_vast_right_wing_movement/; last accessed September 6, 2016).

42. Will Herberg, *Protestant-Catholic-Jew: An Essay in American Religious Sociology* (Chicago: University of Chicago Press, 1955); Ruby Jo Reeves Kennedy, "Single or Triple Melting Pot? Intermarriage Trends in New Haven 180–1940," *American Journal of Sociology* 49 (1944): 331–39.
43. August B. Hollingshead, "Cultural Factors in the Selection of Marriage Mates," *American Sociological Review* 16 (1950); George R. Stewart *American Ways of Life* (New York: Doubleday, 1954).
44. Herberg, *Protestant-Catholic-Jew*, 40.
45. Noah Charney, "Critics call it evangelical propaganda: Can the Museum of the Bible convert them?" *Washington Post*, September 4, 2015 (https://www.washingtonpost.com/opinions/2015/09/04/f145def4–4b59–11e5-bfb9–9736d04fc8e4_story.html?utm_term=.ac7da69e0105; last accessed February 14, 2017).
46. https://www.museumofthebible.org/news/passages; last accessed February 14, 2017.

CONCLUSION

1. https://www.museumofthebible.org/news/president-george-w-bush-talks-bible-museums-dallas-event; last accessed February 14, 2017.
2. Noll, *Scandal of the Evangelical Mind*, 66.
3. Steve Green and Todd Hillard, *The Bible in America* (DustJacket Press, 2013), 75.
4. Ibid., 98.
5. Ibid.

BIBLIOGRAPHY

Baden, Joel and Candida Moss. "Can Hobby Lobby Buy the Bible?" *The Atlantic*, January/February 2016.

_____. "The Curious Case of Jesus's Wife." *The Atlantic*, December 2014.

Bagnall, Roger. *Everyday Writing in the Graeco-Roman East.* Berkeley: University of California Press, 2011.

Bahat, Dan. "Does the Holy Sepulchre Church Mark the Burial of Jesus?" *BAR* 12 (1986): 26–45.

Bailey, Sarah Pulliam. "Birthright for evangelicals? Hobby Lobby family funds new Israel trips." *Washington Post*, May 8, 2015.

Banks, Adele M. "Hobby Lobby president's Bible curriculum shelved by Oklahoma school district." Religion News Service, November 26, 2014.

Barkay, Gabriel. "The Garden Tomb: Was Jesus Buried Here?" *BAR* 12 (1986): 40–57.

Barton, Bruce Fairchild. *The Man Nobody Knows.* Indianapolis, IN: Bobbs-Merril Company, 1925.

Bazelon, Emily. "What Are the Limits of 'Religious Liberty'?" *New York Times Magazine*, July 7, 2015.

Beacham, Roy E., and Kevin T. Bauder, eds. *One Bible Only? Examining Exclusive Claims for the King James Bible.* Grand Rapids, MI: Kregel, 2001.

Bean, Lydia. *The Politics of Evangelical Identity: Local Churches and Partisan Divides in the United States and Canada.* Princeton: Princeton University Press, 2014.

Belluck, Pam. "Abortion Qualms on Morning-After Pill May Be Unfounded." *New York Times,* June 5, 2012.

Biondi, Lee. *The Dead Sea Scrolls to the Bible in America.* Biblical Arts of Arizona, 2004.

Bowler, Kate. *Blessed: A History of the American Prosperity Gospel.* New York: Oxford University Press, 2013.

Brakke, David. *The Gnostics: Myth, Ritual, and Diversity in Early Christianity.* Cambridge: Harvard University Press, 2010.

Brinkman, Paul. "Holy Land Experience to unload furniture, statues amid financial turmoil." *Orlando Sentinel*, July 20, 2016.

Brodie, N. "The Lost, Found, Lost Again and Found Again Gospel of Judas." *Culture Without Context: The Newsletter of the Illicit Antiquities Research Centre* 19 (2006): 17–27.

Brown, Emma. "GOP platform encourages teaching about the Bible in public schools." *Washington Post*, July 14, 2016.

Burleigh, Nina. "Newly Discovered Dead Sea Scrolls Are Skillfully Crafted Fakes, Experts Suspect." *Newsweek*, October 18, 2016.

Byrd, James P. *Sacred Scripture, Sacred War: The Bible and the American Revolution*. Oxford and New York: Oxford University Press, 2013.

Canedy, Dana. "A Biblical Theme Park in Florida Begets Ill Will." *New York Times*, February 3, 2001.

Chancey, Mark. "Can This Class Be Saved? The 'Hobby Lobby' Public School Bible Curriculum." Report from the Texas Freedom Network Education Fund, May 2014.

Charney, Noah. "Critics call it evangelical propaganda: Can the Museum of the Bible convert them?" *Washington Post*, September 4, 2015.

Clifton, Eli. "Hobby Lobby's secret agenda: How it's quietly funding a vast right-wing movement." *Salon*, March 27, 2014.

Collins, John J. *The Dead Sea Scrolls: A Biography*. Princeton: Princeton University Press, 2012.

Dachs, Gisela. "Otto Michel: Freund der Juden?" *Die Zeit*, January 19, 2012.

Darakjian, Gareen. "Pepperdine professors and students get a never-before-seen look at ancient religious artifacts using an innovative imaging technology." *Pepperdine Magazine*, Summer 2013.

Davenport, Stewart. *Friends of the Unrighteous Mammon: Northern Christians and Market Capitalism, 1815–1860*. Chicago: University of Chicago Press, 2008.

Dayton, Donald W. and Robert K. Johnston, eds. *The Variety of American Evangelicalism*. Knoxville: University of Tennessee Press, 1991.

DeConick, April. "Gospel Truth." *New York Times*, December 1, 2007.

Dochuk, Darren. *From Bible Belt to Sun Belt: Plain-Folk Religion, Grassroots Politics, and the Rise of Evangelical Conservatism*. New York: W. W. Norton, 2011.

Elgvin, Torleif, Michael Langlois, and Kipp Davis, eds. *Gleanings from the Caves: Dead Sea Scrolls and Artefacts from the Schøyen Collection*. London: Bloomsbury, 2016.

Fabrikant, Geraldine. "Craft Shop Family Buys Up Ancient Bibles for Museum." *New York Times* June 11, 2010.

Fea, John. *The Bible Cause: A History of the American Bible Society*. New York: Oxford University Press, 2016.

_____. *Was America Founded as a Christian Nation? A Historical Introduction*. Louisville: Westminster John Knox, 2011.

Fieldstadt, Elisha. "Liberty University President Jerry Falwell Urges Students to Carry Guns." *NBC News*, December 5, 2015.

Fitz Gibbon, Kate. *Who Owns the Past? Cultural Policy, Cultural Property, and the Law*. New Brunswick, NJ: Rutgers University Press, 2005.

Flaherty, Colleen. "Banking on the curriculum." *Inside Higher Ed*, October 16, 2015.

Franks, Christopher A. *He Became Poor: The Poverty of Christ and Aquinas's Economic Teachings*. Grand Rapids, MI: Eerdmans, 2009.

Gill, A. A. "Roll Over, Charles Darwin!" *Vanity Fair*, February 2010.

Gloege, Timothy. *Guaranteed Pure: The Moody Bible Institute, Business, and the Making of Modern Evangelicalism*. Charlotte: University of North Carolina Press, 2015.

Goldberg, Jeffrey. "Were There Dinosaurs on Noah's Ark?" *The Atlantic*, October 2014.

Goodstein, Laurie. "A Noah's Ark in Kentucky, Dinosaurs Included." *New York Times*, June 26, 2016.

Green, David. "One judge away from losing religious liberty: Hobby Lobby." *USA Today*, September 1, 2016.

Green, Steve K. *Inventing a Christian America: The Myth of Religious Founding.* New York: Oxford University Press, 2015.

Green, Steve and Todd Hillard. *The Bible in America.* DustJacket Press, 2013.

Grimaldi, Carmine. "The Obsession with Biblical Literalism." *The Atlantic*, August 21, 2016.

Ham, Ken. *The New Answers Book 2*. Green Forest, AR: Master Books, 2008.

Hankins, Barry. *Francis Schaeffer and the Shaping of Evangelical America.* Grand Rapids, MI: Eerdmans, 2008.

Hatch, Nathan O. *The Democratization of American Christianity*. New Haven: Yale University Press, 1989.

Herberg, Will. *Protestant-Catholic-Jew: An Essay in American Religious Sociology*. Chicago: University of Chicago Press, 1955.

Hindman, Sandra. "We Are Storytellers First." *Fine Books and Collections*, Autumn 2013.

Hinton, Carla. "Mustang Schools still plan Bible class, but not with controversial Green scholars' curriculum." NewsOK, December 11, 2014.

Hollingshead, August B. "Cultural Factors in the Selection of Marriage Mates." *American Sociological Review* 16 (1950).

Jarus, Owen. "Are These New Dead Sea Scrolls the Real Thing?" Live Science, October 10, 2016.

_____. "25 New 'Dead Sea Scrolls' Revealed." Live Science, October 10, 2016.

Jenkins, Tiffany. *Keeping Their Marbles: How the Treasures of the Past Ended Up in Museums . . . and Why They Should Stay There.* Oxford: Oxford University Press, 2016.

Johnston, David. "Munificence and Municipia: Bequests to Towns in Classical Roman Law." *JRS* 75 (1985): 105–25.

Kearns, Cristin E., Laura A. Schmidt, and Stanton A. Glantz. "Sugar Industry and Coronary Heart Disease Research: A Historical Analysis of Internal Industry Documents." *JAMA Intern Med.* 176 (2016): 1680–85.

Kelly, Casey Ryan, and Kristen E. Hoerl. "Genesis in Hyperreality: Legitimizing Disingenuous Controversy at the Creation Museum." *Argumentation and Advocacy* 48 (2012): 123–41.

Kennedy, Ruby Jo Reeves. "Single or Triple Melting Pot? Intermarriage Trends in New Haven 180–1940." *American Journal of Sociology* 49 (1944): 331–39.

Klasfeld, Adam. "Looted 200 A.D. Sarcophagus Returned to Greece." Courthouse News, February 10, 2017.

Knowles, David. "Hobby Lobby accused of anti-Semitism over lack of menorahs, Chanukah decorations." *New York Daily News,* October 1, 2013.

Kraft, Robert J. "Pursuing Papyri and Papyrology by Way of eBay: A Preliminary Report." Report given to the 25th International Congress of Papyrology in Ann Arbor, MI, August 3, 2007.

Krosney, Herbert. *The Lost Gospel: The Quest for the Gospel of Judas Iscariot.* Washington, D.C.: National Geographic, 2006.

Kruse, Kevin M. *One Nation under God: How Corporate America Invented Christian America.* New York: Basic Books, 2015.

Layton, Bentley. *The Gnostic Scriptures: A New Translation with Annotations and Introductions.* Anchor Yale Bible Reference Library. New Haven: Yale University Press, 1995.

Leach, William R. *Land of Desire: Merchants, Power, and the Rise of a New American Culture.* New York: Vintage, 1993.

Levinthal, David. "Spreading the Free-Market Gospel." *The Atlantic*, October 30, 2015.

Lindsay, D. Michael. *Faith in the Halls of Power: How Evangelicals Joined the American Elite.* Oxford: Oxford University Press, 2007.

Locke, John. "Of Property." The Second Treatise of Government.

Long, Burke O. *Imagining the Holy Land: Maps, Models, and Fantasy Travels.* Bloomington: Indiana University Press, 2002.

MacDonald, G. Jeffrey. "After winning free campus, Grand Canyon University says 'no thanks.'" Religion News Service, October 29, 2012.

Markschies, Christoph. *Gnosis: An Introduction.* London: T&T Clark, 2003.

Marsden, George M. *Fundamentalism and American Culture: The Shaping of Twentieth-Century Evangelicalism 1870–1925.* Oxford: Oxford University Press, 1980.

_____. *The Evangelical Mind and the New School Presbyterian Experience: A Case Study of Thought and Theology in Nineteenth-Century America.* Eugene, OR: Wipf and Stock, 1970.

_____. *Soul of the American University: From Protestant Establishment to Established Nonbelief.* Oxford: Oxford University Press, 1994.

Mayer, Jane. "How Right Wing Billionaires Infiltrated Higher Education." *Chronicle of Higher Education*, February 12, 2016.

McBride, Bailey Elise. "School Board Members Met Privately on Bible Class." Associated Press, May 21, 2014.

_____. "Oklahoma District Bible Class: Sinners Will Suffer." Associated Press, April 25, 2014.

McCormick, Richard Cunningham. *The Young Men's Magazine* 1 (1957).

McDowell, Josh. "Living Treasures Hidden Within Ancient Artifacts." *Charisma Magazine,* April 1, 2015.

_____. *Evidence That Demands a Verdict.* San Bernardino, CA: Campus Crusade for Christ International, 1972.

McGreevy, John T. *Catholicism and American Liberty.* New York: W. W. Norton, 2004.

Messenger, Phyllis Mauch. *The Ethics of Collecting Cultural Property: Whose Culture? Whose Property?* 2nd ed. Albuquerque: University of New Mexico Press, 1999.

Moreton, Bethany. *To Serve God and Wal-Mart: The Making of Christian Free Enterprise.* Cambridge: Harvard University Press, 2010.

Moss, Candida, and Joel Baden. "Exclusive: Feds Investigate Hobby Lobby Boss for Illicit Artifacts." *The Daily Beast*, October 27, 2015.

Noll, Mark. "The Bible in Revolutionary America." In *The Bible in American Law, Politics, and Political Rhetoric*. Edited by J. T. Johnson, 29–60. The Bible in American Culture Series; Philadelphia: Fortress, 1985.

_____. *Between Faith and Criticism*. San Francisco: Harper & Row, 1986.

_____. *The Scandal of the Evangelical Mind*. Grand Rapids, MI: Eerdmans, 1994.

_____. *America's God from Jonathan Edwards to Abraham Lincoln*. New York: Oxford University Press, 2002.

North, Eric M., and Rebecca Bromley. "The Pressure Toward a National Bible Society, 1808–1816." ABS Historical Essay 9. New York: American Bible Societies, 1963.

O'Hara, Mary Emily. "Former Hobby Lobby Employee Claims She Was Fired for Having a Kid." Vice, July 30, 2014.

Oppenheimer, Mark. "At Christian Companies, Religious Principles Complement Business Practices." *New York Times*, August 2, 2013.

Orsini, Pasquale. "La maiuscola biblica copta," *Segno e Testo* 6 (2008) 121–50.

Osborn, Andrew. "Islamic State looting Syrian, Iraqi sites on industrial scale—UNESCO." Reuters, July 2, 2015.

Pagels, Elaine. *The Gnostic Gospels*. New York: Random House, 1989.

Pattengale, Jerry. *Consider the Source: Young Scholars and the Timeless Truths of Christianity*. New York: Barge Canal, 2000.

_____. *Straight Talk: Clear Answers about Today's Christianity*. Marion, IN: Triangle, 2004.

_____. *Why I Teach: And Why It Matters to My Students*. New York: McGraw-Hill, 2009.

Pilkington, Ed. "Hobby Lobby investigated for trying to import ancient artifacts from Iraq." *The Guardian*, October 28, 2015.

Quecke, Hans. "Eine koptische Bibelhandschrift des 5. Jahrhunderts III (P.Palau Rib. Inv.-Nr. 183)." *StudPap* 20 (1981): 7–13.

_____, ed. *Das Johannesevangelium saïdisch: Text der Handschrift Palau Rib. Inv. Nr. 183 mit den Varianten der Handschrift 813 und 814 der Chester Beatty Library und der Handschrift M 569*. Rome: Papyrologica Castroctaviana, 1984.

Ramey, Corinne. "Meet the Creationist Group Building a Life-Size Noah's Ark." Curbed, July 8, 2015.

Rappeport, Alan. "Hobby Lobby Made Fight a Matter of Christian Principle." *New York Times*, June 30, 2014.

Robinson, James M. *The Secrets of Judas: The Story of the Misunderstood Disciple and His Gospel*. San Francisco: HarperOne, 2007.

Sabar, Ariel. "The Unbelievable Tale of Jesus's Wife." *The Atlantic*, July/August 2016.

Savage, Sean. "World's oldest siddur slated for future D.C. Bible museum." Jewish News Service, November 10, 2013.

Schroeder, Caroline T., in Tony Burke, ed., *Fakes, Forgeries, and Fictions: Writing Ancient and Modern Christian Apocrypha.Proceedings from the 2015 York University Christian Apocrypha Symposium*. Eugene, OR: Cascade, 2017.

Schwartzman, Micah, Richard Schragger, and Nelson Tebbe. "The New Law of Religion." *Slate*, July 3, 2014.

Shabi, Rachel. "Looted in Syria—and sold in London: the British antiquities shops dealing in artefacts smuggled by Isis." *The Guardian*, July 3, 2015.

Solomon, Brian. "Meet David Green: Hobby Lobby's Biblical Billionaire." *Forbes*, September 18, 2012.

Stark, Rodney. *Rise of Christianity: How the Obscure, Marginal Jesus Movement Became the Dominant Force in the Western World in a Few Centuries.* San Francisco: Harper San Francisco, 1997.

Stephens, Randall J., and Karl W. Giberson. *The Anointed: Evangelical Truth in a Secular Age.* Cambridge: Harvard University Press, 2011.

Stewart, George R. *American Ways of Life.* New York: Doubleday, 1954.

Takla, Hany N. "The Massacre in San Jose—The Sale of Dismembered Manuscripts of Christian Egypt on eBay." In *Synaxis katholike.* Edited by Diliana Atanassova and Tinatin Chronz, 705–16. Vienna: LIT, 2014.

Thomas, G. Ernest. *Spiritual Life Through Tithing.* Nashville: Tidings, 1955.

Tov, Emanuel, Kipp Davis, and Robert Duke, eds. *Dead Sea Scrolls Fragments in the Museum Collection.* Leiden: Brill, 2016.

Townes, Elmer. *How God Answers Prayer (How to Pray).* Shippensburg, PA: Destiny Image, 2009.

Trollinger, Susan L., and William Vance Trollinger, Jr. *Righting America at the Creation Museum.* Baltimore: Johns Hopkins University Press, 2016.

Urbach, Ephraim. "The Decalogue in Jewish Worship." In *The Ten Commandments in History and Tradition.* Edited by Ben-Zion Segal, 161–89. Jerusalem: Magnes, 1990.

Van Biema, David. "Hobby Lobby's Steve Green launches a new project: a public school Bible curriculum." Religion News Service, April 15, 2014.

_____. "Hobby Lobby's Green family postpones launch of public school Bible curriculum." Religion News Service, July 16, 2015.

Vehling, Aaron. "Hobby Lobby Says Scott Cole Defied Court by Filing Wage Suit." *Law360*, October 28, 2014.

Watje, Jon. "School district considering adding Bible course." *Mustang Times*, November 13, 2013.

Waxman, Sharon. *Loot: The Battle over the Stolen Treasures of the World.* New York: Henry Holt, 2008.

Willis, William H. "Duke Papyri: A History of the Collection." *Duke University Library Notes* 51/52 (1985): 35–50.

Wood, Diana. *Medieval Economic Thought.* Cambridge: Cambridge University Press, 2002.

Worthen, Molly. *Apostles of Reason: The Crisis of Authority in American Evangelism.* New York: Oxford University Press, 2013.

Wright-Knust, Jennifer. "Early Christian Re-Writing and the History of the *Pericope Adulterae.*" *Journal of Early Christian Studies* 14 (2006): 485–536.

INDEX

INDEX